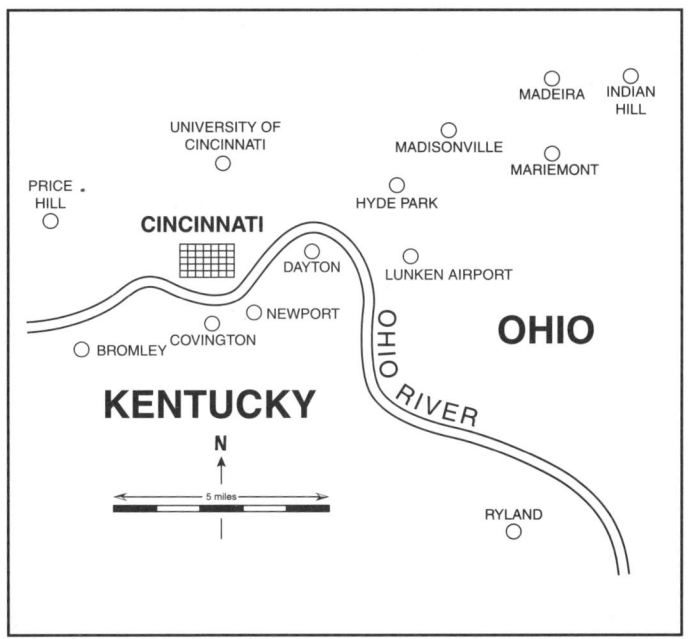

COVER PHOTO:
Tiger driving with Birdlegs;
Left to right: Dick, Bob, Ike,
June Bug, Snake and JC.
in 1929 Model 'A' Ford
Low Boy Hot Rod Roadster

Acknowledgements
Many thanks to my fine editor Dee Garretson, my 5th cousin Kathy Hoeting for her computer expertise and all the many proofreaders including my daughter Kathy.

Additional lifelong thanks to my mother and father for their love and guidance and to all my good friends who changed my young existence into a life of joy.

LIFE ON THIN ICE

A memoir celebrating one boy's life in the '30s, '40s and '50s.

ROBERT LEO GREIWE

Cincinnati, Ohio

Dedication

This book is dedicated to my wife, Kay.
She has the patience to endure, the foresight to maintain the accuracy of the stories and the compassion not to offend anyone. She is the family catalyst and my best friend.

Life on Thin Ice may be ordered
from any bookstore including
Joseph-Beth Bookstore
2692 Madison Road, Norwood, OH 45212
513-396-8960
or online at www.josephbeth.com

© Robert Leo Greiwe 2001

No part of this publication may be reproduced in any material form (including photocopying or storing in any medium by electronic means and whether or not transiently or incidentally to some other use of this publication) without the written permission of the copyright holder.

Foreword

As a young child I loved to sit in my grandmother's lap regaling her with all the details of my tiny world, chatting about my brother and sisters, pets and toys. While we talked, her soft fingers would trickle over my head and face, memorizing my features with her hands. Her blindness limited her to an upstairs bedroom in her house but she never lost the gift of appreciating and savoring the small moments with family and friends. My father had the gift too, seeing endless possibilities for excitement and laughter in life. To witness the grin on his face when he planned a holiday celebration or a vacation was to know we were in for something extraordinary. He passed on to me the idea that you have to find the excitement in living instead of wishing and waiting for life to happen.

I embraced my father's example so completely he probably regretted his philosophy when I carried it too far in my own search for amusement. Growing up in the calm and quiet of the Midwest during the 1940s and 1950s, I thought I needed a few firecrackers and fast cars to liven up life. My friends and I took too many chances and found ourselves in more trouble than we ever planned, hurtling around on thin ice nearly sliding out of control. We thrived on our harebrained stunts, though, laughing through them all.

Eventually, I did manage to grow up, finding a balance between the realities of life and the pursuit of laughs and thrills. The stories in this book, my father's and my own, intertwine in a tapestry tied with threads of family, good friends and laughter. Like most memoirs, the actual events were thrown up in the air and juggled a bit until they dropped into a coherent story.

My drawings at the beginning of each chapter capture the look of midcentury cartoons and flavor of the stories.

The photographs that go along with some of the stories started more than 60 years ago when my parents gave me a Kodak camera for Christmas. I felt even then the pictures might help me hold onto the moments. After all, in the best of lives, our memories entertain and enrich us. Even when the people who helped make the memories are gone, they live on and give us joy in the stories they leave behind.

Contents

1. The King of Capers 1
2. Mouse Afire 6
3. Gene's Revenge 13
4. Fried on the Fourth 18
5. Holy May Malarkey 24
6. Helga and Harry 28
7. The Trouble with Dogs 31
8. Neighborhood Nuisances 35
9. Father versus Son 39
10. The Oyster Uprising 44
11. The Provocateurs 48
12. Blunder Bob 53
13. The Potato Resurrection 56
14. The Power Peas 60
15. In Search of Brownie Points 65
16. Four Minus Two Equals Four 70
17. Saturday Morning Mudball Club 76
18. Double Whammy 81
19. Secondary Hijinks 88
20. Footloose But Not Fancy 94
21. The Mood For Love 101
22. Captain Dick's Tour Boat 106
23. Requiem For A Dead Poinsettia 113
24. Lord Of The Loonies 120
25. The Moonshine Cats 124
26. Win a Few….Lose 130
27. Midnight Marauder 136
28. Testing the Limits 141
29. Blazing a Trail in the Park 147
30. Big Apple Apocalypse 151
31. The Gotham Shuffle 156
32. A Normal Mess 162
33. Switcharoo 166
34. Under Suspicion 170
35. Clan Uprising 175
36. Ugly People 181
37. Grasshopper Bait 186
38. Sigma Chi Sweethearts 192
39. Lollapalooza 198
40. Unsplendor in the Grass 205
41. A View From 4000 Feet 211
42. Greasing a Pig on A Pole 213
43. Box O' Tricks 217
44. Off the Hook 221
45. Looking for "Miss One" 225
46. Piece of Cake 232
47. The Bubble Bursts 236
48. The Last Best Resort 243
    Epilogue 250

The King of Capers (mid-1920s)

My father, Gene, the 'Little King' roared through the 1920's with the best of them. The youngest of five children, he came by his nickname honestly. He grew to 5'4" early and then stopped, apparently deciding he didn't need the extra height to command the world to entertain him. And America was full of amusements then. Modern teenagers can't begin to imagine the thrill of packing ten friends in an open roadster and racing past disapproving elders shaking their heads at youth going to the devil. Young men attracted the female of the species by polishing their hair to gleam like new motor oil, and by adorning themselves with spiffy saddle shoes and Oxford bag pants wide enough to clothe entire families. The young danced and necked and smoked cigarettes and were the despair of their parents.

Every new generation of the twentieth century thinks they are the first to discover the older generation generally bluffs their way through life, but the honor of that discovery should go to the young of the 1920s. They watched the politicians bungle their way into World War I, drag it out to a limp end, and then argue over the remains like fractious two-year-olds fighting over a shabby old toy. The youth decided it was time to make and break their own rules.

With school behind him, Gene bypassed some of the more juvenile aspects of the 1920s. We have no record he ever swallowed goldfish or sat on flagpoles. Of course, my grandfather, J.H. would not have stood for such foolishness. John Henry believed work should order a man's days. As one of the first of his family to be American-born, he devoted long hours to expand his painting and decorating business. His company became well-known for intricate and elaborate church decoration. Maybe the peace and serenity of empty churches attracted J.H. with his five active children.

Gene earned three dollars a week after attending Ohio Mechanics Institute working for his father. Like the rest of the young, though, the important part of life had nothing to do with work. With his best friends, twins "Smiling Jack" and "Bob the Cat", they took in all Cincinnati had to offer.

The Queen City had entertainment for everyone. Stately married couples went off to the Opera, which performed at the Cincinnati Zoo, the monkeys joining in at appropriate moments. The younger crowd rode the Island Queen riverboat from the foot of Broadway up the Ohio River to Coney Island, where they wore themselves out at the Moonlight Pavilion in the steamy evenings shimmying to the new jazz.

Prohibition only made life more exciting. Cincinnati was home to both the Anti-Saloon League and largest bootlegger in the United States, George Remus. Remus, a Chicago lawyer, managed to find ways to sell thousands of gallons of legal 'medicinal' liquor to people who suddenly developed fainting spells, which only shots of whiskey could cure. He also set up an operation to have his employees steal whiskey from his own warehouses and sell it to anyone who wanted it. Three hundred speakeasies filled almost every basement in downtown Cincinnati and Gene explored his share, never letting on to J.H. that here were cellars just crying out to be decorated.

To three young energetic men, Cincinnati was not enough. Gene and his friends planned a long train trip through Canada, which would culminate in a stay at the Banff Springs Hotel, the most famous hotel in the west. The Prince of Wales had made the same trip in 1920, and daily reports of elaborate meals and luxurious accommodations aboard the Canadian Pacific Railroad, with stops for dancing and climbing and golf, fed the dreams of many as the perfect vacation.

The three friends couldn't afford a princely private car, but the car porter sent them to the dining car at all the right moments so they could feast on Gaspe salmon, fresh blueberries and other delicacies while he converted their Pullman seats into comfortable beds each night. Gene and his friends spent most of their time in easy chairs in the observation car,

The Banff Springs Hotel

watching the scenery, or more likely, eyeing any attractive females aboard, listening to the gramophone and telling jokes.

The '20s heralded the writing and telling of some of the worst jokes in the history of the world, including the unforgettable series about the fly in the soup and the more racy traveling salesmen jokes. Every young man had a repertoire and at the appropriate moment could always say, "Heh, have you heard the one about the girl named Marigold? She got her name because that's what she was trying to do."

After almost a week of travel, Gene, Jack and Bob finally arrived at Banff station. Banff is one of the natural wonders of North America, a perfect small valley, surrounded by spruce forests climbing up to snowy mountain peaks. Some say the developer of the Banff Springs Hotel was delusional when he placed his version of a giant Scottish baronial castle on a spur in the valley in the 1880s. The red-tiled, white-balustraded hotel seems to float above the trees, an apparition of a man who was overcome with a surplus of imagination and the fatigue of building a luxury hotel in the wilds of Canada. It does make for an unforgettable site, and at the time when Gene saw it no one cared or thought about the strangeness of such a choice.

When Gene and company disembarked they asked a station porter to call the hotel for a carriage to transport them and their baggage. They were more than ready to enjoy the spot they had heard so much about, so it was to their bafflement when the porter informed them the hotel had no record of their reservation. Gene took over the phone and tried to arrange another room, but a desk clerk with a dubious English accent told him not a single room could possibly be found.

Having more than their share of cleverness and nerve the three friends cooked up a scheme to obtain a room. After all, they had traveled 3000 miles and were not about to be disappointed. At that time every man who traveled to an exclusive destination packed appropriate formal eveningwear including black silk top hats. The three had the porters bring their trunks into the station and here they unearthed the clothes they needed.

Gene and Jack departed first in a carriage hired at the station. The driver left them at the bottom of the wide front steps and a hotel doorman greeted them. Gene announced in a loud carrying voice that the Prince of Liechtenstein would soon be arriving and that they hoped the hotel had everything in order. As the stunned doorman hurried inside to find out why he hadn't been informed of such a guest, Gene and Jack toured around the famous sulfur pools, talking loudly enough for guests to understand a momentous occasion was about to occur.

When they had attracted enough attention outside, they moved into the lobby in time to find a ready-made audience having afternoon tea and listening to music. With lively comments about what the Prince would think of the hotel, they stirred up the guests so much the poor pianist soon gave up his attempt at a recital. The group chatted excitedly about seeing royalty and soon a crowd moved out to the porch to await the arrival of such a illustrious personage.

Unfortunately, Bob the Cat, the newly crowned prince, was late and Gene and Jack started to sweat. Just as they were began to contemplate a quick bolt, an open carriage pulled by a black Clydesdale stallion appeared. Gene and Jack sprang into action and ran up and down shouting, "The Prince is coming! The Prince is coming!" By this time the manager had realized a major problem was in the works. He came out to the top of the steps and stood — a thin, nervous, balding man, wringing his hands, undoubtedly wishing he could ring the neck of whoever had neglected to prepare him for a royal guest.

The carriage stopped, and Bob, seated in royal splendor in the back, stood up slowly and tipped his hat to the delight of the crowd. He stepped grandly out of the carriage and fell flat on his face. Bob, fond of his liquor, had spent the waiting time in town sampling Canadian rye in a saloon. A drunken prince did not surprise the crowd, used to hearing about the decadence and doings of minor royalty. The guests nattered happily, talking of the stories they would be able to tell when they returned home to Omaha and other points south.

As Bob lay there enjoying the steadying support of the warm cobblestones, Jack hurried to his side. He dragged his brother up and brushed off his suit, gritting his teeth at pretending to be a loyal flackey to a twin who deserved a punch in the nose.

The manager descended the steps and introduced himself with a bow. Bob could imitate anyone, even in an inebriated state, so in his best Liechtensteinian accent he looked down his nose and addressed the unhappy man in front of him. "I certainly hope you have der finest staterooms for myself and my attendants."

The manager pulled himself together, except for an uncontrollable twitch of his right eyelid, and replied, "We would be most happy and honored to provide you special accommodations and hope you enjoy your stay as our special guest."

The three grandly entered the lobby; Bob stumbling a bit, as he tried to continue to look down his nose. Gene and Jack hurried him along before he could forget his new birth country and break out a Mexican or a Japanese accent. Miraculously, the hotel managed to find a princely luxury suite and here the three spent their vacation, mobbed every time they ventured into the ballroom, as women just couldn't pass up the possibility to dance with royalty. When their vacation was over, the hotel guests and staff again lined the front of the hotel steps to give them a royal sendoff. The manager did not appear, apparently fed up with the demands of blue bloods. Bob the Cat gave his last royal wave and the three rode off back to the station.

Mouse Afire (late 1920s)

Gene returned to Cincinnati, ready to get back to everyday life. He had a routine: Monday through Saturday morning he did his work and then on Saturday afternoon he picked up a girlfriend or two to go shopping at Findlay Market, located ten blocks north of downtown. The stands were full of cheeses, meats, fruits, vegetables, and Gene's favorites, pastries, and the scent of cinnamon from the freshly baked strudels and stollens filled the entire area, too tempting to pass up.

Neither of Gene's parents could drive an automobile so he was happy to volunteer his services for an opportunity to drive John Henry's 1915 Packard with pneumatic shock absorbers. The girlfriends must have liked the outings too because he never had a shortage of passengers. Findlay Market on Saturdays had the air of a festival.

Everyone came out to do their marketing and visiting was as important as buying. The area still retained a little bit of a European village atmosphere. The early German immigrants congregated around Findlay Market in an area they dubbed Over-the-Rhine, thinking the name would help them overcome their homesickness.

J.H.'s father, Adam, had come to Over-the-Rhine from Germany in 1837. His family struggled to earn a living on a tenant farm in the small community of Haltern in northern Germany. But America beckoned to anyone with ambition and nerve. Adam was 20 when he made the trip and he brought his two younger brothers, Edward and John Henry, with him through rough seas in a crowded disease-ridden

The King all spiffed up ready to go to Findlay Market.

ship. They landed in Maryland, took a wagon to West Virginia and then a flatbed riverboat to Cincinnati. Eventually, they brought their parents and youngest brother Christoff over to live near them.

When they arrived they had little money and no mastery of English. The brothers were willing to work, though, and work they did. They struggled to learn English and to earn enough money to live but eventually all of them started their own businesses, married and had children. Those children all inherited their parents' memories of the struggle to make a new life. J.H. started his own business at 21, and eventually had over a hundred employees.

In later life J.H. appeared to be a stern, upright unsmiling fellow most of the time. He did have a few quirks all his own, though. He loved fast horses and in the days before the automobile took part in a few races himself. He also had a great desire for a long life. He consumed great quantities of oysters, convinced they had some sort of miraculous longevity substance in them. And several times of year he took off to the health spa at French Lick, Indiana, suffering happily through mud baths and drinking vast amounts of the spa's famous 'Pluto' mineral water.

J.H trusted his youngest son's business instincts and though he wasn't one to give out praise, he slowly gave Gene more and more responsibilities.

An inferno and J.H. brought my father and mother together. Years after my father would put his arm around my mother and say "I got her at a fire sale." In 1924, my mother, Mary Liz, moved with her parents into a substantial three-story house on ten acres in Hyde Park, a convenient suburb northeast of downtown. Mary Liz's father, Leo, had worked his way up from Western Union delivery boy to president of a local bank and the whole family was understandably proud of their new home.

The fire started near the living room on a cold night in January. Faulty wiring ignited and quickly burned through the walls, spreading through much of the main floor. The family escaped without harm but the house was not so lucky. The fire trucks roared in from Hyde Park Square and the firemen rushed to run hoses up from Erie Avenue but the cold had frozen the connection at the hydrant. By the time they managed to get water up to the house it was badly damaged. The grand piano fell through to the basement when the living room floor collapsed. A favorite painting of a white Persian cat fell on top of it and was saved from the flames but most everything else on the main floor burned or suffered smoke damage.

The next day the cleanup and rebuilding started. Leo called up J.H. to try to arrange the repainting but J.H. had a spa trip scheduled and was not about to miss out on a chance for a little rejuvenation. He offered to send Gene over in his place. Fate entered the story.

Gene strode up to the door that day unaware of what was about to hit him. He rang the bell, which wasn't working, and then knocked. He was early. An older woman in an apron opened the door. Gene introduced himself and the woman said, "Mr. Van Lahr's not home yet. You can wait in here." She showed him into the hallway and then disappeared. The house reeked of smoke and Gene stood around for a bit whistling softly. The house was quiet except for some faint noises coming from a room off to the right. The door was partway open and he gave it a little push. He looked around the corner and saw a young blond girl on her knees scrubbing the floor. Her hair was tied up in a scarf and she had a smudge on her cheek. He thought she was the most beautiful girl he had ever seen.

He cleared his throat. "Uh, hello." Gene was at a loss for words for the first time in his life. Mary Liz didn't say anything. He glanced around at the disaster. "They sure have got you working hard. This is such a mess for one person to clean." "I can handle it," Mary Liz said and went back to her scrubbing.

Gene started a nervous string of talk. Mary Liz pretty much ignored him. Since he wasn't getting anywhere he finally decided he might as well try the direct approach. "Say," he said casually, "I bet you really deserve some fun after all this work. I'd like to take you out to dinner on your night off."

Mr. Van Lahr came in the room behind Gene. "You must be J.H.'s son. How do you do?" He held out his hand. "I see you have met my daughter."

Boy meets girl scrubbing floors and falls in love. Boy proposes marriage. Girl refuses. Boy compromises

My parents — the King and Queen

and proposes engagement. Girl refuses. Boy stands on his head and does his dog and pony show for five years and girl finally accepts. Not your typical courtship scenario but my parents were never typical. In 1929, Mary Liz couldn't withstand my father's persistence any more and married him in an all-out grand wedding. He was so happy he behaved himself at the wedding and pulled no practical jokes.

The folks moved into their first newlywed living quarters, a nice small three-bedroom house in Hyde Park. Mother liked it. They lived close to their friends, including Dad's best friend, Jack, who met and married Mother's best friend, Mildred. Mary Liz was happy she lived only three blocks from her mother. Their house fit their needs, but Dad was a little less enthusiastic. He lived only three blocks from his mother-in-law.

Mom was a wonderful lady. She had naturally wavy blond hair, blue eyes and a heart-warming smile. At 5'5" she was taller than Dad, and in high heels she seemed to tower over him. She always wore high heels –off to the grocery, cleaning the house, or up to her ankles in garden dirt. She didn't own a pair of slippers, loafers or tennis shoes. Dad couldn't help but look up to her. It's not that she looked down on him, but she was always in control. She was in the catbird seat and being the daughter of a banker, was a tight-fisted manager of family finances. Dad was crazy about her and let her know it with lots of affection and kidding around. She would smile at him and shake her head, probably worried about what he would come up with next.

His first impression of her had been right. She was Miss Tidy. To say you could eat off her basement floor was an understatement. The highlight of Mother's week was Friday. She couldn't wait to get up and organize her cleaning supplies and dive into what she called a 'thorough cleaning day'. Now, naturally, the house was already clean but she approached it as if the circus had come through and set up camp. Nothing got in her way; the phone went unanswered, the mail went unread. It was a daylong happy focus on dirt, critter and cobwebs. She never just cleaned under the sofa. She first moved it out from the wall and then carefully dusted the floor and baseboard. Each week she won the fight against filth. She was *grande*.

Mother had a downright hatred of critters in the house. While dirt was easy enough to control, critters sometimes were either brave enough or dumb enough to challenge her authority. One mouse, one small gray rodent, nearly brought down the entire house. One night, she awoke at 3:00 A.M. to the sound of a strange scratching noise behind the bed. She jumped out of bed, turned on the lights, and started screaming. She knew it was a creature who did not belong. Dad opened one eye, assessed the situation, and knew he couldn't just pretend to be in a deep sleep.

Mother shook his arm. "There's something under the bed, Gene!" she screeched. "Help me look!"
Dad got up and they both peered under the bed. It was uninhabited. Dad made a move to get back into bed but Mother had other ideas. "Pull the bed away from the wall!" she said. He knew better than to argue.

The bed came out and they both looked carefully, Dad was

determined to slay the beast so he could go back to sleep. There was absolute silence. Whatever it was had heard the sound of a brass bed being dragged across the floor and wisely decided to stop its noisemaking for a moment. They looked again, but there were no critters, varmints, or large bugs. Dad stood back, yawning, while Mother crouched down. After a few moments, the scratching started again, inside the wall. Mother pressed her ear flat against the wall, and crept along stealthily, trying to locate the source.

She stopped so suddenly Dad thought she had been bitten by something. "It's a field mouse," the General announced as she jumped up and turned toward her troop, the dream of victory gleaming in her eyes. "I want it out of here!"
Dad could tell by the look in her eye there was no waiting until morning. She was hot on its trail and wanted its tail. He asked, "Are you sure it is right there?" Silly question.

"Yes," she replied firmly, "Get him out or we will never sleep."

Now, Dad was a city boy. Faced with a rodent and a wife on the rampage, lack of sleep and experience marred his judgement a bit. He put on his robe and slippers and went down in the basement to get a hammer and chisel. When he got back to the bedroom, Mother was again crouched down, guarding the wall, in case the creature somehow popped out and made a dash for freedom. "Here," she whispered, pointing at a spot about three inches up from the floor. Resigned, Dad knelt down and carefully cut a six-inch square in the heavy plaster wall. Of course there was nothing there. The mouse was not about to sit around and watch someone cut through the wall in front of his whiskers. He had either scurried vertically up the stud wall or found an opening to move horizontally. He was gone. Case closed.

Or so my father prayed. The next night the scratching started again, and the next and the next after that. That mouse must have peeked its head out every night and watched the luminous clock on Mother's night table, because it had an uncanny ability to start the scratching each night promptly at 3:00 AM. Now why this mouse felt the need to scratch on the wall was not clear. Why he was even in the house was not clear. Obviously a bad choice of living accommodations. There was never even a microscopic wayward crumb of mouse food in the house. Mother wouldn't allow it.

Maybe the poor thing was faint from hunger and confused, trying to find a way to a more rodent-friendly house.

Mother would not admit any mere mouse could get away from her. Each night she sent Dad for the hammer and chisel until the wall behind the bed looked like an army howitzer target. The mouse must have been pleased the humans were making convenient little mouse doors for him, even if they weren't providing any snacks. Finally, after seven nights the scratching mysteriously stopped. Mother was sure the mouse was dead, convinced they had won the war, but Dad told her, "That mouse is just like a kid, when he stops making noise, he's on to something." They needed a cat.

Gene's Revenge (1936)

Other than the mouse damage, that Hyde Park house should have been fine for my parents. My brother, Richard, was born there and I was due two years later. It was a perfect place to raise children; lots of young families lived on the street, it was only a half a block from the streetcar, but best of all, there was a small garden in the backyard. Mother wouldn't spare too much time for any frivolous hobbies but she did love to garden. Flowers, vegetables, fruit, she loved to grow them all and tried to plant any space she could find.

Maybe that garden was too small, maybe the mother-in-law dropped by one time too many, we just don't know what suddenly brought about a major turning point in the history of our family. With the Depression settling in and buying power disappearing, you would think the folks would pull in their ears and sit tight. But instead they got it in their heads that it would be better to raise children out in the country where they could have plenty of fresh air, fresh fruits and vegetables, and lots of land to play.

So Gene and Mary Liz quickly became the proud owners of an old farm house on 14 acres of clay dirt in Indian Hill, an outlying community with a mix of farms and huge manor homes. Our house was on a gravel road four and one-half miles from civilization and the nearest street car line. Gene and Mary Liz decided all they needed to do to make the house livable was to gut the interior, add a new face to the exterior and add a two-car garage. They plunged right in, full of ambition and the will to work.

Mother took time out from overseeing the remodeling to give birth to me on a cold March day in 1932. I distinguished myself immediately by refusing to be anything like my brother.

Our original home at 8020 Blome Road

Richard was a quiet, well-behaved, mild-mannered child. I was not, but my mother did her best to pretend she had two perfect children. Her strategy was to dress us identically, right down to matching hats and socks, hoping no doubt that I would imitate Richard in everything he did. We would appear in our matching white sailor suits and everyone would fuss over us and then in about two minutes my outfit would somehow acquire streaks of dirt and grass stains until I looked like a neglected orphan child.

The Great Depression went from bad to worse. In the mid 1930's, unemployment reached 21%. John Henry's decorating company was losing $85,000 a year. He appointed Dad manager of the company and paid him $50 a week. Then business got worse. The company sold off 33% of its stock to bail itself out of trouble. All the salaried decorators were dismissed. People just did not have money to spend on anything but necessities.

In the early years of the depression people had to find ways to keep their spirits up. They needed entertainment — they needed to laugh, but they also needed money they didn't have. The answer was radio. The old crystal sets with ear phones were tossed aside and the new radios afforded everyone a low cost form of entertainment. Our Stromberg-Carlson console radio was one of our most prized possessions.

While Mother did her mid-day cleaning, she listened to *Ma Perkins* or the *Guiding Light* soap operas. The daily dramas, interrupted by ads for Oxydol and other detergents, kept Mother and millions of other women entertained. The kiddie programs came on in late afternoon to give mothers some uninterrupted time to prepare supper. Richard and I were fans of *Captain Midnight, The Green Hornet* and *The Shadow*. Everyone liked the evening programs the best. We knew what was going to happen on each show. Fibber McGee was always squelched by his wife, Molly. Jack Benny's violin was always out of tune. LeRoy was always giving his great uncle Guildersleeves fits and Red Skelton played host to his good ole country buddy, Clem Cadiddlehopper.

Always identical, except in personality

Dad had another way to keep up his spirits. He loved baseball with a passion and wasn't content just to take in a Cincinnati Reds' game like a regular baseball fan. No, he looked over some of his newly acquired land and envisioned a baseball field. When friends came to visit he would take them to view a four-acre field of ragweed and goldenrod, trying to get them to see a nicely mown grass baseball field. Minor details like who was going to get rid of the weeds, plant the grass seed and then mow the field each week were lost in his enthusiasm.

Somehow it did happen, though. Every Sunday from June to August in the mid 1930's Dad conducted organized baseball games on his very own field of dreams. It became famous throughout the area. Dad's team consisted of friends and relatives and he was always on the lookout to find some competition. Most companies could manage to work up a ball club and the teams were usually well-matched enough to play a good game.

Game days had a set pattern. People arrived around 11:00 Sunday morning. The cars parked in an area off of right field. Women and children hauled folding chairs down close to first base where a huge willow tree provided shade. The usual refreshment for players and male spectators was a keg of beer. Everyone chipped in fifty cents and the keg usually lasted the whole game. I loved the smell of the fresh tapped keg mixed with the scent of the fresh cut grass. The women pretended to watch the game while they chatted, drank iced tea and kept one eye on the children who ran around playing tag.

The day the team from the Sanborne Trucking Company arrived started out hotter than usual. August in Cincinnati is never cool but this day the heat was shimmering off the cars like a line of dancers from a Busby Berkeley musical. Dad's team was already looking a little limp. They weren't in bad shape but most of them spent their work days at a desk and their evenings sitting on their front porches. It quickly became clear that there were no office workers on the team from Sanborne. Those guys were big and muscular. It looked as if they spent their days handing refrigerators to each other. Sanborne took control of the game right from the start. They couldn't run very fast but they didn't need to. They could hit those balls so far the kids had to help find them in the weeds back behind the field.

By the third inning the score was 4-0. Things were looking grim. Not only was Dad's team losing but all the beer was gone too. I guess those big guys needed more liquid to keep their strength up. The heat kept building. Even the flies gave up buzzing. Sanborne's pitcher, Mike Morrisey, quickly struck out Dad's team one more time. As they were switching places, Morrisey walked over to Dad who was at first base and asked, "Do you mind if we eat some of them apples off of them trees over by the white barn?"

"No, help yourselves, fellas," Dad replied. "I've eaten some myself."

Richard and I were sitting on the grass nearby. Richard started to say, "But Dad, won't..." Dad raised his hand and shook his head. I should have known from the smile on his face something was up.

The entire Sanborne team, except for the batter and the guy on deck, made their way over to the trees, picked and inhaled a few apples each and then put a few more in their pockets and came back. I saw Dad motion to his friend Gus in the outfield who then trotted around to each of their players for a brief conversation. None of Dad's team touched the apples

In the fourth inning Morrisey came up to bat. He stood and

tapped the bat on the ground a few times and then raised it up. Then he put it back down and stood very still with a puzzled look on his face. He looked down at his stomach and then up again. I was lying on the grass by this time, idly watching him when I saw his face start to change color. It was amazing. The green tint started near his nose and worked its way out exactly the shade of a squashed lima bean. He turned to say something to the catcher and then threw up. The rest of the team didn't look so great either. They tried to carry on the game but their ability to run after balls or run the bases was somewhat hampered by the delicate condition of their intestines.

Five innings later Sanborne had no more hits, no runs, no players standing straight, and Morrisey was calling for a respirator. He said to Dad, "I thought you said you ate some of them apples over by the barn."

"I've tasted them."

"Well, we got sick from them and I don't like it."

"I didn't much care for them myself. Pretty sour, aren't they?"

Fried on the Fourth (1937)

My taste buds were aching for the cherry pie just out of the oven when the Little King bounded into the kitchen waving his money clip and grinning. Mother had just given him the buy sign. She seldom flashed this signal, but when she did, Dad became ecstatic. You might go as far as to say that he had that rare disease 'buyitis'. A week never passed without him showing up at the house with pastries, ice cream, and turkeys. Dad loved to eat and thought the rest of us should be absolutely delighted with a gift of a bird and a sponge cake.

Sometimes the purchase of these items was more than distressing for Mother for two reasons: she hadn't given him the buy signal and we didn't need most of the purchases. He could not be convinced that the majority of his selections were unhealthy. She always did her best to handle him with kid gloves. Tactfulness and sensitivity to his feelings were important to her approach. In communicating to him on this subject, she was always a woman with few words, "That junk is going to kill you."

Calories were not her main concern that summer day. The Fourth of July ranked right after Christmas with both Dad and me, and Mother knew just how many fireworks we could bring home. Dad grabbed the phone receiver and I knew he was going to call his friend, Mr. Denier, who owned a store about two miles west of us. To make a phone call from the sticks of Indian Hill was not a quick dial. As a matter of fact, there was no dial. Each phone required a ten-inch square transmitter box with a crank handle placed next to the telephone.

Dad cranked the lever four times, picked up the receiver, and held it to his ear. I was close enough to hear the operator in Madeira ask, "Hi, Gene. What number do you want?"
"Hi Florence. Connect me to Sycamore 7691."

The other end of the line answered and Dad said, "Hi, Clarence, this is Gene. You got fireworks this year? Good, we'll be right over."

While Mother focused her attention on the conversation I nabbed a deviled egg from the feast multiplying on the kitchen table, because I couldn't figure out any way to get at the pie unnoticed. Dad spotted me as he hung up the receiver and said, "Come on, Bobby, everybody is waiting for us."

Mother warned, "Now don't overdo it, Gene." Dad just smiled.

Outside, my dad's friend, Smilin' Jack and some neighbor kids had already climbed into Dad's '37 Ford Phaeton convertible with my sister, Madge. Though there were only five children in the car, the backseat could barely contain us because we were hot to hit the firecracker trail. Nothing beat being allowed to make as much noise as we could.

Gene with his explosive experts

We arrived at Mr. Denier's tiny country store on Montgomery Road without managing to lose a child out the back of the car. In his 20' by 30' shop he managed to cram in an amazing array of stuff. Flour stood next to nails and other doodads and the smell of licorice blended nicely with the spicy scent of pipe tobacco. Usually, I headed straight for the jawbreakers and jujubes but that day the candy was nothing compared to the fireworks outside on his open porch.

The incredible array took careful examination. I almost bought the Chinese crackers. I passed them up, though, because I knew from previous experience they were too unpredictable. You would light them, throw them and run like crazy only to have them fizzle out. The Black Cats looked good. They were wrapped in thin black paper with a gold cat and some mysterious Chinese characters on the back. Even if they turned out to be duds I could save the paper.

The sparklers were fine at night, but otherwise boring. Really only for little kids but I got a few packs anyway. Mr. Denier had some twirlers you nailed to a tree that would spin different colors of fire. I had to have some of those. Some new five-inch high rockets looked great too because they supposedly shot a packet about 100 feet in the air and then exploded out a white parachute which floated to the ground. Some of the repeaters were good; they also threw an explosive way up in the air. Roman candles were a necessity. And last, I had to stock up on lots of your basic two-inch noisemaker firecrackers.

I tried to pick a good variety that would make lots of racket and last a long time. Back inside, with my arms full I saw Dad and Uncle Jack looking over something at the counter but I was too excited to pay attention. All the kids gave our choices to Dad and Jack and then we ran back to the car to plan the all-important order of lighting.

When we got home we raced around to the back of the house, avoiding Mother and Jack's wife Mildred in the kitchen, in case they would nix some of the fireworks as being too dangerous. The rest of the afternoon was one long burst of noise. Even though we lived in the country with few neighbors, you could hear the sound of explosives from every direction through the afternoon and into the evening. The smell of burnt explosives seemed to permeate the air all day.

After a while I needed a slight change. I pulled Richard to one side to confer with him. "How about we find some old tin cans and see what happens when a firecracker explodes in them?"

Richard gave a nervous glance at Mom who sat in a lawn chair chatting with Aunt Mil and keeping an eye on my sister, Madge. "I don't know, Bobby. That sounds kind of dangerous."

"Oh, come on. Let's go down behind the barn. We can throw them down the back hill. Nobody will even notice." He sighed and followed me, unable to resist the lure. We scrounged up a few empty tin cans and loaded the explosives. Those 2-inch firecrackers made a terrific reverberating racket when they exploded in the can.

After two lobs a rabbit lurched out of the tall grass that grew in clumps along the foundation wall and stumbled toward us. I don't think he even saw us, he was so dazed by the explosion. We watched him hop lopsided toward the barn and then as he gained his balance back he veered off down towards the creek. We were going to stop anyway but then we heard Mom yell, "Quit whatever mischief you are up and come eat!"

I realized I was famished. We devoured the fried chicken and molasses rich-baked beans as if we had worked all day. I also managed to eat a few more deviled eggs and some Jello salad, since I needed to regain my strength for the evening show.

As the darkness grew we got out the Roman candles we had been saving. We carefully lined them up in a row, lit them and then dashed back out of the way. The resulting burst of sparkling colors dazzled me. In reality, the candles only shot up about ten feet but to my young eyes it looked as if the stars had descended into our back yard. The puffs of pearly smoke from the liftoffs spread through the air and added to the strange dream life our yard was taking on.

When the last of the smoke cleared we decided we needed nourishment again so we headed back to the moms to get plates of cherry pie topped with vanilla ice cream. As we finished up and lit the few remaining sparklers, we watched Dad and Jack prepare the main surprise of the day. They first took some rags, tied them in knots, and then soaked them in kerosene. Then they brought out the balloon made of red and blue striped paper with a wire basket attached to the bottom. Jack held the balloon while Dad loaded the basket with the kerosene fuel. When he lit one of the rags, the hot air from the fire rose up into the balloon and it started to inflate. It grew slowly until it was at least ten-foot in diameter. We thought it was enormous.

As Jack tried to hold onto the balloon without getting singed, Dad added the final touch. He wrote down the balloon's origin, time of liftoff and our phone number, and put it in a little metal capsule attached to the basket. Jack let it go and we watched it soar. The kids jumped around in the grass, the dew cooling our bare feet as we did our own version of a crazy send-off dance. We watched until the flame in the basket was only a tiny speck in the dark sky, and then suddenly all the children, myself included, drooped with exhaustion. Jack and his family left, and the house became quiet again.

This night, as on other hot, sticky nights, Mother and Dad set up World War I army surplus cots for us on the screened-in porch. We collapsed into those canvas and stick beds without a fuss. I barely had time to hear the nightly chorus of crickets and tree frogs before I fell asleep.

About midnight, the ring of the telephone startled me out of sleep. The phone never rang at night. Since we had only one phone and it was in the kitchen, Dad had to hurry to get it. Mother followed, anticipating some sort of family disaster. I got up, pretending I needed a drink of water but really to find out what was happening.

Dad answered the phone. "I can't hear you. Who is this? You live in Florence, Kentucky? You say you got the balloon with the note? Hey, that's really great." Dad smiled and gave me the thumbs up sign. "My family will be very excited about you calling." Then Dad stopped talking and the smile faded. There was a long pause. He finally spoke, "I'm sorry. I'm really sorry." He also mentioned the word 'restitution'. I didn't know what that meant but it sounded bad, real bad. Mother's face was not looking so great either at this point.

Dad hung up the phone. Mother asked, "What was that all about?"

"Well, our balloon made it all the way across the Ohio River and down about 30 miles to Kentucky. Into the hill country. Must have been a good steady wind to go that far. It landed on a Mr. Weir's chicken coop. Must have been an old one because I guess it went right up in flames. Unfortunately, by the time Mr. Weir got the fire out, about a dozen of his future fryers ended up being over-baked instead."

He leaned back against the counter and crossed his arms. I started to giggle but Mother silenced me with a look. The corner of Dad's mouth headed up in a twitch but he wisely kept quiet. Mother stomped around the kitchen for a few moments, her slippers slapping down hard on the linoleum.

When she finally spoke, she laid down the law. "Absolutely no more balloon launches ever." She glared at him, daring him to disagree. He knew better.

On the way back to the porch, I said to Dad, "It's too bad about the man's chicken coop but today was a super fun day, thanks to you, Dad."

He didn't say anything until I climbed back into my cot and then he whispered, "Always remember that famous chicken saying, Bobby. Better to fly and fail, than to sit in a stew."

Holy May Malarky (1938)

Mother said, "I can't believe that's our Bobby."

"Take one long, last look, it might be the only time you see a halo over that rascal's head!" Dad replied.

I marched down the sidewalk dressed in a ridiculous burgundy velvet pageboy suit trimmed with white lace. Shiny black patent leather shoes and long white stockings made my legs itch and my feet hurt. A floppy renaissance-style velvet hat completed the total indignity of it all. My freedom on the farm had ended the previous fall when I got sent to school, but I had no idea then I would be forced to sink to this.

The May Procession highlighted the year for the nuns at St. Mary's School. The event was an annual liturgical celebration of the Virgin Mary entering heaven and the nuns prepared for it as if the performance would help them ascend to heaven too.

Little Bo Hassel and I were selected from the first grade class to walk directly behind a senior high school girl, Anne Marie Martin, chosen to crown the Blessed Virgin Mary. Our job was to carry her ten-foot long white dotted Swiss veil the nuns had so carefully made. The good sisters chose the two of us because we were the only pure blond towheads in our class.

Blondness may have been my only virtue in the eyes of the nuns. Sitting still was next to impossible for me and trouble found me even when I didn't look for it. I liked my teacher, but I just wasn't patient enough for stationary education. Up until that day, though, I accepted the fact I had to go to school. I accepted the fact I had to wear a uniform of gray knickers and a tie each day. No one ever told me part of the deal included being dressed up like a china doll and marched around town.

The long parade turned left up Shady Lane, left again and up the steps into St. Mary's Church. We struggled to keep up with Anne Marie. My hands gripped her veil as tightly as if I were on the winning end of a tug of war game because the nuns had given us dire warnings against dropping the ends and letting it get dirty. I am sure at the end of the day Anne Marie had a ferocious headache from Bo and I yanking back on the veil the nuns had anchored so firmly to her head. That must be why she held her head at such an unnatural angle and her smile looked painted on exactly like the statue of the Virgin Mary.

We marched slowly down the center aisle of the huge stone gothic church. The nuns had stressed that the commemoration was to be joyful but quiet, very quiet, once we entered the church. In other words, no talking. Organ music reverberated, parents of all the children filled the 600-seat nave and 16 nuns sat in the front two rows to enjoy the show they had spent so much time planning and rehearsing. The grand Monsignor waited with hands folded on the top step in front of the main alter. He was tall and elegant and looked like a cross between Neville Chamberlain and Douglas Fairbanks. Standing in front of the stained glass window backlit by a kaleidoscope of color he looked about as holy as anyone I had ever seen.

Bo and I trailed Anne Marie with her crown up the sanctuary stairs. She knelt in front of the Monsignor and bowed her head, probably saying a prayer of thanks that her neck was free from our death grip. We took our places eight steps down below her just like we had practiced. I thought about picking up the end of the veil and flapping it to get a little air but decided against it. The other part of the procession took seats on the right and the left.

The stage was set. The music stopped and the great one said a few prayers. The music started, then stopped, more prayers, then more music, then more sermon. This went on forever. I was going nuts; I couldn't move, I couldn't breathe. It felt like it was a 100 degrees in there. The lace around my neck itched. The nuns had warned us not to scratch or pick at

Front row: Maddie, Bo Hassel, Bob, Rosie and Ann at St. Mary's May Crowning

any part of our body because everyone would be watching us. I tried to count the colors in the stained glass but that didn't distract me for long and the sickly fragrant incense smell made me want to sneeze. I needed a respite, a variation on this theme, anything to break the monotony.

I looked sideways at Bo. He stood, smiling sweetly at nothing, acting as if there was no place he would rather be. I just hadn't been able to bring myself to like him much that school year. He was usually too good to be true, always helping the teacher clean up after art projects instead of trying to make paste balls to stick in the girls' hair like the rest of us. But what I did next was simply a nervous reaction. Bo didn't drive me to it. There was no thought or reasoning. I had this instant impulse.

I reached over and grabbed little Bo in the ribs. I just wanted to see if he was still alive, sleeping or just playing as dead as he looked. I quickly found out.

Bo first let out a shriek of torment followed by a quick burst of laughter from the rib tickle. The Monsignor was not looking. He faced the altar with his arms raised in some sort of consecration event but he turned around quickly when he heard that unnatural noise. He didn't deign to look directly at us but I swear I saw smoke rise from his ears. The look he threw at the nuns clearly placed the blame on them for letting us incorrigible children ruin the solemnity of his service.

I was shocked and frozen at Bo's outburst. It was all a mistake. To make matters worse, I instinctively turned my head to look at the nuns. They had drilled me not to turn my head. Thirty-two eyes of fire under black hoods were focused right on me. I had big problems. I prayed my mother didn't hear or see us in the dimness of the nave. I still believed in miracles.

After the ceremony we marched out of church and the procession led the way back down the street. Bo cried and sniffled all the way. I bit my lip hard because I knew what was coming. We marched into the first grade classroom. Eight nuns were already waiting for me. The principal walked into the room last, her habit swirling around her like a small tornado. She glanced around, caught my eye, picked up the nearest yardstick and came at me. Meanwhile, outside, Dad must have sensed my dilemma and asked mother to bring the Packard up to the front gate so he could go in and fetch me.

Her right hand held the yardstick and her arm quivered. The site of that stick paralyzed me and I stood frozen, unable to squirm for the first time in my life. She was getting close when Dad walked up behind her and said, "It was a wonderful procession, Sister. Now if you'll pardon us we will take our Bobby and return his wonderful costume tomorrow."

When we got out the front door, I said quietly, "Thanks for saving me, Pop."

He replied, " I'm not sure I did the right thing because tomorrow you are going to have to face the music."

The Little King gave an accurate prediction as always. The next few weeks my nerves vibrated like strings on a banjo every time a nun picked up a ruler.

6

Helga and Harry

I also had to fight my own battles at home. The nuns were in charge of me for eight hours a day but when I got home a new drill sergeant was hired to torment me.

During the Depression, poor families from the hills of rural Kentucky and Tennessee flocked into Cincinnati in hopes of finding work. Young, unmarried women looking for housekeeping jobs were paid $5.00 to $7.00 per week to live in, clean, cook, and take care of unruly children. Our first housekeeper, Helga, reminded me of a tough barnyard cat, thin, but all bone and muscle. She worked like a fiend, cleaning to Mom's exacting standards while she sang her favorite song, "May I sleep in your barn tonight, mister, for it's cold laying out on the ground. And the wet winter night is upon us and tomorrow I'll be homeward bound."

Helga came from a family of nine in Indiana, and had developed her own special way of dealing with small children like myself. If I didn't toe the line for her, she would simply smile and slam me against the kitchen wall until my eyeballs felt like they would pop out of their sockets. Her philosophy was that children should hear no evil, speak no evil, see no evil and never, never track mud in the kitchen.

I knew I couldn't go to the parents. I knew the Little King would just say, "Well, I'm sure you deserved it. Mind her and your life will get easier." Minding her was possible in theory, but in practice I just couldn't find it in me to cooperate. It was kind of entertaining to think up ways to irritate her and I managed to do it at least once a day.

When Harry, Dad's outside helper, suddenly started hanging around inside the kitchen, I had hopes Helga would ease up on me. Even at my tender age I could recognize a romance starting when I found them holding hands and drinking coffee at the kitchen table one Saturday night. Harry was a man of few words, tall and skinny, looking like two of him should fit in his overalls. He and his brother Herman had come out of the St. Aloysius orphanage to work for my grandfather at the paint company and both brothers were always willing to earn a few extra dollars. In the kitchen, Harry seemed content to sit, hour after hour, putting away gallons of coffee, just to be in Helga's presence. I couldn't even begin to imagine what he found so wonderful.

Maybe his silence finally got to her because she thought up a good test of his devotion. She found a long thin board about 18" long, gave it and a carving knife to Harry and told him to make a hand paddle she could use on me.

And use it she did. My tail was more often red than white. Plus, Helga was smart enough to know I wasn't above trying to get rid of that paddle. She took to hiding it when I wasn't around. After a few beatings, for perfectly innocent mistakes like being too busy to come inside when she called, I decided I couldn't stand it anymore. She didn't comprehend there was no way I was going to behave to her standards. It wasn't in my nature. We were approaching a dead end draw. Either Helga had to go or the paddle had to go.

I couldn't think of any good reason I could give my parents to send Helga away. She kept the kitchen spotless and she could cook. I knew I shouldn't even try. Therefore the paddle had to go. But first I had to find it. I figured it had to be in the kitchen, and it made sense it would be somewhere above my reach.

One night after my mother and Helga had a daylong cleaning frenzy, I knew they both should be sleeping very soundly. I tiptoed into the kitchen and pulled a kitchen chair around to look on top of all the cabinets. I had almost given up when I spotted it. It was hidden in the coils on top of our 1934 Frigidaire. I snatched it, jumped down and quietly opened the back door and then ran like crazy down the back yard to the creek. I heaved that torture instrument right into the water and snuck back into bed, gleeful because I had solved the problem. With the logic of a seven-year-old I thought Helga would just give up.

My glee was short-lived, though. Next day when I brought a perfectly clean toad into the kitchen Helga reached for the paddle and had a fit when she couldn't find it. I took off outside again, thinking she would cool down. Didn't happen. Harry was summoned to make a new paddle and he did as ordered. I threw that one into the creek too. Strangely, at first, Helga didn't realize I was the one taking the paddle. Poor Harry carved three more paddles, each of which promptly went in the creek as soon as darkness could cover me. Harry surely must have thought the road to true love was awfully demanding because eventually he did crack. He told Helga she had to stop cooking up schemes just to get him to come see her more often.

Mother took Helga's side and blamed Harry for using the situation to see Helga every Saturday night. Helga finally caught on and blamed me, but I played innocent and refused to speak no evil, a strategy that would serve me well in the future.

The Trouble with Dogs (1939)

I thought I couldn't wait for summer to be free of nuns and rules until I woke up the first day of summer vacation and realized I had nothing to do. Other than my brother, Richard, there was not another boy my age within walking distance. Richard and I got along fine but we couldn't understand each other at all. It was hard to imagine we were even related. Not only was Richard quiet, neat and polite, his idea of a good time was to sit in the living room and listen to opera on the radio. This I viewed as worse than trying to sit still in church. I had acquired a little sister a few years back, but Madge didn't interest me too much. She liked to play with dolls all day and if I teased her too much I got into trouble. Outside could be interesting but I wasn't crazy about the bugs. And a new problem developed. From spring until September, being outside made my eyes water and my nose fill up. I just figured everyone had the same problem, but when I helped cut the grass it was much worse and sometimes at night, breathing was tough. It didn't occur to me to mention it to my parents so I just sniffled along.

I got a new baby blue Schwinn bike for Christmas with white wall tires and Texas handlebars. It was a great escape vehicle. I rode up and down the road in front of my house, logging several miles, counting the bumps in the road. After a while though, I was still lonely.

One Saturday, The Little King took a break from his gardening and sat on the porch watching me do laps. He must have felt some pity for me because the next Friday he brought

The Trouble with Dogs 32

Even my new bike did not completely relieve my boredom.

home a pure-bred collie to keep me company. I was in heaven. We named him Kydoo, for no good reason that I can remember, but it sounded perfect then. He was the friendliest dog I had ever seen and also the dumbest dog I had ever met. I'm not even sure he ever really learned his name. Every time we called him he would look around as if we were talking to some other dog. Either way, I dearly loved that dog. I realized that I was a little smarter than he was, which gave me a mental boost.

Dad explained to Mother we needed a watchdog, but Kydoo's ability to guard against intruders was non-existent on our 14 acres. Everyone who came to the door was a long-lost friend. The only creatures he considered intruders were squirrels. He chased them until he was tripping over his tongue. The dog had no territory. The only territory he claimed was the area where his four paws were standing. Unfortunately, he assumed that all other dogs and cats in the neighborhood had the same non-protective nature and frequently came home with a scratched and bloody nose.

When the dog got older, we thought he would get wiser, but it seemed like just the opposite happened. On our road, a car would pass every 15 to 30 minutes on average. This didn't seem to be frequent enough to imprint on his brain. Each time he saw a car driving by he would stare at it as if he had never seen a car in his life. Then he would erupt in a frenzy of barking.

Some cars he chased, some he didn't. It depended on the sound of the motor. The Model A Fords confused him the most. Their exhausts sounded like the gobble-gobble of a very large turkey. These drove him wild because he could never link the sound with the car driving by no matter how many hundreds of time it happened. Instead he would run crazily around the yard, nosing under bushes looking for the turkey he knew was hiding from him.

He ignored farm pick-ups. They were noisy but for some reason unworthy of his notice. It was the quiet automobiles that were the problem. He was deeply suspicious of them. Did he think they were enormous squirrels? Whatever he thought they were, he knew they were sneaking somewhere they shouldn't be. He would crouch low to the ground; convinced he was invisible in the 3-inch grass. Then, when the car would pass the driveway, he would speed toward it, not running along beside it as most dogs did, but instead trying to run in front of it. Maybe some primeval herding instinct came out in him. A few old ladies would see him coming, swerve to avoid him, and almost kill themselves so as not to hit a seemingly blind dog. Many an upset driver reported this to Dad and the Indian Hill Ranger police force. One day he underestimated an opponent and tried to stop a speeding Hudson Terraplane sedan. His left paw got in the way of the tire and left him with a long-term limp.

Kydoo's best friend.

One time in his life he turned into a watchdog. One weekend the entire family left for three days and Dad thought Kydoo would be happier if we let him run free in the yard while we were gone. We decided we could put enough water and doggie crunchies to keep him satisfied. He never commented, so we assumed he was happy. When we arrived home after the long weekend, we were amazed to find Kydoo was standing guard over Mr. Jackman, one of our neighbors, who was in the process of stealing vegetables from Dad's prize garden.

Mr. Jackman had always been pretty unfriendly but we never suspected he had larcenous tendencies. I guess we were stunned because we just stood there watching him. As soon as the dog saw us, Kydoo forgot he had a dangerous criminal under guard and ran toward us wagging his tail as fast as he could. The neighbor took off running across the baseball field, his long Ichabod Crane legs tangling in the tall grass, tomatoes spilling out of his baskets. Dad took off after him, shaking his fist and yelling, "If I ever catch you over here again, I'm going to hang you out to dry, you idiot!"

Kydoo gave a half-hearted bark to reinforce Dad's curses and then turned back to me, satisfied he had done his job, ready to go back to a dog's life.

Neighborhood Nuisances (1940)

Kydoo did a pretty good job of keeping me company those summers but I missed playing baseball with my friends. They were all in Hyde Park, miles away from me. My other problem was cash. The extreme lack of money. My mother didn't think I needed an allowance. I couldn't convince her I needed money to take the bus to town to find a decent ball game.

Late one Friday afternoon, I was riding in the back of mom's car down Blome Road when I spotted a cardboard sign that read "Wanted-Grass Cutter". This was the answer to my problem. I could mow grass to earn the money I needed for a bus ride. The next day I rode my bike down early, thinking there would be lots of people waiting for the job. The driveway was a quarter mile long and at the end was a small, shabby wooden house in the middle of a two-acre field of dandelions and chickweed. Okay, so it was big, but I reassured myself that they couldn't be too picky about their weedy yard. One hour with a gas-powered mower would knock this job down quick. No one was in sight, so I knocked on the screen door. An old woman in a putrid yellow cotton floral housedress opened the door. She didn't have a sweet, grandmotherly look to her. In fact she looked amazingly like a witch – a Wizard of Oz wicked witch. I almost ran, then I told myself to stand my ground.

I managed to squeak, "I'm here about mowing."

"Fifty cents and you can start right now," she muttered. From the size of the yard, it should have been a two-dollar job, but she didn't look like the type you engage in debate.

Who knew what she might do with children who gave her trouble? She probably had a pack of flying monkeys she kept in her attic.

"The mower is in the barn. Yell out back when you're done." She slammed the door shut and I decided I would get this done fast. On my way to the barn, I realized I forgot to ask her where she kept the gasoline. It wouldn't have done me much good because sitting in the barn was an old reel push mower. I hadn't cut a blade and already there were two strikes against me.

Two and a half hours later I was one beat puppy. My tongue was flapping and my tail was dragging. I wanted my fifty cents and I wanted to be home. I went around the back of the house where the old woman was muttering at her garden. She was probably putting spells on the weeds to make them wither and die. "I'm finished, Ma'am," I said, politely, considering my body was ready to melt into a puddle.

"Let's see." She walked to the front, with me trailing her. She stood and studied that lawn like she was the head groundskeeper at Crosley, the Cincinnati Reds' baseball field.

"Did you crosscut it?" she asked.

"Crosscut it?" I never heard of this.

"Well, you cut it first in a side to side direction. Then you need to finish by giving it a final cut front to back."
Cutting grass wasn't supposed to be complicated. "For fifty cents?" I asked.

"Yes sir, young man. Are you going to finish or what?"
I stood there, my nose running, my eyes bloodshot from the pollen attacking me, and she wants another two and a half hours in the heat. Fifty cents for five hours. A grand total of ten cents an hour. Such a deal.

I thought of a lot of good things I could say but I didn't because I knew the old witch would call my mother and complain about my bad manners. Then a bad day would get worse. I had to make a decision.

"Lady, keep your fifty cents and give it to the next kid. He deserves double pay for double duty. Or you could put the fifty cents towards the purchase of a new gasoline mower. Or..." I stopped before I got her too mad. By the look on her face I decided it was time to cut my losses and run. Baseball would have to wait.

On my way home I tried various curse words out on the

old witch. I was running through possible revenge schemes when I rode by a kid I didn't recognize; who stood in the front yard of a big brick manor house. I slowed down and circled around, staring at him. We didn't get new kids very often in the neighborhood and I thought this could be interesting. He stared back.

I stopped my bike and said, "You live here?"

"Yeah, my dad is the caretaker of the big house. We just moved here. We live next to the garage in that little gatehouse."

Freddy's garage and gatehouse.

This sounded great. Imagine living in a cozy gatehouse cottage. I wondered if I could get my dad to put in a cottage next to our garage. "What's your name?" I asked.

"Freddy."

Freddy didn't look like much. His ears stuck straight out from his head and he was so covered in freckles that they had blended together; his skin resembled a giraffe more than a kid. Beggars couldn't be choosers, though. He was a potential friend.

"I'm Bob. You want to play ball?"

"Sure, I've got a basketball."

We went down the driveway and I studied him on the way. On closer inspection I wasn't so sure I was seeing freckles. He was about the dirtiest kid I had ever seen. The grime under his fingernails alone would have driven my mother into screams. I speculated on the last time he had seen the inside of a bathtub. Now I was as fond of dirt as the next kid but I wasn't allowed to have it hang around on me indefinitely.

The dirt didn't bother me as much as his nose. It was running and I wasn't sure he even knew it. "Got a cold, Freddy?"

"Nope", he said and that was the end of that conversation. Okay, so he didn't talk much. Still, he did look close to my age.

We got to the end of the driveway. There was a wire ring rigged up above one of the garage doors. "Wait here. I'll get the ball."

Freddy came out with the ball. By the wide grin on his mouth I could tell this was the highlight of his day. Maybe it would be mine too.

"Catch," he ordered and tossed the ball to me. I caught it on the second bounce and was ready to shoot one, when my fingertips sent a message to my brain. This ball felt strange. I looked down on it and saw my fingers were right. This was no ordinary ball. It was slightly irregular in shape, a light brown color and had strange lines on it going every which way.

"Freddy, what is this thing? I've never seen a ball like this."

"It's my basketball."

It was no basketball but it was obvious he loved it.

"What's it made out of?"

"My daddy butchered a sow yesterday. He took that out of her and blew it up for me."

"What do you mean, he took it out of her?" This wasn't sounding good.

"It's a pig's bladder. It's great, isn't it?"

Father Versus Son (1941)

The depression eased but since I couldn't remember any other times I didn't notice much difference. The adults had serious discussions about Roosevelt and the aggression of the Japanese and Germans. I caught snippets of talk about French Indo-China and Russia, but they were only places on the map the nuns expected me to learn. On December 7th of 1941, the adult world suddenly became real and important.

That Sunday afternoon I was contemplating the possibility of a new baseball glove appearing for Christmas, listening with one ear to our Philco radio, when the broadcaster broke in with the news about the attack on Pearl Harbor. In no time flat, the entire family clustered around the radio. We listened anxiously over the next hours as reports came about additional attacks on Manila and Burma. The radio became our link to the world and we hardly moved from it over the next few days. President Roosevelt's speech to the nation may have fortified the country but it scared me. When he said, "Every single man, woman, and child is a partner in the most tremendous undertaking of our American history," I didn't know how I would live up to what might be expected of me.

I worried for my Dad. I worried that he would be drafted, sent far away and be killed. I worried mother would be a widow. I worried there would be no money for us orphans to buy food. How would we survive? I was so worried I could hardly stop thinking about it. Then the Little King got a letter from the draft board. It said, "You're too short, you're too heavy, you're too old, you're 4F" and I stopped worrying. I always had tremendous faith in my dad and if he said we were going to be okay I believed him. We had no close relative drafted into the war, but my Dad's nephew by marriage, Bobby Thompson was sent to Europe in the army and Mother's second cousin William Clark was sent to the Pacific war zone. We hoped and prayed for them.

I started worrying again when I realized the adults were still worried. The first six months of the war looked grim. On every front the Axis were attacking. Germany controlled France and was hundreds of miles inside Russia. Italy dominated the Mediterranean and was swarming across North Africa to the west, Egypt and the Suez Canal on the East. The Japanese were all over China, and threatened the entire South Pacific region. We poured over the war pictures in *Life* magazine each week trying to make sense of it. I'll never forget a picture of two little kids playing on a temporary teeter-totter attached to the deck of a navy transport ship heading for Pearl Harbor. The picture was taken a few days before the attack but published weeks afterward. I wondered what happened to those kids. I also studied the aircraft silhouette identification pictures of enemy aircraft in case Cincinnati ever came under attack.

Major rationing started in the spring. It was the first aspect of the war to directly affect me. Sugar was first to go. Mother got a ration book each month for sugar and she had complete control over the sweets. I think Dad suffered as much or even more than I did. He loved cakes and pies and the low-sugar victory cakes Mother patriotically served just didn't quite live up to their promise.

I wanted our family to do our part for the war effort but when the Little King enthusiastically embraced the 'Vegetables for Victory' idea I lost some of my enthusiasm. I knew I hated the heat, the bugs and the sneezing and here was Dad planning out a huge victory garden.

I firmly believed a garden should be a nice little plot of vegetables where the adults could entertain themselves while the kids were off doing more important things. Dad had a different idea. That spring of 1942 he planted an acre and a half with no mechanical equipment to plow, furrow or turn under. Harry, Richard and I were the labor. Dad had us plant onions, radishes, carrots, lettuce, tomatoes, corn, string beans, squash, rutabagas, red cabbage, lima beans, pumpkin and asparagus. But he didn't stop there. We already had 12 apple, cherry, pear, and peach trees but he decided we couldn't live without 15 rows of red raspberries. Fifteen prickly painful rows 60 feet long were planted.

For the first time I dreaded the end of the school year. That summer fruits and vegetables were my nightmare. The raspberries were the worst. When they ripened, those seedy little devils produced 30 quarts a day, every day. We couldn't begin to consume that much fruit so we packed them up and sold those supposedly rare little rubies to the local grocery for ten cents a quart. A dime was a humbling reward and an insult to my precious time wasted picking them.

Dad finally hired Harry's brother, Herman, so the two of them could help us with some of the heavy work on Saturdays, but there was still Monday to Friday to live through. In late June Harry received his 1-A draft notice so we knew he only had a few more weeks before he had to report. I could predict how the rest of the summer would run without him so I decided to revolt. One evening I sat down to dinner and announced to everyone present, "Our farm is like a garden of evil."

That started a major lecture. Mother put down her spoon and said, "Bobby, this victory garden is our contribution to the war effort and you are old enough to pitch in. Children in China and Europe would be thrilled to have the food we have."

I knew I couldn't win an argument once hungry children entered the discussion so I resorted to negotiation. "Okay, how many hours do I have to work every day in the heat cutting grass and working in the garden? I haven't had a chance to do anything fun this summer."

"Don't be so lazy." I could tell by the tone in Mother's voice I wasn't going to get out of much. "You have to give me three or four hours a day. No more argument. Eat your dinner." End of discussion.

Even with all our sweat the garden didn't flourish. Every vegetable looked puny. Dad hadn't thought much about the quality of the dirt. When he started the garden he thought dirt was dirt. And then he took to reading about soil. We didn't have soil, we had clay. If I dug a foot-deep hole anywhere in the garden I would create a small orange clay-lined pond that would hold water almost long enough for mosquitoes to take up residence. Any sensible farmer would have started running

Father Versus Son 42

for the bottom lands. Not my daddy. It was one more challenge.

Saturday, July 11, 1942, was the memorable day when I decided never again to do anything with gardening, farming, growing vegetables or enriching the fine earth. Dad decided we had to have manure. Only manure could give us the kind of flourishing victory garden Dad saw in the magazines. He was in high spirits once he hit upon the solution. I think he felt it would turn his garden around just like the war seemed to be turning around for us in the Pacific.

With the victory at Midway, the American people felt the attack on Pearl Harbor had been avenged. The U.S. sunk two Japanese carriers and crippled three battleships and four cruisers. The battle at Midway stopped the Japanese threat to Hawaii and gave everyone a tremendous mental boost. I still didn't understand much of what was happening but I did know we won a major victory and the adults were happy.

Dad, Richard, Harry, Herman and I took off that Saturday for a nearby dairy farm on Dad's open-bed Ford trucks. The Little King was so excited you would think we were off to pick up a load of gold. We pulled up to the Miller Dairy on Galbraith Road and there it was on the left side of the main barn. Twenty tons of hot, smelly, steaming fresh road apples. The odor nearly knocked me flat.

Harry, Bush and Herman

We all grabbed pitchforks, some of us less enthusiastically than others. Everyone except Dad of course, who naturally was the supervisor. We stood in a row at the base of the pile, dug in and slung it over our shoulders up into the truck bed. Since Harry was the tallest and strongest, he took the last position in line. At 6'1" he had bulging muscles on his skinny body and looked just like Lil' Abner in his button-up boots. After an hour of throwing manure I made the mistake of needing a short two-minute rest. I walked around to the opposite side of the truck where I hoped I might find a sliver of shade.

When I wiped the sweat out of my eyes I caught a glimpse of the incoming bomb. Before I could duck or react a full pitchfork of manure hit me square in the face. I yelled like a squealing barnyard pig. Harry rushed to my aid and tried to convince me how sorry he was for the overthrow. Richard was rolling around on the ground shrieking louder than I had ever heard him laugh before. I felt like kicking a little manure his way. Herman used his shirttail to try to clean off my face. I had done more than enough for the war effort that day.

10

The Oyster Uprising (1942)

Helga left us and married Harry before he went to boot camp so we lost one housekeeper and gained another. Ruby was a tall, good-looking redhead with personality and spunk but she couldn't see dirt even if it looked her in the eye.

She did have one big redeeming factor. She was the most amazing mouse catcher I have ever known. Since we didn't have a cat, there were dozens of field mice who found their way in and out of our house, especially in the basement. When it turned cold in late fall, I swear those mice would wait their turn in line just to come in and warm their little backsides around the old coal furnace. Mother was not quite as hysterical about them as she had been in Hyde Park but she still had an execution order out on any who showed themselves upstairs.

Ruby had their number. She would manage to corner two or three of them, take a swipe at one with her left hand, catch it and then take a swipe with her right hand and catch another. It was incredible. They would wiggle around in disbelief as she marched them out of the house down to the creek. She would fling them both up at the same time and they would fly through the air and come down with a splash like little Japanese kamikaze pilots dive-bombing the frogs in the creek.

Ruby's cooking didn't come close to her mouse-catching. Mom tried to get more inventive with her own cooking as the war went on but we weren't very appreciative of her efforts. She loved bread and tried to create endless versions of bread dishes. She would shape it like sticks, roll it into balls, dice it for croutons and even mash a slice in the waffle maker to make a fake waffle. No matter what geometric shape it acquired, it was still just bread.

The worst was bread pudding. For some reason Richard and I both hated raisins and Mom made bread pudding with lots of raisins. We called the raisins 'poonies' and tried everything we could think of to get out of eating the little dried up shriveled bits. Mom knew we didn't like them but she made sure we finished every last bite of that dessert before we got up. She would always say, "See, you can do it if you set your mind to it." I would walk out of the room without answering because I always had a mouthful of poonies tucked under my tongue waiting to be spit out in the backyard.

I put off sitting down to Friday night suppers as long as possible because they involved some sort of non-meat, church-sanctioned food. Plus, I liked to listen to the radio late in the afternoon when *Amos and Andy* came on, followed by *Abbot and Costello*. I loved Bud Abbot; he reminded me of my dad. He always put on an unsuspecting act, but you knew he knew a lot more than Lou Costello.

One Friday afternoon I was lazing around my room listening to my Crosley radio when I caught a whiff of something bad. Pretty soon the whole house reeked with the sour aroma of oyster soup. I hated oysters as much as I hated raisins. Maybe even more.

Ruby called up the stairs, "Get down here, you little shrimp. Dinner's been ready for five minutes and it is getting cold!" I dragged myself down because I knew she would come up and drag me down if I didn't go.

Everyone was sitting around the table eyeing the big bowl in front of Dad. Mom's idea of oyster soup was to mix milk, a little pepper and butter, and a lot of oysters all together and heat it up.

I sat down and considered my options. "None for me, thanks." I thought the politeness angle might work.

"Now, Bobby," Dad replied, "A few weeks ago you ate a big bowl of oyster soup."

"I know. I was a good kid and I shared half my soup with Madge. I gave her the oyster half."

"I don't want your old oysters tonight," she said. She gave Dad a sweet smile. I wanted to kick her under the table.

The Oyster Uprising   46

Bobby, Madge and Richard

Richard turned in his chair and looked out the window. He was never one to argue with or contradict the parents. He turned back in his chair, took a deep breath and announced in his normal polite manner, "There is no way I am eating any part of that mealy mess."

Madge and I looked at each other like the earth had turned upside down. Here was the model child acting like, well, acting like me. Mom's eyebrows reached for the ceiling. Dad decided to take himself out of the battle and see where the chips would fall. They fell hard. Mom made one of her profound statements we had heard before. "You won't leave this table until you finish all the oysters in your soup." Richard sat perfectly still.

I thought I would show my support so when dinner finished an hour later, Richard and I were still sitting there. I was going nuts; I couldn't decide if oysters were worse than sitting still in a chair while life outside beckoned. I looked down in my bowl. There were only three of those slime balls partially submerged in gunk and I decided to be brave. I threw them down quick trying not to think about them. As I got up I heard Richard say, "I'll eat them but I will get sick." I sat back down because I wanted to watch this.

Mom said, "Don't be silly. You won't get sick. Finish them now." Richard gulped the soup down, stood up, and walked around the table to Dad who was hiding out from the struggle by pretending to read the newspaper. Richard started to say something and then he threw up all over Dad's shirt and tie and the newspaper.

The Little King had a royal fit, not at Richard but at Mom. I took off but I heard as I went out the door, "Don't you ever, ever, make them do anything like that again." Thanks to Richard my oyster soup eating days were finished. Now I just needed to convince him to throw up some raisins.

The Provocateurs (1943)

I didn't look forward to the nuns beating the tar out of me, but by the end of the summer it seemed better than the farm. The first day of school I changed my mind when I put on my school uniform. "I can't stand these gray corduroy knickers. They itch. I've been wearing them for four years and they look stupid." I knew I wouldn't get much sympathy from Mom but I had to air my complaints.

"Listen, Bob, next year when you enter the sixth grade they may not require them," Mother answered. That didn't do me much good for fifth grade.

Fabric was already in short supply. The war posters in store windows told us to "Use it up, wear it out, make it do or do without." For growing children it meant wearing clothes that shrunk until you could barely squeeze into them. We did our part to wear things out. After a summer of eating all our delicious homegrown vegetables I could barely get into my last year's' clothes. And on top of the knickers, I had to wear a white shirt and tie. I grumbled my way into my clothes, grabbed my satchel, my roller skates and checked my pockets. One cotton hankie, a key to adjust the roller skates, no money, one bologna sandwich and an apple in a brown paper bag. Mom wouldn't give me any money because she said I didn't need it. Our opinions on that differed but my opinion didn't count for much.

I had forgotten how tough it was to sit still in the same classroom, with the same nun teaching us. The calendar may have said September but in Cincinnati we still steamed like it was August. That old brick school building absorbed the heat of the day until I thought I could imagine we were some of those children in the missionary schools in China the nuns were always running on about. Thirty-nine kids around me wiggled and squirmed and were all itching for twelve noon.

Kenny Hoffman sat behind me. About eleven o'clock he whispered to me, "Bobby, let's jump the back wall at noon and go down to Hyde Park Square for a hamburger."

I could almost taste a hamburger from the diner but then I remembered. "Can't, no money," I whispered.

"Don't matter," he says. "I got two nickels." Two nickels, enough for two hamburgers. I couldn't pass up an offer like that.

We could have walked out of the front playground but that was too visible. The back wall under the trees was more isolated. We strolled casually around the rear of the school and when we rounded the corner took off running. The wooden fence looked like a breeze. We hit it at a run and reached the top. There was a problem. A section of old rusty wire fencing ran all along the top of the wall. I knew the nuns weren't really worried about keeping the enemy out; they wanted to keep their kiddies in. We managed to squeeze our way under.

No problem. We were tough. What were a few scratches on a mission to get a hamburger?

After lunch we headed back to school and savored the lingering taste of fried onions on the hamburger. Kenny was first to go under the wire, then me. Getting through the wire should be easy again; all my clothes fit tight, nothing baggy to snag. They were so tight I was starting to wear them out from the inside. When that tiny metal barb caught the back of the pants a 9" slit popped open and exposed my little white bottom. Kenny looked and said, "Don't matter." He took me down to his locker and fitted me into an old pair of his knickers he wore to play baseball. We went back to class. Sister took one look at me in those dirty pants and I got hit with a hundred-word composition on the topic, "Never neglect your knickers."

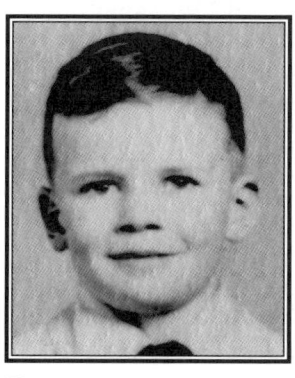

Kenny

I walked out of school at 2:30 PM and said to Kenny, "Does matter."

After school I was supposed to walk two and a half miles to my Grandma's house and wait for Mom to pick me up. The #69 Madisonville streetcar ran the route between the school and Grandma's house but I had no money to ride it. That was the purpose of the roller skates. I tightened the two front clasps around my shoes with the special key I carried and started the journey. After two miles, I lost interest in skating and just happened to be passing in front of my classmate Obie's house. He just happened to be goofing around on the front porch. I stopped to check things out. There was a 20-foot deep gully cut in the rear of his back yard for a single train track that had a great attraction for me.

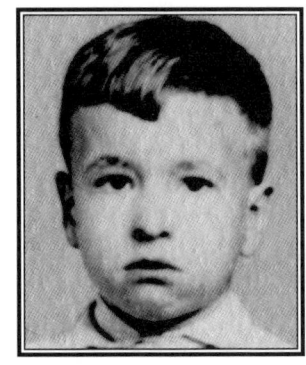
Obie

I took off my skates and the two of us slid down the embankment and walked the tracks till we arrived at a trestle bridge about a quarter mile long and about 50 feet off the ground. We debated whether we should cross it. If a train came and we were caught half way, there was no escape. We decided we could always lie flat on the wooden ties between the rails and the train could pass right over us. No problem. It happened in the movies all the time.

We decided to chance it. There were no distant train sounds. We went on our way pretending to be soldiers sneaking into enemy territory when we heard an old iron horse steam whistle. It sounded pretty close and suddenly we weren't so sure we wanted to attempt a movie stunt. We darted back to the end of the bridge and hid behind some bushes to see what was coming. It was a long, slow local freight and the flatbeds were stacked with truck bodies. We knew it was headed to the GM plant in Norwood where they were assembling army trucks.

I thought if this was Germany and we were saboteurs ready to take out the Nazis' wartime production, we would jump on this train and ride it right into the factory to do our job. Maybe we needed some practice in case the war lasted long enough for us to be drafted. There was a slight curve in

St. Mary's School in Hyde Park

the tracks ahead and soon the engine was out of sight. It was a really long train and we still couldn't see the caboose with the watchman. We looked at each other. I said, "Let's go." We went.

We ran along the gravel next to the tracks. Obie was ahead of me. We each grabbed a three-rung ladder of the side of adjoining boxcars, swung our legs up and straddled the ladder. This did work just like we saw in the movies. We hung there feeling the wind on our faces and the track clicking beneath us. Saboteuring work was easy. We would be ready to do our part when we got to Europe. The train started downhill and began picking up speed. We looked at each other and Obie yelled to get off. An overpass loomed ahead of us. We jumped, rolled, and got a little scraped and dirty. Well, a lot scraped and dirty.

While we were brushing ourselves off we spotted three hobos under the concrete bridge. They had a little fire started and they were heating a large can of Campbell's pork and beans. When they saw us they started to yell, trying to scare us off. I guess they thought we were intruding on their formal dinner party. Then they started to throw stones. They were protecting their pork and beans at any cost. We couldn't let a bunch of hairballs intimidate us so we picked up some gravel and pelted them with a dozen stones.

Those geezers went bonkers and ran towards us. We took

off as fast as we could. Pictures of my parents crying over my crumpled body went through my head. They chased us a hundred yards before they realized they had to make a choice between dinner and a couple of kids. Lucky for us, they chose the beans.

I left Obie at his house and made my way to Grandma's house. Richard was already there sitting on the porch. He looked me up and down but didn't say a word. When Mother pulled up, I hopped in the back seat fast so she couldn't get a good look at me. When I was sure she was focused on the traffic I leaned over the front seat and said, "Mom, which would you rather have happen? I fall out of a big tree or I tear my knickers?

Mom said without thinking, "Naturally, I'd pray that you tore your knickers." She caught on quickly and looked at me in the rear view mirror.

I smiled. "Mom, I think your prayers have been answered."

Blunder Bob (1943)

Our teacher that year should have chosen a different profession. As the year went on she lost more and more control. We came up with one way after another to torment her. The best scheme came close to the end of the school year. Each day a group of us would drop our pencils one by one, up and down the rows. They would hit the floor with a satisfying clatter and bounce around. We varied the time of day and tried to look innocent each time.

Sister did not seem to know how to deal with this. The long school year must have worn down her faculties because she didn't do anything. After a week or so she seemed to be waiting for the pencil dropping and would twitch and jump as if machine guns were about to go off.

The final straw came the day someone left a wiener dog on her desk made from a sausage and some toothpicks. Sister discovered it on her desk after lunch and just seemed to go crazy. It was an amazing sight and the racket brought the principal in to calm things down.

Eventually, I took to noticing a pretty little brunette in class named Maddie. She had been in my class all along but suddenly I couldn't stop admiring her and I decided the time had come to ask her out. Other kids were arranging dates and I didn't want to be left behind. At recess I went up to her on the playground trying to ignore the giggles of her friends and asked, "Would you like to go to Sefferino's Roller Rink Saturday?"

"No thank you," she answered.

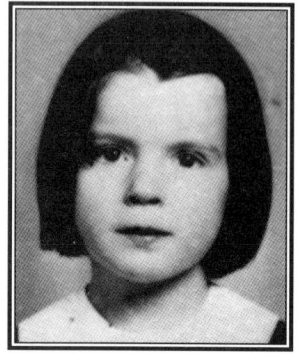
Maddie

"No, you don't want to go or no, you can't go?" I said.

"I can't go," she said. "I have a date with Tony."

I was floored. My little buddy, Tony? He was a shrimp, kind of a funny little guy, but surely no girl would want to roller skate with a midget.

"Where are you going?" Her friends giggled some more.

"He said we are going to a matinee movie downtown. Why?"

"Never mind," I said and tried to walk away like I didn't care.

I went and grabbed Tony by the scruff of his neck. He confirmed the plans and I asked him how he was going to get a ride to go to a movie downtown.

He hadn't thought that far ahead. Fifth graders aren't known for long-term planning. I came up with an instant scheme. "Tell you what, Pal. I'll get my dad to drive and we can take your date to the roller rink." At this point he should have realized this was not a good deal for him.

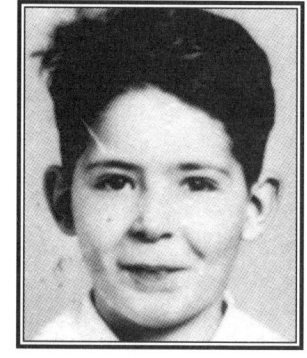
Tony

With that settled my next problem was Dad. How was I going to convince him to give up half his Saturday for three kids?

I waited until after dinner when he was good and relaxed.

"Dad, you know my friend Tony that we call Dodo? Well, he and I are taking Maddie who lives on Mooney Avenue roller skating on Saturday. Will you drive us?"

He said, "They live on Mooney?"

This seemed unimportant to me but I said they did.

"I know them. That's Walter and Madge's daughter. Why, Maddie's mother and I dated years ago."

It was a stroke of luck. He agreed to take us.

Just before the war started, Dad had been lucky enough to purchase a new 1941 four door green Packard sedan. It looked like a big streamlined fat olive toad with four black feet and it made a spiffy taxi for my first date, even if I was sharing it with little Tony.

On the way into Hyde Park to pick up Maddie, I needed to have a long serious talk with the Little King so he wouldn't spoil my date. The first few minutes were crucial to convince Maddie I was the one she should find interesting.

"Heh, Pop, we're going to pick up Maddie first and then swing back to get Tony." He gave me a funny look like he didn't understand the pickup rotation, because he had to double back to do it my way.

I jumped in with more instructions. "Now when she gets in the backseat of the car I don't want you to kid around with her or make any of your jokes. In fact I don't even want you to talk at all or even look at her, O.K.?" I held my breath waiting to see what he would say.

Gene was a great father; he always went along with the gig. "Okay, sport, I won't say a word. I'll be the perfect chauffeur."

We pulled up to her house. I got out of the car and wiped my sweaty hands on my pants. I knocked on the door and was disappointed when Maddie's younger sister, Kay, opened the front door. She was cute, with lots of little blond curls, but she was only a little kid. As I stood there waiting on the front porch I felt like this was an important day in my life. It would take me 15 years to find out why.

Maddie came out, but I was too nervous to look at her. We went down the steps to Dad's Packard and I opened the back door for her. As soon as he heard the rear door close, Gene kept his promise and stayed on his best behavior. He put the car in gear and pulled away. The Packard rolled down the street, my date leaned forward and said, "Pardon me sir, but Bobby didn't have time to get in the other back door and he's still standing back in the street."

The Potato Resurrection

I did manage to have my date with Maddie but things went downhill after that. I knew summer would be bad. Our house was close to nowhere and nobody. I had no money for the streetcar and 'the garden of the dammed' grew right outside my bedroom window.

At dinner a few days after school let out Dad looked at us and beamed. "I know you kids want to make some money, so your mother and I have thought of a way you can learn responsibility and earn $100 each."

I nearly fell out of my chair. A hundred dollars was more money than I could imagine. Visions of a new bike and a Red Ryder B-B gun flashed in front of my eyes. Then I came back to reality. What horrible responsible thing would I have to do to earn that much money?

Mother and Dad sat smiling that sort of parental, 'this is going to be good for you' smile. Dad said, "If you work a full five days a week every week this summer in the garden and cutting grass you will earn one hundred dollars."

I should have known it. There was no escape from the garden. If Adam had been forced to weed Eden he would have begged God to kick him out. I wished I could think of something terrible enough to do for my parents to ban me from their garden.

Naturally, Richard jumped up and shouted "All right!" There was something seriously wrong with that boy. The parents beamed at him and then they looked at me.

Mother said, "You know, Bobby, you have to work three hours every day in the garden anyway. Five more hours a day for a hundred dollars is a good deal. You'd better grab it."

The desire for filthy lucre was taking over. For a hundred dollars I could do anything. I could buy anything, maybe even an electric train. I could go anywhere. Then I remembered the heat and the bugs. "Let me think about it."

I sat back and contemplated my thoughts. This was a huge decision. It meant trading my whole summer for some cash. Both parents were yakking at me from both sides but I didn't hear a word they said. Committing myself to this project meant no more bike trips with my dog, no more splashing in the creek to cool off, and no more just goofing off. I was halfway through my favorite book, *Seckatary Hawkins,* and I wanted to find out if the fat little guy with the clubhouse on the Ohio River would get out of his predicament in the cave and find the treasure. I still had three *Classic Comics* I hadn't even opened. I had my brother's half-finished jitney in the barn and if he wanted to race in the soap box derby we would have to finish it. I had important things to do.

The soap box jitney

"What's it going to be, Robert?"

Whenever Mom called me by my formal name, I knew either she meant business or I was in serious trouble. In this case it was both. I knew I was going to hear a lecture on poor children in some obscure part of the world being grateful for a nickel. I started to feel guilty. Mom and Dad were both good to me and I didn't want to aggravate them. But I just didn't want to do it. I thought I could let them down gently so I said, "Thanks for the offer but I don't think I can this summer.

Maybe next summer."

Dinner ended in a dead silence. The disappointment from the parents oozed out and filled the room. I escaped but the next night it started again. We had barely started to eat when Dad tried another tactic. "Here is an offer you can't refuse, Bobby."

"I hope it's not about the garden, Dad." I thought I would nip this in the bud.

"It is, but don't worry. I think you'll like it. I'm going to buy you boys a few bushels of potato spud seed. We'll give each of you a good plot in the garden and plow the dirt so you can plant the seed. If you take care of the potatoes and harvest them when they are ready, you can keep all the money you get from the sale."

This was starting to sound good. I didn't know what price you could put on a potato but it had to be darn good because everyone ate them. Right? A little warning signal clicked in my brain but I decided to ignore it. This sounded pretty easy. Once those seeds were planted I would just have to do a little weeding, no all day stuff, and then the money would roll in. I would be liquid. I agreed.

Richard and I each planted ten rows fifty feet long. When we were done I was pleased. The garden looked good, the summer was just beginning and the hard work was done. A couple of weeks later the young plants broke through the surface along with lots of weeds.

Dad came out early one Saturday morning to inspect. "You boys better take care of your potato patches or they won't grow," he warned. With visions of the money to come in our heads, Richard and I eagerly plucked out weeds like a couple of rabbits in a carrot patch. Two hours later the pollen, heat and flies were so bad I decided I needed a break. In fact, I decided I needed a break until harvest time.

I went back to bike riding and comic book reading. Soon the weeds became so dense in my patch I couldn't really detect the potato plants. Richard sweated and weeded every day. His area looked like an illustration of the perfect potato patch in an issue of *House and Garden*. Neat straight rows, full of uniform 12-inch tall potato plants with white flower buds.

By the time harvest day arrived, he didn't have a weed higher than an inch. We rented a horse and plow, dug in and turned the taters over and out. We did my patch first and underneath all the weeds my potatoes looked great. I was already spending the money. Dad slapped Richard on the shoulder. "If this lazy kid got this crop, I can't wait to see yours."

When we started on Richard's patch, a bunch of puny golf balls appeared. We kept going and more and more golf balls showed up. Not a single potato large enough to bake. Richard glared at me like we had somehow mixed up the plots. Dad held up examples of each. "Richard, I didn't even think about it but because it was a dry summer, Bob's weeds shaded his plants and yours dried out. You shouldn't have weeded."

I was vindicated. Weeding was a bad thing.

Dad spoiled my glee quickly though. "No problem, boys. We'll still get a decent price for all of them and you can split the money." I just couldn't win.

The Power Peas

Gasoline rationing during the war severely curtailed our vacations. I would rather travel than eat. Give me a choice of bikes, trains, cars, any wheels, or a big steak dinner and you can forget the meal.

I thought my summer was going to be a bust until Mom saved me. She suggested Dad take me with him on his annual trip to the Grand Rapids Furniture Mart. Actually, what she really said was, "Bob is driving me crazy hanging around the house. Take him with you." Mom had another baby, a girl, in February of '43 and I think I was wearing her down. She needed school to start again to keep me out from underfoot.

The painting business that Dad's father started in 1881 evolved into a decorative painting company 20 years later. Homes, theaters, churches, restaurants, steamboats and hotels were all clients of his artistic personnel, who hand decorated with painted murals, stencils, glazing, gold-leafing, or any conceivable effect that would enhance an interior ceiling or wall. It was a natural progression for Dad to introduce decorating with carpets, draperies, and eventually furniture. To keep up on trends, Dad had a good excuse to make a yearly visit to the only central furniture market in the United States at Grand Rapids, Michigan.

Dad's offer to take me was a real hummer. I couldn't wait to get out of town. I packed all my clothes and considered the necessary standard equipment needed for a trip. My old B-B gun was impossible, too obvious. Firecrackers would be difficult to light in a car with the windows down all the time. The

Grandpa and Dad's decorating company

only possibilities were the sling shot and a bean shooter. I didn't use a sling shot much but I decided to take it along as backup. That left the bean shooter. I had been pondering some of the design problems with mine. Maneuvering large, oval-shaped beans into a rubber hose shooter took time and skill and you only got off a few at once. Whole dried peas were the answer. I could put of dozen of those morsels in my mouth and with one mighty blow spray out the whole bunch. I could safely conceal a pea-shooter in my pockets and it would make little or no noise when I blew those missiles through it.

A quick three-mile bike ride to the town of Madeira supplied me with all the goodies for less than a dollar. The hardware store had the hollow rubber quarter-inch tubing and the grocery had a one pound box of Del Monte whole dried peas. I was set.

We left on a Monday morning in the Packard with Dad's friend, Joe. Joe was a minor stockholder in Dad's business but he mainly went on trips with Dad because they had a good time together. They looked like the comics' characters Mutt and Jeff when you saw them together. At 5'4" Dad was Mutt, Joe at 6' made an identical Jeff. Joe even had Jeff's little Hitler mustache on his face but I always thought his head was too small for his towering figure. Even though I thought Joe was a pinhead, he had a good, relaxed attitude about everything.

After a few hours on the road headed north, I had no idea

where we were, and I really didn't care. I read Burma Shave signs until I thought I could make up my own. Some advertising genius in the '20s had come up with the idea of sticking these little red and white signs all over the U.S. to advertise their shaving cream. In series of six signs, each spaced 50 yards apart, you could spend an entire car trip reading a peculiar form of American poetry always ending with 'Buy Burma Shave'. You knew you had been in the car too long when one of them stuck in your head and refused to leave:

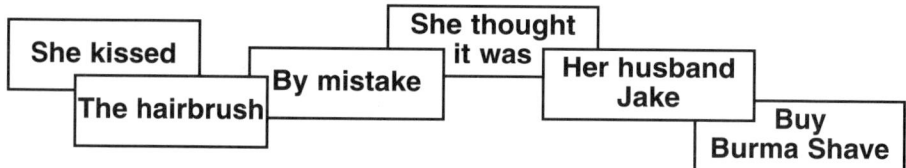

I stopped reading them and sunk to just counting how many signs we passed. I had forgotten how boring it was to ride in the back of a car through the cornfields of the Midwest. The conversation up front didn't interest me and my right hand started to fiddle with the bean shooter.

What was I waiting for? At 55 miles per hour all the windows were down to keep cool and the traffic was moderate. I was ready. Next time we passed some geezer, he would get a pea spray job on his windshield. We came up on a '36 Ford convertible with a guy and his girlfriend out for a leisure ride. I leaned on the edge of the window and put my head down like I was tired. Then I brought the peashooter up and angled it out the window slightly, bracing it on my forearm. We passed and I hit the car with 10 rounds of pea ammo but I missed the windshield and caught the side of the driver's head with a couple of misdirected shots. I hoped maybe he wouldn't feel it because he had such a thick bunch of greasy hair.

Joe and Dad didn't even notice. I crunched down in the back seat, turned around and inched my head up to sneak a peek at the Ford. Bad news. The Ford was weaving from side to side.

A minute later the Ford passed us and gave Dad a bad look. "What's their problem?" Joe asked. Shortly after that pass, they slowed down to 35 mph and Dad was forced to pass them again. I shouldn't have done it but I gave them another pea blast. This time Joe spotted me. He just smirked.

They wouldn't give up though. The convertible cruised by

again with the same foul expression on their faces. Once past they backed off again. My old man was getting agitated and he looked like he wanted to ram that car.

Joe turned around and said, "Gimme that bean shooter and whatever you're shootin'." Dad looked back at me and then at Joe. "What's going on in the back seat?"

"Don't worry about it," Joe said. "Gene, just pass that jerko again." Dad happily obliged, tromping on it and pulled around the guy going full throttle. When we were neck and neck, good ole Joe gave the poor sucker a blast of a whole mouthful right in the guy's kisser. Gads, he couldn't miss, we were only three feet from the guy. The guy probably thought big Joe was some kind of dangerous nutcase, a grown man blowing peas out the window, because after that he slowed down and dropped back until we didn't see or hear from him again. On the other hand, I heard from the Little King and he ordered me to can the peas.

When we arrived in Grand Rapids we checked in downtown at the Pantland Hotel. They were holding only one nice room reservation so I ended up in a crummy little space on the eighth floor by myself. After dinner and a walk we checked in early for a good night's sleep. Since I had done nothing all day but sit in the back of the car, I wasn't ready to go to sleep. I had to get rid of the peas because I promised Dad I would, and when I promised him I kept my word.

The big question was how I could rid myself of them creatively. Dad hadn't given me any specific orders. My window faced a side street and I could see five yellow DeSoto cabs lined up below, waiting for a call from the head honcho at the front door of the hotel. Business was slow. No one wanted a cab at ten o'clock in Grand Rapids. I thought about aiming at them but decided it would be more challenging to attempt a moving target. I emptied the box of peas by shooting at all the other cars and trucks passing below. In a few minutes all I had left was the box.

The cabs below were still at a standstill. Cabby #5 was out of his car and leaning on #4's window in deep conversation. He was certainly a possible target. He stood not only directly under my window but he was huge, bearded and mean looking, kind of like Popeye's archenemy Bluto. I could see his scraggly beard and I was sure he had a squint in his eye.

I filled up the empty pea box with water, took a few extra

rubber bands from my slingshot supply, wrapped them around the newly created water bomb and let her fly. Little droplets of water trailed behind her, shimmering in the glow of the streetlights as the box arced out and then descended. It was a beautiful sight. I held my breath waiting for it to make contact. It came down straight and true and smacked on the shoulder of the elephant man, busting opening and spraying water around. The cabby grabbed his shoulder like a bullet had hit him. He looked down at his wet sleeve as if he expected to see blood spurting from his arm. It scared all the drivers and the rest jumped out and gathered around him. One of them had the presence of mind to start scanning the windows to locate the perp. I drew back slowly away from the window, hoping he hadn't spotted me. My lights were already out so I got in my pj's and hopped in the bed, trying to breathe calmly.

About ten minutes later I could hear two house detectives out in the hall talking and closing doors. I feared my day was here and I shivered in that hot bed. I had seen too many movies where the tough-talking detectives roughed up the little guy in the stairwell. My door opened after a faint knock and with my eyes shut I could feel the glimmer of a flashlight beam pass over my face. I tried to look angelic and asleep and it worked because the door closed. The two mumbled a bit out in the hall but it sounded like I was going to get off scot free. I fell asleep in a cold sweat, thinking I couldn't wait to be back home safe and sound in my own bed.

In Search of Brownie Points

Once we came back from the Grand Rapids trip, I was still faced with a long, long summer. The mosquitoes that year were fruitful and multiplied, and the 17-year locusts emerged to keep them company. The cicadas crawled out of the ground and up into the trees, clinging in lumpy masses to the branches, rubbing their hind legs together to create a brain-numbing, shrill racket. Sometimes they would fly around to find a less crowded tree but locusts must be blind because if you were standing in their way they would fly right into you.

Watching their ugly brown bodies zinging around the yard gave me a better understanding of the poor Egyptians in the Bible when they had their own plague of locusts. The worst part of our affliction was they loved the sound of the lawn mower. To them the hum of the motor must have sounded like one big 'king bug' calling his subjects because each time that engine started, those creatures swarmed it. I thought it was pretty funny the first time I saw Richard outside jumping around in some sort of Indian war dance, swatting away as little brown creatures tried to perch on him. It wasn't so funny when it was my turn on the mower.

Mom came through again in August when she signed me up for camp. Fort Scott Camp saved the summer for many Cincinnati parents. Fifteen miles northwest of the city was close enough to go pick up a sick child in an emergency, but far enough away to make the kids feel like they were on a wilderness adventure.

When the big day arrived I was tingling with excitement

and nothing could discourage my upbeat attitude as we approached the camp. The car bumped across the small iron bridge spanning the Big Miami River. The murky waters revealed a few abandoned beer bottles and a recently deceased raccoon but it didn't dampen my spirits.

Dad said, "You know I never went to camp, Bobby, but it sounds like you are going to have one fine time. Baseball every day, new friends, what more could a fellow want?" Dad was right; I felt kind of sorry for him because he had to go back to boring old grown up things.

After we unloaded my gear, Dad shook hands with the camp director and then clapped me on the shoulder. "Have a good time, Sport. I'll see you in two weeks." I was so excited to get started on the camp life, I didn't even look back at him as he walked away.

A flagpole stood in the center of camp, surrounded by 20 cabins that held eight boys each, a dining hall, a barn for handicrafts, a dorm for the high school counselors, a swimming pool down the hill and a 15-holer set behind the cabins. Not a 15-hole golf course, but an outhouse for rustic campers.

I quickly learned the main challenge of Fort Scott. If a kid accumulated 100 points he received the epitome of camp life, a beanie. Normally I wouldn't have given a hoot about a beanie cap but somehow confined to those woods without my normal distractions, a beanie cap seemed to be the pinnacle of my desires. You could instantly recognize those who were the camp superstars by their brown beanies with a red stripe. Some kids stayed at camp all summer so they had ample opportunity to earn a beanie. This was obviously unfair because us regular campers had only two weeks to win points.

I set about pondering the system. It took 100 points to get a cap and points were given for excellence in all phases of camp life from cleanliness to sports. I felt sure I could accumulate some points for things like baseball but I knew I would have to scramble to get the magic 100. There was no way I was leaving camp without a beanie.

Each morning after reveille our cabins were inspected. The cleanest cabin in the camp got to be honor cabin of the day and all its inhabitants received five points. Usually we scrambled to hide comic books and dirty socks under pillows and blankets to get the place looking shipshape. I did a pretty good job of keeping my bunk area clean but my cabinmates weren't as concerned about gaining points. A piece of a candy wrapper was enough to doom the whole cabin. One of kids, Clyde Sims, caused the most trouble. He had a secret stash of Aunt Janes, peanut butter flavored candy in yellow wrappers.

Every night after lights out he would pull out a handful and quietly try to open the wrappers. The sound of that paper rustling and the slow slurping like a cow chewing cud nearly drove me berserk. I would lay in the dark picturing the wrappers gently falling like new snow around the bunk, piling up in drifts, sure to cost us the honor cabin award. Each morning we would gather up handfuls of those wrappers but one or two always escaped our notice, but not the sharp eyes of the inspection team.

Every day we swam, learned archery and made Indian headbands but even at camp we weren't able to forget the war. The second week of camp two army officers on leave came to teach us to march. Everyone at home thought the war would be over long before we were old enough to be drafted but at Fort Scott they acted like it was a junior boot camp. The officers grouped us in small platoons and immediately started shouting marching orders: "To the right flank, march, to the rear, march."

Until that moment most of us could have told our left side from our right side, but when some angry-looking guys started barking at us we fell apart. We bumped into each other and stumbled over blades of grass and clods of dirt. Every time a boy got his feet crossed up or missed a command, he was yanked out of line until there were only six of us remaining. We were put through ever more rigorous steps by the captain until I was drenched in sweat. It got down to me and one fellow named Timmy. I was short but Timmy was downright scrawny. He reminded me of one of those greyhound dogs, all bones, shivering with the fear of being noticed. I wasn't so crazy about being noticed at that point either. The captain shouted "To the left-flank" and I turned right. That was it. I was out. Timmy got named a sergeant while I was stuck with the rank of corporal.

I was now ten points shy of my dream and desperate. Two days before camp ended we were ushered into the screened-in dining hall along with the same black hovering mass of mosquitoes that seemed to follow me everywhere I went and slept. The head counselor, Michael, got everyone's attention after three minutes of screaming. Michael was the perfect counselor, always with whistle ready to blow, rocking up and down on the balls of his feet, ready to order somebody to do something. "There will be additional points awarded for courageous performance in a series of individual sports championships." The room buzzed. "Who wants to participant in a horseshoe championship?" Sixteen hands went up and his assistant wrote all the names down on a clipboard. "Now how about archery?" Twenty hands went up. "Now who wants to get into the tennis championship?" No hands went up. I figured, what the heck, if I'm the only one in it I can't lose. I threw up my right arm.

Michael pointed in my direction and said, "O.K, I have two tennis players over here." I spun around just to see some tall skinny kid bring his arm down. The die was cast, but at least I made the finals of the championship. I was sure I could get enough points.

After the signup we stayed to enjoy a camp meal of sauerkraut, baked beans and German sausages all washed down with a big glass of red Kool-Aid. The sauerkraut looked a little grayish but I was so hungry I ate everything. I felt like my pump was primed with good food to give me the energy I would need for the next day's battle on the court. We sang our camp songs and went to bed. I woke up about an hour later. All of the sudden I felt a suspicious gurgle in the depths of my stomach and could sense a volcano of molten sauerkraut and beans about to explode.

I wasn't alone. It was a depressing scene to see all the guys fighting their way out to the privy behind the cabins. It was an even further challenge to the intestinal endurance of 160 campers to wait, jump, and holler for their turn at the 15-holer. They should have awarded points for patience.

The next morning I met my tennis partner 'Skinny Jimmy' on the championship court. I thought I felt bad but when I looked at Big Jim, I saw he was pale and had bigger sauerkraut problems than me. He was so dehydrated; a strong wind could have blow him off the court or into the net. We played a painful game; slow motion tennis on a court that expanded to the size of a football field. The locusts zinged around faster than the balls.

After the match as I dreamed of my beanie Jimmy said, "Congratulations on winning, Bob. I hate to lose and I'll remember this for a long time." Jimmy was a nice guy but I had this strange feeling. I felt good about winning the battle but sometime in the future I might lose the war.

Tennis at Fort Scott Camp

16

Four Minus Two Equals Four

While I loafed through the summer the parents brooded over my education, or rather, the lack of it. They rapidly came to the conclusion I wasn't living up to my potential at St. Mary's. I didn't know if I had much potential, because the ability to blow peas out of a moving car and hit a target didn't seem to count for much in the adult scheme of life. Plus, I thought things were going pretty well. I had lots of friends, the nuns were manageable and in the fall I would see Maddie again.

Unfortunately, Mom and Dad focused on a school named Summit. It had a reputation as a highly disciplined school and worst of all, the boys and girls inhabited separate classrooms with any contact strictly regulated. I didn't want to go but like most children of the time I didn't have a say, so in September off I marched.

The grounds of the school impressed me, because the smooth green athletic fields and the oak trees shading the buildings gave it the appearance of a small college campus. The sprawl was in luxurious contrast to the cramped classrooms and small concrete play yard at my other school. The main building, built of brick and stone, had five stories and looked vaguely exotic to my eyes, like it came straight out of France or some other far away European place.

The first day passed in a jumble of details and new rules. I had four bright male teachers and one wonderful nun, Sister Mary Lucille. The Headmaster and football coach, Mr. Werner, was a big, broad, tough disciplinarian, but at least he was rumored to have a good sense of humor.

After classes ended I walked to the front of the school to wait for my bus. The one major advantage I had discovered so far was Summit's bus service. I wouldn't have to walk to Grandma's and wait for a ride home. The buses lined up behind the boys' school, loaded up and proceeded around to the front of the campus to collect the girls. I waited. As each shiny new blue Studebaker bus filled and passed us, I fully anticipated the next ultramarine chariot would be mine.

"Wait, boys, and stand back, this next bus is yours," said Sister Helen, who among other things was the official director, dispatcher and dictator of the school's bus system.

An old 1934 Packard limo pulled up.

I said "What bus?"

"Don't get smart, Mister. You will ride in the front seat." I didn't know whether to laugh or cry, but I certainly was amazed. The chrome and the black paint were in good shape but the car itself, with its two side mounted tires, reminded me exactly of one of Joseph Goebbel's Gestapo cars.

I climbed into the front seat next to my new classmate, Dick, who sat next to the driver. Two other boys climbed in the back but I was too busy looking around to notice them. I ran my hand over the mohair upholstery and the sleek rosewood trim not believing this was really a bus.

As we drove around to pick up the girls, Dick and I started to get acquainted with our driver, Mr. Castelluccio. Lots of refugees were flooding into the larger cities in the U.S. and he seemed like a recent arrival. His black suit and black cap gave him a European look that went with the school and the car. He wasn't young – about my dad's age at least – and I knew he was from the old country because he didn't speak much English and seemed nervous as hell. Maybe it was his first day as a bus driver.

We stopped at the girls' school and the rear suicide doors opened. An unknown nun climbed in first. I guess she was going to tell the driver how to get around town. Besides the front and rear seat, there were two fold-up seats in the middle. The girls streamed in.

I craned my neck around. "Where in the world are all these people going to sit?"

"You'll see," Dick said.

"This thing is starting to look like a black sardine can."

"And we aren't loaded yet."

The heat quickly built up as the sun hit the top of the car and the mohair itched like I was sitting on the original goat. The seats let off wafts of what smelled like ancient cigar smoke and some sort of strong alcohol. I began to wonder if some former student turned bootlegger had donated the car to the school.

New buses line up at Summit School.

"Just how long does this trip take?" I asked Dick.

"For you and me, an hour." He settled back and crossed his arms. I thought about a nice walk to Grandma's house.

The doors slammed shut. I counted 23 sardines. I already missed hopping trains in the afternoon. It was going to be a long, boring ride. I glanced at Dick again. He had dark curly hair, a rectangle-shaped head and kind of a scowl on his face. I wasn't sure if he and I would hit it off.

Dick jabbed me with his right elbow and signaled me to watch him. He opened his hand to reveal a bunch of gumdrops; then he shoved them in his mouth and chewed for about 20 seconds. Casually, he pretended to wipe the sweat off his face while ejecting the gummy mess into his hand. He turned and gave me a grin I will never forget.

By now, Mr. Castelliccio was quite busy figuring out which way to turn, up-shifting, braking, down-shifting, and struggling with both arms to maneuver the ancient auto. He made a hard left onto Madison Road and needed more power so he down-shifted to second. As soon as he put his hand back on the wheel, Dick's arm crept out and placed that slimy glob on top of the floor-mounted gearshift knob.

I watched it, fascinated. Pinkish-green iridescent goo oozed down over the knob like a tiny jellyfish searching for saltwater. It was just about to slide off when Mr. C. got up to speed, firmly grabbed the knob and shifted to third. His hand stayed comfortably on the knob. My heart beat faster. Now what? A right hand turn was coming; he downshifted back to second and tried to take his hand off the stick shift. It happened. And that's when he realized he had something awful stuck to his hand. He tried to shake it off and swerved, narrowly missing a telephone pole.

"Mama Mia," he yelled, just like Italians in the movies.

The poor man took his left hand off the steering wheel to try to remove the stuff. The car snaked down the road in the absence of any attention. The girls began screaming and the nun called out, "What's going on up there?"

This was the first of many times I would see Dick invent an answer to a tough question. He put one hand on the steering wheel and steered while Mr. C. threw the sticky mess out the window. "Nothing, Sister. I think there was a bee in the car but it's gone now."

Mr. C. took over the steering wheel and gave us a quick sideways glance like he had the devil's own children in the car. I could see the whites of his eyes as they rolled around in their sockets before he turned back to watch the road. I guess he needed that job pretty bad because he didn't say a word.

The next day we stood outside waiting for our bus. I could tell Dick would shape up to be an interesting friend but I was a little worried how far he would go.

"Let's face it, Dick, that was pretty funny yesterday but we owe Mr. C. He didn't get us in any trouble and his hands are probably still shaking. The main problem here is too many fricken kids in that bus. I don't want to be stuck in that thing all year."

"I have a great new plan. Maybe we can eliminate some students from the bus."

"Now you're talking. Who will be the lucky ones?"

He lowered his voice. "The two biggest guys take up the most room and that's Mike and his brother, Tank." He motioned to two boys standing about ten feet away. They were definitely large, very large, army tank large, with matching chubby cheeks.

We kicked around some ideas but couldn't come up with anything that didn't involve getting in a lot of trouble. We more or less forgot about the problem until a week later when we loaded into the bus but no nun appeared to supervise. I guess she'd decided Mr. C. knew the route and that the bus was too crowded to leave room for any real trouble. On this trip Dick and I shared a middle fold-up seat built for one. When we left the grounds the noise level started to climb. I liked girls but a bunch of them stuffed in a car all chattering away about who said what was enough to get on any man's nerves. We were about two miles from Mike and Tank's house when an idea flashed in my head.

"Dick, I've got it!" I whispered.

"Got what? Speak up. I can't hear you."

"Listen, it's about Mike and Tank so keep it down." They were sitting in the back seat together, quietly, as if someone had shut them off for the ride. They had turned out to be nice enough guys, but it didn't matter. We had to be ruthless.

"We want to get rid of them, here's the plan. You and I get everybody in here all stirred up and crazy making noise. It will drive Mr. C. bananas. Then I'll show you the rest."

In the next few minutes we laughed, poked and joked until everyone was whooping and hollering. Mr. C. hunched down his shoulders and drove grimly on. As soon as the two brothers climbed out of the car, I passed the word for everyone to clam up. "Everyone be quiet now so Mr. C. thinks it's Mike and Tank."

We brought the car under noise control. An innocent silence fell among the remaining students as if we all were a bunch of Pollyannas who would never dream of creating a commotion.

The next day we repeated the whole routine. Mike and Tank sat in the back looking bewildered, and when we got to their house they scrambled out to get away from us. But it was the storm before the calm for the two big guys. Now that everyone was in on the joke it was harder to keep quiet because they all wanted to whisper about it. I could see Mr. C. was starting to think some bad thoughts about those brothers.

The next afternoon when our limo arrived at the girls' school, Sister Helen was waiting for us. She had a stone face that day to rival some of the statues of martyrs in the church.

I had never noticed quite how large she was. She had to top out at six foot at least. The right rear door flew open. Sister Helen grabbed the two brothers and in one jerky swoop had them flying out of the back seat before they knew what hit them. She took one in each hand by the back of their necks and shook them until I thought the buttons would fall right off their shirts. She looked like she was shaking two giant bulldogs. Their cheeks wobbled back and forth and I almost expected them to growl.

Mike and Tank were normally well-behaved guys who never got in trouble. They didn't know what to do. The sister stood there and gave them another shake, expecting a confession. Mike mumbled, "We, ah, er, didn't do anything, Sister."

"You call being a troublemaker nothing? You call practically inciting a riot nothing? Even nice Mr. Castelluccio says you two are responsible for all the noise and misbehaving on the bus." In her fury she gave them one more good shake. "Now, I'm telling you two for the last time, if it ever happens again, you're off and out for good. You'll have to find your own way to school. Now get back in there."

Mike and Tank looked at each other in total confusion as they climbed back in the limo with their tails drooping. I gave Dick a little punch and thought after this day we would have them out.

At the last minute, Sister Mary crowded in behind them and plopped down. "Good afternoon, children. I understand we are having problems keeping quiet on this bus. I will endeavor to help you remember how young ladies and gentlemen behave." She added brightly, "Perhaps we should use this time to reflect on our many blessings compared to the suffering going on in the rest of the world."

Now we had a chaperone no one wanted and she took up a lot of room. Nineteen pairs of eyes glared at us, surely wishing us in Purgatory. Luckily for Dick and me, no one told on us.

I sighed. "It was wishful thinking, Dick," I whispered.

He nodded. "Yeah, chalk that one up to experience. We'll just have to work out another plan."

17

Saturday Morning Mudball Club (1944)

I adjusted pretty quickly to this so-called sissy school. I got my ears trimmed back in the class boxing program and my fanny kicked nine ways sideways in football. For our first game with Cincinnati Country Day School, I started at center. I was glad they had recognized my potential so quickly. The opening kick-off ball hit me in the chest and it bounced back up and right into a Country Day linebacker's arms. After he caught it, I ran over to tackle him but tripped and tasted mud. The headmaster booted me out for the remainder of the game.

But even though failures in the sports area mounted rapidly, I did make some great friends. Besides Dick, I met a fellow classmate nicknamed Hap. Apparently, he had been such a happy kid from day one, his mother nicknamed him and it stuck. I knew right away he could be counted on for some fun. He and Dick were best buddies and had the same mindset. He was also Maddie's first cousin and I thought he could make sure she heard a lot of good things about me at family gatherings.

The best part of the new school year was to be invited to Dick or Hap's house for the weekend or invite them to my house. One Friday night Hap invited us both over. We played a little ping pong after dinner, and then Hap played a few tunes on the piano for his 85-year-old Grandma, Annie. After Hap's 20-minute concerto, we went up to his room to read comics and play with his brown, shorthaired Airdale, Nifty. Nifty was a good dog who didn't seem to mind being tossed around by two kids. In the fracas we put a rubber band on his tail and forgot about it. He didn't complain.

Saturday morning we woke to the sound of gunshots. I could hear Hap's mother raising hairy hell, which was surprising because she was normally a sweet, quiet lady who didn't complain about things. She sounded a lot more mad than scared. We jumped out of bed to see the excitement and tracked the shots to the bathroom. This was turning into a good weekend. We never had gunshots in the house at home. Hap didn't seem worried so I followed him down the hall.

Hap's dad was a large man and the son of a preacher from Tennessee. He stood in the doorway of the bathroom with a 22 pistol, aiming and firing at some villain. Hap's mom stood next to her husband screeching in his ear. We peered around the corner and saw it. A crazed squirrel with a wild look in his eyes dashed around the bathroom. I've never seen a squirrel run across a ceiling but that thing ricocheted around as fast as the bullets. Hap's dad managed to nick the corner of the sink but as far as I could tell the squirrel was uninjured.

The window stood wide open but the fact that a southern gunslinger was shooting at him must have confused the little guy, because the squirrel couldn't seem to see the opening. Finally he got a lucky break. He was dashing across the window ledge making for the bathtub when he lost his footing and fell out the window. We heard him scrambling down the roof as if he knew he was escaping from a guest of honor place in a squirrel pie.

Hap's dad went over and leaned out the window to try one last shot but Hap's mom yelled, "Don't you dare! The neighbors have probably already called the police." He reluctantly pulled his arm back in. I hoped the squirrel would stick to trees after this.

Hap's mom was looking pretty upset. Her face got redder and more scrunched up as she took stock of the war damage in her bathroom. It didn't seem likely she would make us some pancakes anytime soon. Hap grabbed Dick's arm. "I think we should get out of here," he whispered. We took off back to his room, threw on our clothes, and escaped.

We stopped on the front porch and watched it rain. "What should we do?" I asked.

"Let's go up on the White Cliffs of Dover and heave a few mudballs." In the early 1900's men and machinery made a deep 40' cut in a hill to level out Erie Avenue. Up on top of these miniature cliffs you could stand and take perfect aim at the autos and the streetcars. Timing was everything. It was like throwing a football pass to a moving target. After a lot of misses, we had a few direct hits and the splats were nice and satisfying. In about 15 minutes we heard police sirens coming down Erie. They were either headed to a fire or after us. We decided there was only a slight chance they were after us but to play it safe, we disappeared down the neighborhood back paths.

Dick and Hap were best friends

Hunger drove us back to Hap's house. As we came down the hill, we stopped dead in our tracks. A black car with dual spotlights was parked in front of Hap's house. "It can't be for us," I said. "They didn't even come up on the cliffs. The neighbors must have complained about your dad's shooting."

As we got closer we could see the cop talking to Hap's dad. "Do you think he is going to handcuff him?" I asked. That would make my weekend.

"I don't know. He might be here because of us. Let's duck out back until he leaves."

Five minutes later he was gone and we casually strolled in the kitchen door. Hap's dad came in and stood with his hands on his hips. At least he had put away the 22. "Y'all the dumbest three harebrained youngsters I ever did come across."

"What happened, Dad?" Hap asked innocently.

"I'll tell you little runts. That policeman who was just here chased y'all over the cliffs and you didn't even know it. He must have gotten a description and an address because he came right down here to find you. I swear to God I can't understand you three. If you are going to throw a mud ball at a police car you better learn to run faster."

Right then and there I knew Hap's dad was a kindred spirit. That was exactly what I would have liked my dad to say. He and the Little King could be friends just like us.

That afternoon we walked about two miles over to the Oakley Movie Theater. We loved war movies, especially the ones where the GIs shot down or blew up the enemy so we were excited to see *Guadalcanal Diary.*

Two months previously the mayor of Cincinnati had dedicated a new program for the collection of scrap metal in the war effort. The neighborhood movie houses agreed to provide a location to drop off scrap metal and to give out free matinee tickets to anyone bringing in a large donation. When we arrived at the theater there was a pile of metal at least eight foot high. We tossed in the bags of tin cans Hap's mother had given us and went in even though we were a half-hour early.

A live kiddie talent show was about to begin. Local gifted child expert Harris Rosedale stood on stage acting as M.C. A few mothers and grandmothers sat up front, but the rest of the theater was empty except for Hap, Dick and me.

Mr. Rosedale flipped the switch on a turntable, carefully laid down a '78' record and turned up the sound. He ushered the first little girl on center stage to begin her version of the Bo-Peep Ballet. The second child came out with a tabby cat on a leash and they both did flips, the cat needing some extra coaxing to exert himself. The next contestant sang *Auf Wiederseh'n Sweetheart.* Considering she had a mouth full of braces she did a decent job in German. The one boy in the show came out with a purple ukulele and sang *The Banjo's Back in Town.* I hoped they would choose a winner soon because I didn't think I could stand much more talent.

The final little girl waddled forward to Harris's microphone. Mr. Rosedale announced, "Our final act in the competition will be Irma Sue who will sing and tap to *Yankee Doodle Dandy*". The record started and the pudgy little miss curtseyed and bounced into her routine. Fifteen seconds later she was in trouble. Her rhythm didn't match the rhythm of the song and the floor was slick enough that her tap shoes kept sliding out from under her. I felt sorry for her. She pasted on a brave smile and kept going. Finally, the music ended and she gave another curtsy.

Mr. Rosedale lined up the five contestants. He explained, "When I raise my hand over the performer's head, you may applaud according to their abilities and the person with the most applause will be our winner. I leaned over to Dick and Hap, "Are you thinking the same thing I am thinking?"

They nodded and Dick said, "There are so few people here I think we can pull it off." We sat silent through the first four entries. When he put his hand over Irma Sue's head we went nuts. We clapped, whistled, stomped our feet and made cat call noises. The mothers and grandmothers turned and glared at us.

Harris walked up to the mike, adjusted the height and said, "I am happy to announce our new winner. Miss Irma Sue!" We felt we had done a good deed for the day but since the movie was about to begin the theater filled up quickly for the main attraction. The Pathe war news came on first to give us our only visual explosive action shots of the Pacific and European struggles. The Disney cartoons always followed the war news. It was the perfect time and Dick whispered, "Follow me."

The three of us loved fireworks so when Dick pulled out a one-inch firecracker in the men's room we eyed it happily. Our minds worked together. Dick reached in his pocket and extracted a bent up cigarette he had filched from his dad. By sticking the fuse in the tail end of the cigarette we knew we had quite a while before it burned down enough to ignite the fuse. He lit the cigarette, placed it behind the door and we strolled casually back to our seats.

I was just settling in when a loud pop resounded from the men's room. General disarray and confusion followed as bewildered ushers scurried about for answers.

Since no one came forward to claim responsibility, the movie restarted and all was forgotten in the blasts and explosions on the screen as the Army Air Force got a direct hit on a Japaniese fuel depot.

Five months later, the rubber band did its work and the dog's tail fell off.

Double Whammy 1945

The war ended more quickly than we ever imagined. Everyone thought it would take at least another year of heavy fighting to take Japan, so when President Truman announced Japan's surrender after the two atomic bomb attacks, our country went wild.

WKRC in Cincinnati held microphones out their studio windows so those of us out in the sticks could hear the bells and whistles of the people celebrating in the streets in downtown. Workers ripped up paper and threw it out the windows of the Carew Tower to make a confetti shower for the people dancing below. I wanted to be there but no one volunteered to take me and I didn't think my bike would make it all the way.

Like the rest of American kids, I had lived so long with the war in the background I had a tough time remembering when it wasn't happening. I didn't know what it meant for us but since the parents were happy I was happy too. Plus, more immediate to my life was the fact that the end of the war coincided with our annual vacation to northern Michigan. Normally, it was the hands down, absolute best time of the year for me and the end of the war added an extra bit of excitement. We had all been in a feverish sweat of August anticipation, both literally and figuratively, of the trip to the Portage Point Inn. The biggest problem was saving enough gas rationing stamps to get us there for the 1000-mile round trip.

Dad took care of his responsibilities. He delegated me to clean up and simonize our pea green '41 Packard. His other job was worrying about the tires. You couldn't buy tires during the war so he prayed the old re-capped tires would hold up through the trip.

Mom's job was the packing. The little King told her she was the best packer from Cincinnati to Green Bay. She believed him. She could roll, fit and stuff more clothes in a two-suiter than Lowell Thomas could jam in his world traveler four-suiter. Her problem was she packed a clean shirt and underwear for every one of the 16 days plus the required coat and tie attire for dinner. The packing ordeal started three weeks before the trip when she crammed her mother's old steamer trunk full of duds for herself and the big guy. That was hauled off to the B&O train station and would be waiting in their room in Michigan when we arrived.

The big day of departure arrived. Richard and I shared the back seat with my sister Madge, the lunch cooler, two bags of sweaters and a box of 25 *Life* magazines, 20 comic books and five *True Romance* beauties. My baby sister Conky was two and a half years old and sat up front with Mom and Dad. Mom was 4 months pregnant with her fifth child and seemed a little frazzled. It never occurred to us that going on a long car trip with four kids in an unairconditioned car might be a little wearing on a pregnant woman's nerves. The rest of us were upbeat and Dad was raring to go.

We took off down Blome Road and our worst fears came true. The car hunkered down and bounced off the axle every time we hit a slight sway in the road. The springs were compressed to the limit with the combination of bodies and luggage and we realized we were in for a bumpy ride. The King was ready to croak but he knew better than to criticize Mom's heavy packing. We had notions of going back home, but Dad, optimistic as ever, said "Wait 'til we get on the main Route 22. It might smooth out" and it did.

Four hours and two pit stops later we stopped at an official Ohio State Picnic Area, which consisted of one picnic table under a maple tree ten foot from the edge of the road. As the cars and trucks went racing by we were given our choice of chicken or peanut butter and jelly sandwiches and Neihi orange soda. The best part about lunch was when it was over. I don't know what was worse, the dust and flying gravel from the traffic, or the heat and flies.

I wanted to be on the road again and on our way. The

thought of two weeks without chores and parents who were going to ease up a bit on watching my behavior was great. Back in the Packard, I got hot and sluggish and kicked the back of Dad's seat for entertainment, even after he told me five times to "knock it off or I'll knock your head off." We slowed down, stuck behind a sheep truck. Mom suggested a really exciting game of counting cows. This has to be one of the stupidest games ever invented. Cows are not all that interesting. Since they all look alike it felt like you were counting the same cow over and over, and some farmer kept moving it down the road ahead of us.

Some of my friends who spent time in the country had told me all about cow-tipping, but I was never fortunate enough to have the opportunity. Supposedly, if you snuck up on a sleeping cow and pushed gently on its side it would fall right over. I didn't think I could get Dad to stop while we tried it out so I didn't bother to suggest it.

A few more miles into southern Michigan and things began to liven up and get interesting when Dad got agitated at the slow traffic. He tried to pass a farmer's slow chicken coop truck four times before he gave up. The flying feathers were bad enough but the droppings weren't dropping. They were getting swooshed up in the highway air currents and coming to roost on our windshield. Dad brought out some four-letter 'King's English' words I had only seen written on walls. Fortunately the pig truck we followed through the next town was short-lived. The heat, kids squawking, bladders ready to burst, boredom, and everything else blended together for the family car trip. I loved it. We were on vacation.

We stopped in Grand Rapids at the Pantland Hotel. I swore to myself that this time I would stay out of trouble at the hotel. I hadn't even packed a pea-shooter. We hit Grand Rapids at the right time. The day had been designated as the official V-J day of celebration even though people had been celebrating all week. It was an exciting surprise to see the main streets blocked off and the swelling crowds directly around our downtown hotel.

After dinner the manager let us out on the front balcony to watch the crowds. We had one of the best seats in America. By 9:00 PM there were thousands milling about cheering, drinking and all having the best time of their lives. Conga lines snaked around as people broke out dancing and every-

V-J celebration in downtown Grand Rapids. Pantland Hotel is in the background.

one seemed to have a bell or a whistle. I wanted to be down there with them in the worst way but I knew it was a no go.

I roamed around the balcony and found a roll of thin wire in the corner, probably left by the house electrician. I started to fool with it and decided it would probably reach the sidewalk. Nobody noticed me because they were all too busy watching the crowds so I had the leisure to ponder what to do with the find. I leaned over the rail and spotted a big, bald guy standing directly under us leaning his back against the hotel with his hands in his pockets. He was a tempting target. I thought about tickling the top of his head with the wire but was afraid he would figure out what was going on. He had this enormous cigar sticking straight out of his chompers like he was smoking a torpedo.

I couldn't stay away from the cigar. I made a small loop in the wire and carefully lowered it a few inches from the top of his head. When the moment was right, I swung the wire outward, lowered it in the same motion, hooked his cigar and gave the wire a quick yank. The sparks flared, the cigar went flying and this guy thought some mysterious tornado just hit him. He never did figure out how that lit-up smoke exploded out of his teeth. I decided not to press my luck and stayed out of trouble for the rest of the evening.

We arrived at the Portage Point Hotel the next day. It was a large old wooden hotel built at the turn of the century with a big front porch full of mothers and grandmothers in rocking chairs. Steamboats from Chicago, Milwaukee and other points south brought guests who didn't want to drive. We kids ran free until dinner time and then after dinner we went out again on our own. It was perfect.

I quickly found a new friend, Wally, and we roamed around together. The place to hang out at night was called the 'Casino', located next to the hotel. It was as far from the casinos of Monte Carlo as you could get. There were no tuxedos or beautiful girls. The main attractions were a ping pong table,

Portage Point Inn

a juke box, a dance floor and a bar with a strong smell of spilled beer. The juke box played Duke Ellington, Glenn Miller, Benny Goodman and Count Basie all night long and I couldn't think of any other place I'd rather be.

That first night the only girl in the place was a Chicagoan named Tammy. Wally and I introduced ourselves and took turns jitterbugging with her. Tammy was a large girl with blond hair and enough make-up to go on stage. If you squinted a lot she faintly resembled a young Betty Grable. Well, maybe not, but when you are 13 dancing with a 16-year old, she looked like a dream to me. She kept flipping her hair back and giving me a look that scared the wits out of me. I thought she was a little too aggressive for my own juvenile taste but then what did I know? Not much, I soon found out.

We all sat down at a table and had a coke. I couldn't think of anything witty to say and Wally just sat there like a kid slurping up every last drop in his coke bottle.

Tammy leaned close to us and said in a low voice, "You guys ever kiss a girl?"

My throat constricted with total disbelief and amazement. I thought about bluffing but then I knew I couldn't even get a word out so I just shook my head 'no'. I glanced over at Wally and thought his eyes were going to pop. He shook his head too.

"Tell you what, I'll teach you guys to kiss but you gotta promise to keep your hands off me, you know what I mean?"

This time our heads bobbed so fast up and down they must have looked like they were on a spring. My first rational thought was that my mother would kill me if she caught me. We would have to be careful.

I managed to squeak, "Where should we go?"

"My dad's Hudson is parked across the street in the hotel lot. I'll only teach you guys one at a time. Soon as you learn how, you're out and the other gets in the car."

Wally got out a nickel, called heads in midair and lost. I won and my heart started thumping, trying to break out of my chest. We all strolled out of the Casino towards the parking lot, Wally and I trying to saunter along casually looking like nothing was going on, bumping into each other and tripping over the gravel.

Luckily the lot was out of sight of our rooms and pretty far away from the Packard. I hoped Mom would be too occupied with putting my sisters to bed to worry about me. Tammy and I got in the car and I quickly locked all four doors, in case Tammy changed her mind. Wally stood outside resembling a kicked dog and since he was killing the mood, I rolled down the window a crack and said, "Wally, get lost for about 15 minutes." I rolled up the window and turned away so I couldn't see him.

I didn't have a watch but I was sure when that little jerk started tapping on the window it had only been about two minutes. I rolled down the window.

"Time's up," he said, looking kind of red in the face.

I decided I didn't need a new friend. Besides, I was in the car and he was out. "I'll let you know when time's up." I rolled up the window.

He came back again and tapped on the window. I rolled it down and up so fast I didn't give him time to talk. Tammy just sat back and smiled, happy to have two kids in a frenzy over her. The next time, Wally tried to put his hand in the window but when he realized I would happily break his fingers to stay in that car, he gave up and went away mad.

I was loving every second with my teacher and knew I was a natural. Humphrey Bogart couldn't have done better. I decided I needed a little positive reinforcement, though, so I asked Tammy, "How is it? Am I any good at necking?"

She got a compact out of her pocket and started to repair her lipstick. "Bobby, you're one year away from being a great kisser. At the rate you are going, next year you will be two years away."

Secondary Hijinks (1946)

Attending the Summit turned out to be a cakewalk compared to the next four years of law and order I was about to experience. In the seventh and eighth grade, every kid had this magnificent image of high school where the girls and guys streamed out of the front door after school laughing and planning the afternoon's fun events. They would proceed to the school parking lot, throw a couple of books in the back seat, hop in a convertible and head to the local malt shop to feed nickels in the jute box and start swinging in the aisles.

When my time came for enrollment, the Little King gave me one of his royal proclamations that could spell trouble in my impending castle of learning. "Bobby, I want you to take this upcoming Xavier High School entrance exam. Richard is doing fine there and I'm sure you would too. "X" has a good national ranking; it would be a real feather in your hat if you passed and spent 4 years there in preparation for college."

I groaned inside. Sure, Richard could attend 'X' because he could memorize anything, no matter how dull. I wasn't sure I wanted to be set up in a place where I would constantly be compared to him. "Dad, you know I'm not a good student. Besides, what difference would a high score make if I follow an artistic career like you?" I thought this appeal to our obvious similarities might work.

The King replied, "My mind is made up, don't confuse me with the facts."

I tried a different tack. Besides tough classes, the other major problem with 'X' was the lack of girls. I tried a psychological angle. "How can I grow into a mature adult if I am surrounded by a bunch of guys just like me, without the good influence of some girls?" I asked Dad.

He didn't fall for it. "The real question here is how can you study and concentrate if your are surrounded by good looking girls?"

It was just my luck. I passed that lousy test by a minimal margin. My life was set for the next four years. There was no turning back. The parents said go and I went. And worse again, my two best friends Dick and Hap had abandoned me; it felt like forever. Hap went to Country Day High and Dick's parents sent him all the way up to Connecticut to a private all boys school. Probably to get him away from the fine influence I had on him.

The first week was a real doozy. Everything I wished and envisioned about high school was just the opposite at 'X'. Instead of a nice new red brick colonial campus surrounded with grass and trees, the three-story stone and brick high school squatted in the middle of downtown. The school and adjoining church were built about 1860 and you could tell the contractors on the job were aiming for eternity. Sometime in the early part of the century the school was modernized enough to have three bathrooms put in the basement. Other than that, it looked unchanged. The desks still had the inkwells and the tops were carved with the names of generations of prisoners like me. The total athletic field consisted of a slab of concrete between the school and Sycamore Street.

I tried to have a positive attitude. The guys seemed friendly but diligent. It took a while to sort them out because everybody looked the same in their white long-sleeved shirts and ties. Everyone lugged briefcases stuffed full of books and I quickly found out why they all looked as if they were carrying their own personal libraries in those heavy saddlebags.

Most of the teachers were Jesuits. Half were priests and most of the others were scholastics in the process of their learning experiences before induction into the priesthood. Even the lay teachers took their jobs seriously. They meant business from 8:00 AM to 3:00 PM and were determined to cram some knowledge into us.

The principal, Father O'Brien, inspired fear in all of us. He stood about 6'2" tall and had heavy black eyebrows with eyes to match and a mouth that hadn't smiled in any of his 45 years. When he strode down the hallways with his black robe flying behind him it was as if he was on a God-given mission to bring learning to us puny ignorant beings whether we wanted it or not. I quickly decided I would try to avoid crossing him.

Latin I dreaded. Hearing priests chant it at mass didn't give me an overwhelming desire to learn it. Some previous student, probably long since crumbled to dust, wrote on the flyleaf of my Latin text: "Latin is a dead, dead language. It's as dead as it can be. It killed the ancient Romans and now it is killing me." I could easily envision it withering me away too.

On the steps of St. Xavier High School

The first freshman kid I really noticed stood out because he sported a gold zoot chain and a cashmere sweater over his white shirt every day. He swaggered around like he owned the place and I pegged him as the son of a big donor to the school, even though he had the unlikely name of Willard. The freshman class was divided into five groups and the students stayed in their own classroom for all subjects. The teachers rotated between classrooms, leaving a 60-second unsupervised void of time between subjects. At the end of the first week Willard carefully timed that moment to go to the door and take a quick glance out in the hallway. He picked up a chalk eraser off the blackboard ledge and cocked his arm. "Hey, Husemueller", he yelled to a kid in the back of the room, "You've been pitching out so much noise and crap all morning, see if you can catch this."

Willard never saw it coming. When Willard's arm was

cocked back ready to throw, Father O'Brien loomed behind him, grabbed his throwing wrist, spun him around, and glared down on him. We all cowered in our seats in case the principal smote Will dead right there. Father O'Brien let Willard shiver for about a minute and then he said 'Out". That was the last time we saw Willard at 'X". We quickly got the message that it made no difference who you were or where you came from, step out of line once and you were dismissed. Out of school forever. I don't know if the school was trying to impress us, but it did. That day set the tone for the next four years.

    I got stuck sitting in front of the most deranged kid in school. We had to sit in alphabetical order and D.J. was right behind me all day. He twitched and jerked and squirmed all over the place so that the front of his desk was always bumping into my seatback. Worse yet, he mumbled to himself constantly, keeping up a running commentary on the subject, the teacher and the students. Since he couldn't sit still or keep quiet, whenever the teacher left the room he had to start in on someone and he quickly figured out how much he annoyed me. I tried to ignore him but since I couldn't leave my seat it was tough. The pace of the classes was so fast, it required almost more concentration than I could muster. With D.J. behind me it was like having a freight train chasing me all day long.

    One time he leaned forward and hissed, "Hey, Bob, I can show you how to get a 100 on your Latin test tomorrow." I already knew how he got good grades. He could write amazing amounts of information on the heel of his shoe, on his wrist or even on the face of his watch. His favorite spot was the fingernails of his left hand. He managed to get Hamlet's dying epilogue spread across those five nails for a Shakespeare exam. He twitched so much during exams that even though the teachers walked around looking for signs of cheating, he didn't hold still long enough for them to realize his scheme.

    I turned around and said, "I don't need it. And why don't you stop spazzing around all the time? What's wrong with you. Do you have fleas in your underwear or something?"

    After that he found a new way to drive me crazy. He would lean over his work and drone quietly enough so the teacher couldn't hear, "Bob, abob, sob, mob, cob, job, lob, nob, rob, fob, Bob, abob," over and over while he set up a rhythmic bumping of the back of my chair. I couldn't tune it out and I feared I would start to get as loony as he.

One day he snookered me good. He pulled out a 2" horseshoe-shaped magnet and claimed he could make my watch stop. I had just bought a Big Ben pocket watch for a dollar at Pickerings hardware store. It had a pendulum like a hammer jack and I was sure it was up to the challenge. "Okay, D.J., if the watch stops, it's my loss. If it keeps running you owe me a dollar."

He took the watch in one hand and with his other put the magnet against the backside of the chrome case and slowly turned it 360 degrees. He shook it and then put it to his ear. A devil-be-damned grin spread over his face and he handed back a timepiece that remained silent and timeless forever.

That was the last straw. I swore I would have nothing to do with him ever again until I could get even. A few days later he placed a small glass vial filed with brown liquid on my desk. I knew something was up. I took off the cork top for a second and jammed it back on. Even in that short second I realized I had a potent stink bomb sitting on my desk. We had made hydrogen sulfide gas in chemistry class that morning and somehow D.J. had taken some of that sulfur and made reeking sewer muck. I sat there and pondered my options. It was time to take a gamble. If I succeeded I could get D.J. off my back. If I failed I would be in major trouble.

When the bell rang, we closed our Latin books and the priest left the classroom. I jumped up, went to the gray metal waste can in front of the room and poured the entire contents all over the trash. Before I could return to my desk, the guys in the front row had already garnered a whiff of that juice and they started to groan. Thirty seconds later the Jesuit Scholastic English teacher, Mr. Braatz walked in with Shakespeare under his arm and dropped poor William on the floor. Something was sure rotten in the state of Denmark.

"Who in God's name is responsible for that sulfur smell?"

Everyone sat quietly, hands covering their noses. No one turned around to look at me. I felt a rush of gratitude that no one was going to snitch on me. Five seconds seemed like sixty. I stood up and said, "I'm very sorry but I'm responsible for pouring that material in the waste can."

"Why on earth did you do that?" Mr. B. asked. "Are you

nuts?"

"No, someone put it on my desk. I had no idea what it was and just decided to throw it away."

"Who gave it to you?"

I didn't answer. I just turned around and looked vaguely in the direction of my desk. D.J. sat slumped in his chair.

Braatz got the hint. "David, did you give that vial to Bob?"

"Yes sir."

"And who gave it to you?"

David straightened up and replied, "No one. I made it in chemistry class. Mr. Brennan said if we made a noticeable chemical contribution in the class we would get an 'A'."

One of the guys up front said, "You numbskull. He said 'notable' not 'noticeable'."

20

Footloose But Not Fancy (1947)

Mom found me one Saturday out sitting on the front step feeling sorry for myself. "What are you doing today, Bobby?" she asked. What did she think I was going to do? At 14, without wheels, on a muddy October day, there is nothing to do. Zippo Zero Zilcho. When I answered with a mumbled 'Nothin' she said, "Grandma is coming over this evening and it would be nice of you to wash her car."

I perked up immediately because I had hit the age where I was obsessed with cars. I loved cars just like my Dad did. We liked to discuss the designs and colors of the new models and admire the older classics. Like most young teenagers, I counted the days until I could get a driver's license. Richard and I had one big advantage over our city-bred peers. At age 15, we could obtain an unrestricted driver's license because of the burden of transportation needs out in the country. But at 14, 15 was an eternity away.

When Grandma parked, I washed her black 1941 Buick until it sparkled like a new bowling ball. I polished the chrome and cleaned the mirrors and then I went back and repolished the chrome. I couldn't find another spot to clean. I walked around the car and kicked a few tires. The car just sat there expectantly. I opened the driver's door to wipe the edge of window frame clean and saw the key in the switch, and then I walked around the car again.

There were no signs of life coming from the house so I went back and checked the key. It was still there. I swear it lured me into the driver's seat. I had never driven on the road before but my confidence was high. The engine started smoothly and quietly. Still no signs of life from the house. Kydoo whined a little as if he couldn't believe I was going to take off. I eased the car out the drive for a five-minute joy ride. No problem. Grandma didn't miss it and I had a great little driving fling. I gained a lot of confidence on the operation of a car.

The next week Richard and I were late for school one morning. I waited for him in the front seat of his '40 Ford worrying about a math test. I didn't know why he was taking so long. In the spur of the moment, kind of like an aggravation reflex, I pushed the starter button. The car was in first gear. It lurched forward, crushed three bikes and crashed through the back wall of the garage, sending wood bits flying everywhere. I got so upset I climbed out of the car and threw up. It was one of those moments when I wished I could turn back the clock five minutes. Luckily, Dad had already gone to work.

When Mother saw me kneeling on the grass, my face a pasty greenish white, she was so worried I was hurt, she didn't yell at first. The next few months I tiptoed around knowing I had better not get in any trouble if I wanted to ever leave the house again.

I couldn't stop thinking about that misfortune in Richard's Ford but the memory of that disaster faded and I was still hot to get in the driver's seat of anything that had four wheels.

One Saturday I wandered down to the barn to look for some old *Life* magazines. Mother and Dad had saved them for years but since Mother was suddenly contemplating throwing them all out in a super cleaning effort, I decided I should look at them before they disappeared. In the corner of the barn I tossed aside one of Dad's paint dropcovers, exposing four three-foot high stacks of the magazines.

Right on top was one of my favorite covers. Jane Russell in a skimpy short outfit sprawled out over the cover on a bed of hay while she chewed on a piece of straw dangling from her lips. I guess she was supposed to look like she regularly lounged around barns but even in my limited experience I knew I was never likely to see any girl doing something similar in our barn. A flash of orange color caught the corner of my eye. I flipped the dropcover again and there it was, a forgotten four wheeler, our overlooked and neglected soapbox racer.

It had held up pretty well during storage. I pushed it out of the barn and up on the street. I didn't know why we were saving it; the little car never won any races and Richard didn't care about it. I pondered the best spot for maximum speed so I pushed it two blocks to Kugler Mill Road where there was a good hill to go down.

At the top of the hill I climbed in and gravity let her rip. Halfway down that hill the thrill of the speed overwhelmed me so I pushed hard on the floorboard drag brake. But the hill was too steep; it would not slow down. In fact it went faster. I stopped worrying about Richard's Ford in two seconds. Bigger problems raced toward me. I was headed for the intersection where Kugler meets a main road. Camargo Pike had no stop signs and I was ready to blam through the intersection at full speed.

I can only remember the screeching of tires on my right side. The chrome grill of a blue car flashed by only three feet from my head. The rush of air from the car tore my cap off and I continued straight ahead into the tall grass embankment, coming to a stop among the dried up goldenrod.

I sat for a moment waiting for my heart to start beating again. The driver of the car didn't stop which surprised me but I was glad I wouldn't get some lecture about foolish kids. Finally I climbed out and pushed it slowly back home into the barn and told Dad about the experience. He said, "That thing is too dangerous out on the road. That's why I had it stashed away with a cover over it. Go back down to the barn and hide it. Put three covers over it."

For the next few months I was convinced my parents would ban me from wheels forever. But finally Dad in his wisdom and knowledge of teenage boys decided I was likely to get into more trouble attempting to drive than I would if I had a legitimate car and license. I got the license a few months later and Grandma cleared the way for me to obtain wheels.

In the late 1930s my mother's father bought some acreage of woody hills and dales five miles from the city limits. He built his vacation cottage on the highest peak where you could see some of the taller buildings downtown. 'The Farm' was the family catalyst for all the aunts, uncles and cousins in warm weather.

Grandma was one of those lucky persons who truly enjoyed farming her wartime vegetable plot. Her one-acre garden required a medium-sized barn to store a tractor, miscellaneous equipment, and a 1934 Chevrolet coupe, her 'farm car.' She removed the rear rumble seats and used it to haul everything from potted plants to fertilizer.

After the war Grandma decided to cut back on her gardening and the Chev was relegated to the barn. The spring I turned 15, Grandma happened to mention to Mother she had no more use for the Chev in the barn. Instead of buying it, she suggested I could work a few days doing farm chores and then she would give it to me as a gift.

My heart raced when I heard. For one week I was the most enthusiastic farm worker that land had ever seen. I weeded, cut brush, moved rubbish, and painted as fast as I could. Once the Chev was in my hands, I looked it over and realized it needed a bit of fixing up. The canvas insert on the steel top leaked, the black paint was oxidized, the missing rumble seat area had long since turned into a huge mouse town, the

Bob's rumble seat Chevy

clutch was almost shot, and the mechanical brakes didn't work well. Just a few problems and I loved it.

Dad looked the car over with me. "What are you going to do with that Chev now, Bobby?" he asked.

"Get a job to pay for all the repairs. Do you think I could work for you at the company?"

"I think that could be arranged. It looks to me like you have a long-term project here."

I decided first impressions were most important. The

clutch and the brake problems could be dealt with later. I made a few repairs to the body and bought some black enamel paint. The spoke wheels got a coat of yellow and a white rubber-based paint created the look of snappy white wall tires.

My next step was a trip to the Duck Creek auto junkyards and I managed to find the needle in the haystack. One set of 1934 Chevrolet rumble seats for the grand total of $1.00. Dad followed the progress with keen interest.

Finally, I thought the car was presentable even though it smelled a bit foul and ran even worse.

My first real tryout for the Chev came on a blind date with a girl named Joanie. I had never met her but Dick told me she had won a junior miss pageant and was beautiful. That was all I needed to hear.

I wanted to dress carefully to make a good impression but Cincinnati had been hit with one of its periodic early heat waves and the temperature reached 95 degrees by late afternoon. At that heat and humidity level, the air weighed like a down blanket. A white short sleeved tennis shirt was the coolest thing I could find in my drawers. I tried on a pair of shorts but quickly decided on a scale of one to ten my legs ranked a two and were unlikely to wow my date. I ditched the shorts and covered up the offending limbs with a pair of cotton madras pants. I put on my white bucks but they were as hot and heavy as a pair of work boots so I decided on loafers with no socks.

After looking in the mirror and deciding I had cleaned up pretty well, I slipped downstairs before Mom could question me on my plans. The Chev made it to Joanie's house without overheating so I thought everything was going to be okay.

I rang the doorbell and Joanie's parents invited me in. We chatted briefly while I kept envisioning the beauty who would come to greet me. After a few moments she strolled into the living room and said hello. I didn't know what to say. She sure wasn't dressed for any beauty pageant. Her hair was pulled back in a pony tail and she wore pedal pushers and a white tee shirt that probably belonged to her father. Emblazoned across it was 'See Rock City'. Maybe I was expecting too much considering the weather but a little lipstick would have been nice. A guy can't be too choosy so we jumped in the Black Beauty and took off. "Where would you like to go?" I asked.

"Somewhere we can drink beer and stay cool," Joanie said as she leaned her head out the window and closed her eyes. This girl really did not like the heat.

"How about we go see an old Charlie Chaplin movie called *City Lights* at the Montgomery Drive Inn?" I suggested. I didn't know if a drive-in was right for a first date but I decided it was worth a try.

"Fine, anywhere where it is cool."

We stopped first at Carl's Pony Keg. Pony Kegs were to Cincinnati like carry-out pubs were to England. They were everywhere. An attendant stood on an outside loading dock to take your order. Behind him the cooler door led to a large refrigerated room containing anything anyone would want to drink. The most popular product was the beer, especially the beer made by the four local breweries. They produced the regular 6% alcohol beer but also made a 3.2% for the younger set.

"What kind of beer would you like?" I asked her as we pulled in. "Bavarian, Hudepohl, Red Top or Wiedemann?"

"You pick." I thought to myself she likes beer, she's not particular, she likes drive-ins, the date is going well. She picked her ponytail up off her neck and twisted it up in a knot like she wished she could throw it away.

I pulled up to the dock. I figured if I called the attendant by his name, it would look to Joanie like I knew him and was no stranger to pony kegs. It was legal for 18-year-olds to buy 3.2 beer but I didn't know if I could pass for one.

I said, "Carl, gimme six Wiedemanns 3.2 and a pack of pork rinds and beef jerky."

"Sure, pal," he smirked. He brought out the goods and after I paid him he leaned in and said, "By the way, my name's not Carl, Sonny." I glanced over at Joanie to see if she heard. Her head was back against the seat and she was too hot to notice.

The movie had already started by the time we arrived, but I didn't care and neither did the rest of the audience. We parked close to the back with the rest of the teenagers, leaving the front for families with kids and lawn chairs. We drained that six pack while watching Chaplin barely miss disaster time after time.

When the beer had disappeared, Joanie and I started to

get friendly. After a few minutes Joanie said, "Jeez, does your car have holes in it? I am getting all wet."

I had forgotten about the gaps in the seams of the top and hadn't considered rain. "I think it's just a sprinkle. I'm sure it will stop soon." The rain continued, turning into a steady drumming on the canvas roof. While we kissed, we kept shifting around to avoid the drips until we found a spot if we held perfectly still and leaned toward the dash we wouldn't have any rain dripping down our necks. I came up for air and said, "Joanie, I've got news for you. I have never seen a girl in a tee shirt look as beautiful as you."

She whispered in my ear, "I've got news for you too. If you had been watching the movie instead of looking at 'Rock City,' you would have realized the movie projector busted a half hour ago."

21

The Mood for Love

Mom stopped me as I tried to get out the door. "Where are you off to tonight?"

"Dick and I have dates and we're taking them to Coney Island. He's going to Harbor Point, Michigan, next week so we wanted to go on the Island Queen before he leaves."

"Anybody I know?" she said casually, flipping through the newspaper, pretending to be interested in the classifieds.

"I don't think so." I thought fast. I knew Mom wouldn't be thrilled with details of my new friend, my post-Joanie date, so I thought I should avoid telling her. First of all, she wasn't Catholic. Second, my parents probably didn't know any of the same people her parents knew, and third, I just didn't want to tell her.

"Her name is Gloria Glockenspiel."

"Hmmm... Glockenspiel, I don't think I know that name. Where does she live?"

"In Hyde Park." I thought I had better nip this interrogation in the bud. "I gotta run, Mom, or we will miss the boat. Bye." I slipped out before I could get more questions.

If you asked and put them on the spot, most Catholic girls had a favorite saying: "I never kiss until the third date," was the line and they didn't. I wasn't sure when or where they were taught this but it was one of the commandments of Catholic teenage girls. The whole idea made no sense to me. I didn't understand why a kiss on the third date was sanctified while a kiss on the first would require repentance.

Not so with Protestant girls. No hang ups there. No nuns

lurking in their heads shaking a finger at them. If a girl liked you, she would happily kiss on the first date. If she didn't like you, she didn't bother to kiss you at all. One gal wouldn't let me kiss her on the sixth date. I got the message loud and clear: don't ask me out again.

That Saturday night my date was a lovely little babycake named Marilyn. She was Protestant, fast thinking, beautiful, and I knew she would have no problems on the kissing issue.

After picking up Marilyn I drove the old Chev to the other side of Indian Hill to pick up Dick. I didn't know who he had finally decided to ask out but I hoped she lived nearby so we wouldn't be late. Dick came out and hopped in the rumble seat, folding up his legs, stork-like.

I cranked down the little oval rear window. "Where to?" Dick said, "Hope you don't mind going over to Price Hill. I met this great girl named Dinnie. We can get over there in about 40 minutes."

"No problem" I said, praying the car was up to the long trip.

When we arrived at her house I said, "Dick, hurry up so we can get out of here and down to the boat."

Dick and Dinnie came out of the house so fast he must have speed talked through the parent preliminaries. I thought Dinnie was cute until she looked at my car and said, "Pardon me, I'll be right back. I didn't know we were riding in the rumble seat of this breeze mobile. I need a scarf for my hair."

We finally arrived downtown, and none too soon. I parked at the old riverfront public landing at the foot of Broadway Street and we dashed over to the ticket booth to buy four round trip tickets for 25 cents each. "Last call, all aboard," the steward yelled from his megaphone while the calliope player banged out "Won't you come home, Bill Bailey, won't you come home?"

I had looked forward to this all week. Taking the Island Queen to Coney Island was always one of the highlights of summer. The four-tiered white and green *Island Queen* side-wheeler steamboat was magnificent. Built in the late 1920's she was modeled on the old time steamboats that traveled the Mississippi and the Ohio in the 19th century. About 2200 of those boats had steamed up and down the rivers but eventually at least half disintegrated by collision, snags or explosions. Most of the rest succumbed to the pressures from the railroads but the *Island Queen* maintained the illusion that leisurely river travel still existed.

People crowded all the decks. I knew if the boat was full there would be about 4000 people on board and we needed to

The Island Queen

find a good spot for the trip. We moved to the central ballroom to escape the crowd. The calliope stopped playing, the engines revved up, the steam whistle sounded, smoke billowed out from the twin stacks and we were under way. As soon as the boat slid away from the dock everyone else poured into the ballroom. It heated up and filled with cigarette smoke and got so noisy I couldn't even tell where the music was coming from.

"Let's go somewhere else," Marilyn shouted in my ear. We went outside on the third deck, looked up at the sky, darkening quickly, and saw the wheelhouse parked on top of the Moon Deck.

Dick loved anything mechanical so I wasn't surprised when he said, "Let's go up there and find out if they will let us see how this thing runs."

The first mate stopped us at the door of the wheelhouse but relented when he found out we were interested in the boat. "I'll give you kids a quick peek inside but keep it down because the captain is approaching the Dayton, Kentucky sandbar."

The open door offered us a good view of the small wheelhouse interior. The eight-foot wheel was so large that almost half of it was recessed into the floor. Gauges lined a wood panel behind the wheel and I could see the captain had easy access to pedals on the floor for braking and whistles.

The first mate spoke in a low voice, "See those handles, kids?" On either side of the wheel were 30-inch horizontal handles mounted on three-foot vertical brass shafts coming out of the floor. "Each of those act as a clutch and control the engagement of the port and starboard side wheels that push the vessel through the water." I was suddenly envious of the captain's job. To be in charge of that beautiful boat would take the skill of a real artist. I guess Marilyn wasn't mechanically inclined because she grabbed my hand and pulled me toward the door tapping her foot. Just as we left, the captain yelled into the tube down to the engine room, "Slow engines to five knots," as we approached the sandbar.

We went back out onto the Moon Deck. The damp river aroma was a welcome change from all that pure fresh air back on the farm that the King loved so much. The sun had almost set but there were still bathers on the Dayton, Kentucky beach. I leaned on the rail and watched the flow of the river while the girls chattered with each other. On the ten-mile trip we passed more swimmers, shanty boats where the river people lived, yacht clubs, speedboats and kids fishing in row boats. After an hour the *Queen* slowed, swung north, put its bow gently on the shore, and dropped its gangplank at Coney Island.

An entrepreneurial farmer started the amusement park in his apple orchard in the 1870s. He attracted crowds with his dining hall, dance hall, bowling alley, and mule-powered merry-go-round. Eventually the farmer sold it to a steamboat captain who built a dance pavilion on the site as a destination for the passengers on his steamboat. When the captain's own boat blew up and burnt to bits downtown, he sold the park to two brothers to keep his head financially above water. The Schotts turned it into one of the best run amusement parks in America, adding rides and building the largest swimming pool in the world. It even thrived during the war, after the ration board decided the *Island Queen* and Coney Island were essential for morale. They freed up enough fuel for the steamboat to make the trip back and forth.

The four of us walked up the embankment path through the stone lighthouse building into the park. To get to the Moonlight Gardens we passed through one of my favorite childhood spots, the Land of Oz with its miniature carousel and pony rides. That brought us to the main Mall lined with gingko trees, gardens, the Shooting Star roller coaster, the Wildcat and a slew more.

A few yards off to the west at the other end of the Mall and we were at the Gardens. The open-air dance floor stood in the center, surrounded by a roofed area protecting the tables and the bandstand. "Let's get a table so we can look at the Lake," Marilyn requested so we walked around until we found a spot that had a clear view of Lake Como. I knew it had been built on an old cornfield and didn't resemble the real Lake Como in the least, but I didn't care. It was our Lake Como.

Marilyn turned out to be a great jitter bugger so we spent the whole evening on the dance floor, only stopping long enough to cool off with some swigs of beer. Perry Como crooned away for us, backed up by his big band.

At 10:00 PM the traditional fireworks ended the day for the amusement park rides. The lights of the explosions reflected off the lake, dancing with the crowd. Finally, Perry finished the night with his best selling rendition of 'Lilli Marlene' and the dance floor began to clear.

"The last boat is leaving, let's get a move on," Dick recommended. We hated to leave but in 15 minutes we were back on board and moving downstream. We climbed back up to the Moon Deck. It was a perfect warm night, the moon was at half-mast and it was made to order for romance. The only ripples on the river came from the boat wake behind us.

By the time we disembarked at downtown Cincinnati the clock was moving toward 1:00 AM but we were reluctant to let go of the evening. We walked up the steep cobblestone landing, and turned around to catch one last glimpse of the Island Queen.

I dropped Dinnie off again in Price Hill, a little windblown but no worse for wear. Across town and 40 minutes later Dick was out and we were on our way to Marilyn's. I had it planned out to pull into the long driveway to her house and stop short where the car would be hidden by some large pine trees, in hopes the romantic night would set the mood for a little necking before we said goodnight.

Marilyn snuggled over close to me. The floor-mounted gear shift got in her way so she kicked it and said, "I'm coming over anyway. I had the most wonderful time ever, Bob."

"Good" I put my arm around her.

"And I want to ask you something."

"Shoot," I said, She started to squirm around in the seat like she was nervous, but then again after that long ride anyone would get fanny fatique and start twitching.

Marilyn pounced with her question. She was the type of girl who got to the point real fast. She asked, "Do you believe in free love?"

Without understanding the question or thinking it out, I simply said, "Sure I do." I couldn't make heads or tails out of her question but I couldn't ruin my suave man of the world act. I had never heard of any girl charging for a kiss and wondered if this was some sort of new Protestant dating rule.
I decided it was time to find a different Gloria Glockenspiel with no kiss tariff.

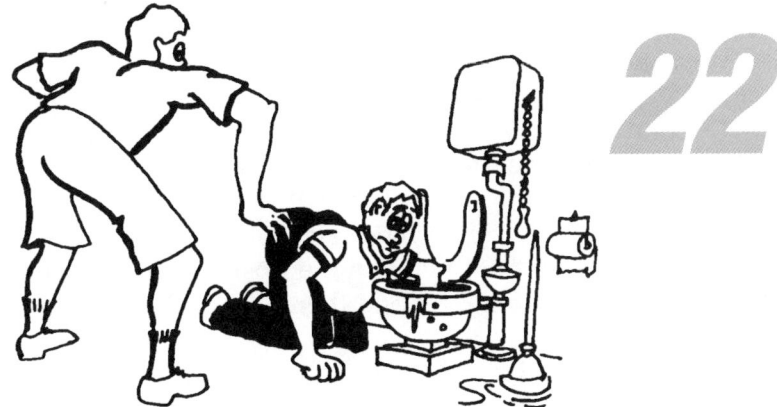

Captain Dick's Tour Boat

To pay for the Chev I needed to start working for Dad. I looked forward to earning some real money and being treated like an adult. Most of all, I looked forward to working on artistic or important projects. The first morning I walked into Dad's office to get an assignment, hoping he would take me with him on a design consultation or let me pick out some paint colors for a job. Dad got off the phone and said, "Bob, I've decided you are going to work in the paint shop. Harry will be your boss."

Harry, Helga's husband, had spent his time in the war spray painting camouflage on jeeps and tanks in England so he ran his shop with the organization and iron hand of the army. He played second fiddle to no one and demanded everyone's full time attention.

Harry led me into the lye boiler room. I had never been inside and as I walked in I knew why. The heat hit me in the face like a volcanic eruption. I was about to mention to Harry it was kind of hot in there when he said, "It's not too bad in here now. I turned off the gas burners at 7:00 this morning so it stopped boiling two hours ago." The room was ten foot square and had two-foot deep vats on three walls filled with steel paint cans encrusted with layers of dried oil paints in bubbling hot lye. My heart sank.

Harry handed me a pair of rubber gloves. "Here, put these on and grab an apron. You can scrub these pots clean with this putty knife. The hot lye should have loosened the paint up by now enough for you to get them clean." He left me to my job.

After a month of scrubbing paint cans I thought I needed a vacation. In fact my fifteen year old brain couldn't comprehend this idea of working day after day in a 140 degree room. On some days I even imagined myself back in algebra class. As an introduction to the job world this boiling misery was too much.

I dragged myself home one evening and collapsed at the kitchen table. Mom handed me a postcard of two girls on a sailboat. I flipped it over and there was Dick's familiar handwriting:

Come up to Harbor Point for a few days.
Grandma says it okay.

I wasn't tired anymore. Dick's grandparents owned a big, rambling house right on the water in Northern Michigan perfect for a summer vacation. I had to go. Since I was gainfully employed or so Dad said, I could only go for a long weekend but that was better than nothing. We planned it so I could take the train up on Thursday night and stay until Sunday morning. The traveling time would about equal the time I spent on the lake but I wanted to go anyway.

Dick picked me up at the train station at Petosky in his '47 Ford coupe. He had new features on his car I hadn't seen before, two official looking spotlights mounted outside. "What are you going to do with those, buddy?" I asked. "No one is going to believe you are a cop."

"Just wait, Bob." We sped off at Dick's usual flat out speed. Once we were on the road he said, "Bad news, Bob. Dad invited the Warden to stay with us." Werner the Warden was the headmaster at Summit and even though I was no longer under his control the thought of being under his eagle eye unsettled us. You couldn't get much past him.

I decided not to worry about it and enjoy the 12-mile ride to Harbor Point. We hit a stretch of road that begged for some racecar moves, up hills, down dips and over curves. When we slowed to a crawl on a two lane road behind some oldsters out for a scenic drive, Dick said, "Open the glove compartment and pull out the shower cap in there."

I spotted the red translucent cap and instantly knew what he had in mind when he covered his spotlight. Up close it didn't look like much but then Dick turned on the spot and began making a spine-tingling noise deep in his throat as he leaned toward the open window. It exactly mimicked a police siren. Those oldsters pulled over and stopped so fast I'm sure they left skid marks on the road.

"Dick, you have more talents than a hog caller," I said. He just grinned.

We parked at the little town of Harbor Springs and took a small 12 seat ferry over to his grandfather's dock. No cars were allowed on the Point, only bikes or horse drawn carriages. Even the deliverymen, the plumbers, carpenters and the hired help had to come by wagon. For quick trips back and forth to town most cottage owners used boats.

I loved Dick's Grandma so much I even called her Grandma but I stayed out of the way of Grandpa Leblond. He was a tough 83-year-old buzzard who came up the hard way. During the two world war years, his machine tool business flourished so by the late forties he was enjoying a semi-retirement. I never said much to him, figuring he wouldn't be too interested in me, and he didn't seem like the type you would want to annoy.

Dick and I spent Friday golfing with his dad, W.J., the Warden, and our friend, Mitch, from the Summit. In the summer everyone who could came to northern Michigan from Cincinnati to escape the heat so you ended up running into

Dick's father W.J., Dick, Mitch and the "Warden".

the same people on vacation that you saw at home. By Saturday we were anxious to get out on the water and do some boating.

Grandpa had three boats and each one held a place in his heart. The best was a '48 mahogany Chris Craft cruiser that was like his favorite son. We knew we wouldn't ever get a chance at it, so Dick said, "We want to go out in the Lyman, Grandma. Is that okay?"

The Lyman was a 16-footer perfect for goofing around the harbor. It had a steering wheel in the bow but the cables were not connected to the rear outboard so Dick ran the boat from the stern with his hand on the engine tiller. We had just opened up on full speed when we were surprised to hear the steam whistle blow. A huge Lake Michigan sternwheeler steamboat was exiting Harbor Springs on their 10:00 A.M. tour. It was about a half-mile away but headed in our direction to make its way around the point and eventually out into Lake Michigan. We idled in place to watch it go by. By the time the big paddle wheeler was opposite us, it was going full steam, leaving a series of perpendicular wake waves about eight foot high off the stern.

With all the engine noise, I could barely hear Dick yell, "Let's go out and get in right behind it."

"Sounds good to me." I hollered back. Dick ducked the boat right in behind that thrashing paddle wheel and turned it 90 degrees so we were headed straight into the oncoming rollers. When we hit the first one the bow rose up, hanging suspended in midair at the very top of the wave and then it dropped eight feet down and slammed on the low point of the second roller. My teeth jarred together and I grabbed the dead steering wheel, clinging to it for dear life.

On the other side, Dick looked like a pin on a hinge. His end of the boat always stayed in the water and didn't suffer the traumatic impact like the front.

I was scared and really desperate to get the hell out of there and quick before the boat swamped. I yelled and motioned to him but he couldn't understand me because of the noise. We finally rode it out. That was more than enough excitement for the morning so we took the boat back to the dock and tied it up. Soaked through, Dick said "Let's go back upstairs, dry off and get dressed for lunch."

"I don't know if I can stand any lunch after that and I think we should go in the back way so nobody asks how we got wet."

After cleaning up I got downstairs first and sat down to help Grandma with a jigsaw puzzle of Yosemite National Park. I could hear Mrs. W.J. helping in the kitchen with lunch preparation and see the old guy lounging in his rattan recliner in the sunroom. Dick's father, W.J., rattled around the porch mixing a spot of gin. W.J. was from England and seemed to find gin and tonic the answer to most questions.

Dick clattered down the stairs. Grandpa roared from the sunroom that overlooked the lake, "How was your boat ride, Richard?" There was something in his tone that caused Grandma and me to make instant eye contact. She set a piece of jagged mountain down and placed her palms on the table as if she was bracing for an earthquake.

"We had the best boat ride and that Lyman is perfect for the harbor, Grandpa."

Grandpa said, "I'm so glad you two enjoyed yourselves this morning but there is one problem."

"What's that?"

He sat straight up in his chair and yelled so loudly the few remaining strands of his white hair flopped wildly up and down. "Where's the damn boat?"

I jumped up from the puzzle table and followed Dick out on the porch. The boat was not at the dock where we left it. Did someone steal it? No one else in the house used the boat. We bolted down the steps and out on the dock to take a look. We couldn't believe it was gone and then I caught a glimpse of something dark. I looked down through the clear water on the side of the dock and saw it. That boat had sunk to the bottom. It rested in about ten feet of water, gently rocking back and forth like a baby's cradle.

Dick spotted it too. "We are in a bad way, Bob. I think that big wake did in this boat. Grandpa is going to be pretty mad."

I nodded. I hadn't been around him too much but I knew Grandpa wouldn't be happy. We walked as slowly as possible back to the house. The rest of the group had already sat down to lunch. Dick's grandpa looked at us expectantly. "Grandpa, do you have insurance on the Lyman?"

Grandpa sat his fork down right in the middle of his chicken salad. "Why?"

"Because the boat sunk. It's right off the end of the dock."

LeBlond's cozy cottage

"Now why would that boat just up and sink?"

"Because the floor boards are cracked."

"Why would the floor boards be cracked?"

"Because we probably hit a big wave in the harbor this morning." The rest of the table watched the exchange go back and forth like a tennis game.

"Dick, I have been coming up here for 40 years and I've never seen a wave big enough in this little harbor to bust up a good lap-plank boat. What did you do to the boat?" He was getting hotter by the second.

"Now simmer down, daddy," Grandma said. "We are just lucky the boys weren't hurt."

He pushed his chair back from the table and went out to survey the damage. Dick and I looked at each other and then followed him out, staying far enough back not to annoy him more.

He shook his head and then stomped back inside. The rest of the day was taken up with the boat rescue operation. A couple of men brought a large fishing boat out with a hook on a wrench and cranked the boat up. We stood watching them lash it to the side of their rig when Grandpa spoke his only words to us that afternoon, "Keep your pea-picking hands off the other boat." I thought it was a good thing I was leaving soon.

The next morning I slept late so I had to rush around to pack. I threw all my dirty clothes into my suitcase and went into the bathroom to collect my other stuff. When I reached for my toothbrush I knocked a bar of soap into the toilet. Just then Dick came banging up the stairs. "Let's go, if we are going to get you to the train on time."

"I just did a stupid thing. I knocked the soap into the toilet. Let me get it out before we go." I knelt down on the white tiles and took a breath before I plunged my hand in the old fashioned deep-throated bowl. I put my fingers around the soap but it slipped away as soon as I tried to grab it. I tried again. It was like trying to catch a fish by hand.

"I can't get the damn thing. It's too slippery."

"Don't worry about it. I'll deal with it later but we need to go."

The train ride took all day. Mother picked me up at the Winton Place train station and after the usual hugs, kisses and greeting she said, "You received a telegram from Dick. I hope nothing is wrong."

I opened the yellow envelope and read to myself: *FORGOT TO DEAL WITH IT stop. MINOR FLOOD STOP CEILING DAMAGE, ETC stop. GRANDPA'S PLUMBER HAD TO DEAL WITH IT stop. GRANDPA SAID HE <u>WISHES</u> HE NEVER SEES US TOGETHER–EVER stop.*

Mom's curiosity overcame her. "What does it say?"

"Just Dick and Grandpa send their best wishes."

"How nice. I hope you send them a nice thank you card."

23

Requiem for a Dead Poinsettia (1948)

It was tough to believe three years had passed since the war ended because there were still remnants of military life everywhere. We still saw men in uniforms, war posters in store windows. The popular music still focused on wartime romance and cars, homes and practically everything else were in short supply because of the skyrocketing demand from returning soldiers who were getting married.

The soldiers inhabited another world from the rest of us. Even the ones who were still in their early twenties looked years older. If a group of them came in a diner, bar, or any other gathering place we just made way for them, always assuming they would not be intimidated by anything.

I watched their camaraderie with each other and couldn't help but reflect on my own friends. My camp buddy, Tim, had been at Summit and was now at St. X and I got to know him better when we started going to a few afternoon football games.

One October afternoon I drove the two of us to a Withrow High School football game in Hyde Park. That following Monday I was walking up the front steps of school when a kid named Sam ran up behind me yelling his head off. He stopped and put his hands on his knees, gasping for breath.

"What's going on, Sam?"

"We were just sitting on the bar stools in the drug store having a Coke and he fell off!"

"Who? What are you talking about?"

"The ambulance just left. They said Tim is dead. His heart

failed."

I sat down on the steps. "Are you sure?" I asked, even though I knew it must be true. I had never thought about why Tim was so small and scrawny. I just thought he would grow later. Now I understood why he always got out of breath in gym class. The day passed slowly as the whole school seemed to talk in whispers.

That evening I sat up in my room, doodling pictures of the rows of cabins at Fort Scott Camp when Mom called up the stairs, "Telephone for you, Bob"

It was Timmy's mother. I didn't know what to say but she didn't wait for me to talk. "Bob, I would like you to select three of Tim's best friends and the four of you to help be pallbearers at the burial on Thursday."

I felt weighed down inside at the thought of a funeral but I said, "I would be honored to do that. Thank you for letting us help. We loved Tim." I choked up.

Wednesday night I went to the visitation at Tim's house. The open casket stood in the living room and about 30 people conversed in hushed tones. The odor of the flowers nearly overwhelmed me. I didn't want to look at Tim so I stalled for time by talking to anyone I recognized. Finally I knew I had to do what was expected.

Two other people stood talking next to the coffin. One of the fellows was a big tough looking soldier in a full dress marine sergeant uniform. He had enough ribbons on his chest to wrap his body twice and even though he wasn't that much older than me in actual years he didn't look anything like those of us who hadn't been to war. I gave Tim a quick glance. The skin on his face resembled the smooth shiny sheen of meringue on a charlotte russe. I felt sick to my stomach so I jerked back, bumping into the Marine.

He smiled and continued his conversation with some older man in a suit. It involved some long story about a jeep, some extra liquid k-rations and an impromptu party. They both laughed uproariously at the end and I glanced around the crowd, hoping the relatives wouldn't be too upset with the soldier's behavior. After a final laugh he held out his hand to me. "Hi, I'm Tim's older brother."

I shook his hand, stunned at his casual lack of concern and then I looked at the lines in his face. I thought back to all the pictures I had seen of soldiers crawling through mud over the bodies of their buddies and knew he had seen too much to let death affect him.

The next few months passed slowly. I was looking forward to Dick coming home at Christmas. Whenever he came back we had to rush out and do something, anything. We believed that each new day was an opportunity for an exciting new chapter we couldn't have imagined the day before

I was cleaning out my car one day in mid-December when Mom yelled, "Dick is on the phone."

I ran in and grabbed the phone. "Welcome home. How is it going?" I asked.

"You don't know how glad I am to be back and not cooped up out in the sticks with a book in my face every day. Anyway, what's going on around here?"

"*Devil on Wheels* is showing at the Mariemont Theater. It's supposed to have an amazing souped up '32 Chevrolet coupe in it." Neither Dick nor I cared about the plot of a movie as long as it had different cars in it.

"I'll pick you up," I said.

"Good, I'll bring some firecrackers."

We had long since graduated from the days of beanshooters. There were four types of firecrackers we favored. Each had its own purpose, the tiny Chinese crackers were useful to get someone's attention, the 2" crackers made things jump, cherry bombs made things rattle, and M80s took care of major demolition.

We headed through Madisonville toward Mariemont when Dick spotted Bart's Florist sign on my side of the street. "Do you know what he did?" he asked.

"Dick, I've heard this story three times. It's old hat." A few years earlier Dick's mother had paid Mr. Bart to plant 200 fancy tulip bulbs for her and not one had come up. The chipmunks and squirrels in Dick's yard looked particularly chubby that year leaving small trenches all over where the varmints had excavated. Clearly Mr. Bart wasn't at fault but Dick didn't see it that way. I wasn't sure what it was about these tulip bulbs that was so important.

"I'm not going to blow my top," he muttered, "but I'm going to use the lighter to set off one of these two-inch firecrackers and blow the back of Bart's flower wagon."

What the heck. We shouldn't have done it; it was a bad

Requiem for a Dead Poinsettia 117

No. 69 streetcar in Madisonville

idea. Fortunately, it made a bad landing in the gutter but bounced up on the sidewalk just as Mr. Bart walked out of his shop with a box full of potted red flowers. We were following a slow streetcar ready to make a left turn on to Whetzel Avenue and I turned around just in time to see the explosion and see Mr. Bart blow his top.

"Step on it," Dick yelled, hunkering down in the seat. Mr. Bart spotted us trailing the streetcar and ran after us, juggling a few remaining pots of Christmas poinsettias. Bits of red petals fluttered behind him like confetti at a New Years' Eve party. We escaped but I had a bad feeling he got our license number.

Dick whistled happily as we headed to the movie. I wasn't so sure we were in a position to celebrate but what was done, was done. Plus, we had a movie to watch. There were a slew of hot rod movies out and they all had pretty much the same story line. The local kids hung out on their particular California beach and life was peachy until the bad guys with the mean looking cars showed up and upset the balance, poaching the girls and spewing sand on the lesser cars. They all raced up and down the beach with each other until finally the bad guys were chased off somehow and the girls came to their senses.

After the movie I said, "Let's go look at some hot rods at Frisch's Drive-In." I was fired up to see some really good 1930s Fords and they all came to cruise at Frisch's Mainliner on the weekend. The owner, Dave, gave his restaurant a terrific art deco streamlined look with lots of chrome and neon. The parking lot completely surrounded the eatery so the cars could enter one side, make a slow circle of the lot, exit, and then repeat the same trip again to show off their works of art.

We pulled up and waited for a carhop to take our order outside. There were only 12 seats inside and these were usually occupied by older people. The other benefit to Frisch's were the goodlooking carhops. They wore coral-colored jackets, short skirts, little pinched army hats, and chrome coin changers around their waists. "What will you have, fellas?" the waitress asked.

We both ordered fries and Frisch's trademark double decker 'Big Boy' hamburger with tarter sauce 'through the garden' which meant piled high with shredded lettuce, a slice of tomato and onion. When our order came, Dick bit into his with relish. "You just can't get one of these burgers out East," he said. We settled back to watch the motor show. Because the lot could get rowdy sometimes, the owner had hired the only kid he could find who wanted to be a security guard. Jack was pretty young to keep order but he looked very snappy in his uniform, almost like the sergeant of the carhops. At 5'10" and 125 pounds dripping wet he did somehow manage to keep the rodders under control.

Half an hour later we took off from the drive-in and made the mistake of backtracking right through the center of Madisonville to check out the scene of the crime. The red bits were gone and the store was dark. I breathed a sigh of relief but when we got past the city limits red flashing lights appeared behind us.

"Maybe you have a taillight out," Dick said as I pulled over, but from the feeling of dread inside me, I knew it was something worse.

I rolled down the window and the Madeira police chief leaned in. "Howdy boys," he said, jovially. "Finally gotcha, hey? Mr. Bart got this warrant out for you two so I'm going to follow you back to the Madeira police station."

"It must be a mistake, sir. We were at a movie."

"Don't try to pull the wool over my eyes, boys. You just do what I say and come into the station." He walked back to his car without waiting for an answer. Dick and I gave each other a remorseful look and obeyed his instructions. There was no escape this time.

As we drove off, herded along by the Plymouth cruiser following us, my mind was churning. No one ever remembered the police chief's last name because everyone just referred to him as 'Tag-em Willie'. He took his job very seriously as if the slightest bit of slacking off would cause the upstanding citizens of Madeira to turn to a life of crime. Most of the time he liked to direct traffic, sometimes turning off the only stoplight in town so he could stand in the middle of the intersection blowing his whistle and waving his arms around. No matter what the weather he always appeared in his starched beige police shirt with epaulets on the shoulders and a pair of silver captain bars on the flaps. We never knew what decoration would appear on him; it seemed to depend on what new items he could find in the uniform catalog to award himself. I also knew that with so little excitement in town, Willie would stop at nothing to be able to make a real arrest.

I also knew when we got to the station he would search the car and find the incriminating evidence. "Dick, I'm going to speed it up a little just before I make the left turn at the end of Madison Road. Open your window and grab the brown fireworks bag." Willie was now 50 yards behind and just after we made the turn Dick gently tossed the bag of crackers out into a heavy growth of weeds.

By the time Willie turned in behind us, we were driving along sedately. When we reached the station, we parked and followed him meekly into the station. One of the deputies, who had been lounging with his feet propped up on a desk straightened up and looked at us in surprise, as if he couldn't believe there were potential criminals in a town like Madeira. It was a quiet burg with a grocery, a hardware store, a drug store with a fountain and a railroad track that ran through the center of town next to a lumberyard.

Willie sat down behind his own desk, taking his time as he got out a pencil and an official looking form. "Okay, boys where are them firecrackers?" he asked.

"What firecrackers?" Dick tried to put on an innocent face but I didn't think it would fool anyone.

"Don't jerk me around. I mean business, I know you have them. Charlie, go out and go over that car of theirs with a fine tooth comb and find those firecrackers."

I glanced at Dick and without saying a word, we knew we had to tough it out. With my fingers crossed behind my back I prayed Willie wouldn't call our parents. I knew the adults wouldn't manage to keep a clear perspective of the fact that one cracker wasn't the end of the world. We stood there quietly while Willie sat at his desk filling out the form. I tried to read it upside down but all I could make out was the word 'firecrackers'. In about five minutes Charlie came back without the evidence. He put his hands out and shrugged.

Dick and I held our breaths. We weren't going to incriminate ourselves. I thought, if we can just hold on to our nerves we might get out of this.

Willie slammed his hand down on the desk. "You boys ain't going scot free because we are going to make a record of this and we'll be watching you two real close. You know you did it, Mr. Bart knows you did it, and I know you did it, so get out of here but look out, because my day will come."

As soon as we let the door of the police station shut behind us we raced back to the car. I said, "Those firecrackers have got to go. They are dangerous and they always seem to get us in trouble. Where should we go?"

Teenagers have short memories. The fear we felt in the station had turned to exultation. "Go back to those weeds in Madisonville so I can find my brown bag. You don't think I'm going to leave those red beauties back there to rot and fizzle?" Dick asked.

When I got home, Dad and Mother sat waiting for me in the living room, dressed in their pajamas and robes. The fear returned. Dad spoke, "We got a call from the Madeira police chief. He said you and Dick almost blew a wagon load of Christmas flowers half way to the North Pole with some kind of bomb."

From the tone of Dad's voice I could tell he saw the humor in the situation. "He exaggerates, Dad." I said, hoping to get a smile out of him.

Before I could explain, Mother had her turn. From the expression on her face I knew she didn't find anything funny about it. "I want you and your friends to get rid of all firecrackers forever. Those things have been a problem since that chicken coop in Kentucky, and I'm not blowing smoke when I tell you that you are docked for a week with no wheels."

Lord of the Loonies

I should have gone to bed early that Friday night. All the memory work at St. X was draining me and clouding my judgement. Hap and I had planned a nice quiet evening at the movie but even that didn't happen.

"Bad news, Bob," Hap said. "I got one foot in the grave and the other on a banana peel."

"How's that?"

"Remember last week when we were driving down Columbia Parkway and I sort of accidentally ran that old geezer into the curb? I've got to tell you that it really opened up a can of worms for me and I'm prohibited from using the car."

"Who exactly was that old geezer?"

"He was traffic court Judge Gusweiller," Hap replied.

Bad news. He hadn't looked that official when we passed him. "In that case I'd say you're getting off pretty easy considering it wasn't quite accidental. But any hoo, let's start walking. It's only six blocks to the movie."

"I got a better deal", Hap replied. "Four of my buddies from Country Day School are meeting and want us to go with them."

"I'm game. Where are they?"

"At Pritch's grandfather's house. We are supposed to meet them outside the garage."

"Why? What do they have planned?"

"I don't know but Pritch is calling the shots tonight." We met the other four at the garage near the street. I could barely see the main house through the heavy grove of pines on the hill but it was huge. "Who exactly is Pritch?" I asked.

"His grandfather used to be governor," Hap replied, "but once you meet Pritch, you'll never believe he's related."

I could see what he meant when we found Hap's friends. Pritch was a small weasly fellow with a pale face and long, spidery looking hands. About every five seconds his head would jerk to the right like he was possessed. Everyone else pretended not to notice so I tried not to either. For some reason Pritch was dressed like he was going to school in a blue blazer and a striped tie. I thought it was strange dress for a weekend night. Besides the twitch he was nervous as hell and kept pacing around like he was planning something. The other fellows seemed okay but I wasn't sure the night was going to shape up into anything interesting.

We hung around the front of the garage for a while until it was good and dark. One of the other kids, Walt, said, "I'm getting bored. Let's do something."

Pritch motioned to us to gather around him. He spoke in hushed tones. "Grandpa keeps an old '39 Cadillac in this garage and the chauffeur always leaves the keys under the driver's floor mat." We opened the creaky pair of wooden garage doors, Pritch backed it out and we closed up shop behind him. Walt climbed in up front, Hap and I sat in the rear seat with a liquor bar between us and Steve and Harry sat in the fold-down seat in the center.

As soon as Pritch got on the street, he turned on the headlights and tromped it. We headed for the bars in northern Kentucky and in the 15 minutes it took to get there, I don't remember him ever using the brake pedal once. He was good at timing the green lights and if he needed to slow down from 50 mph he would double clutch and downshift to second. We bought beer at a variety of bars and drove around in the limo drinking and telling stupid jokes.

At 12:30 I told Pritch I promised my mother I'd be home by 1:00 AM. "No problem," Pritch said. "Let's drink up and hit the highway."

Instead of taking me back to Hyde Park to my car, he raced me directly home. It was standard practice in our house to kiss Mother goodnight, whatever the hour. She couldn't sleep soundly until all were kissed and accounted for. Pritch turned off the headlights before turning into our driveway.

"O.K., Bob. Make it quick. We'll wait."

I went clopping loudly into the house and down the first floor hallway to my parent's room. Mom smiled at me sleepily and I felt guilty. "Goodnight, dear," she said.

From there I went bouncing up the steps to my second bedroom and closed the door. Two seconds later I tiptoed down the stairs and out the back door.

At 2:00 AM we were down on Wooster Pike at Frisch's eating 'Big Boy' hamburgers, fries, and finishing off some of the remaining variety of Bavarian, Hudepohl, Wiedemann and Red Top six packs of beer. Before we left the lot Pritch found a rag in the glove compartment and decided it would be a good idea to wrap the rear license plate to conceal our identity just in case the cops started chasing us.

At 3:00 AM we were buzzing through Mariemont when we all got the shock of the night. Some cop with red lights and siren blaring was only 15 feet off our tail and motioning us over. He was too close for Pritch to run as planned. I pictured all of us in jail on ten counts of speeding, drunk driving, stolen car and whatever. I thought Pritch's head was going to jerk right off his shoulders he was so nervous, but then again we were all pale and shaking. Hap and I shoved all the empties into the bar cabinet just in the nick of time. The officer put his flashlight beam in the back first and then in Pritch's face. "Hand me your driver's license please," he ordered.

Pritch complied but didn't say a word. After examining the document the policeman said, "Your license seems OK now tell me how you got it."

"I don't understand," Pritch said.

"And you probably don't understand why I stopped you."

"No sir." At least he sounded polite.

"Well, let me tell you."

I sat in the back seat and thought this was going to be catastrophic. Spending one night with old Pritch was like opening Pandora's Box and being unable to close it.

The cop proceeded, "I just can't understand why you think you can drive around at 3:00 AM with covered license plates. There is a law against hiding your license number."

Pritch was quick to answer. "I can't believe those guys did that. Officer, we just came from a party and got in a scuffle with a bunch from the other side of town. They did this so we would get in trouble, sir." At least Pritch had something in that twitchy head of his.

The officer said, "Take the rag off and stay out of trouble. Next time you won't get off." I couldn't believe it. Maybe the combination of the blazer and the limo convinced the cop Pritch had friends in high places.

By now it was around 4:30. We were still driving around but getting punchy. We headed west on Erie Avenue, going about 95 mph and approached a red light at Hyde Park Square. Even though there were no cars on the road we were still going way too fast. I knew Pritch would not hit the brakes and he couldn't downshift with the car flying along. I held my breath as he went right through the light and weaved his way around the grassy center island.

Naturally there was a police cruiser parked on a side street. The cop was wide awake and punched on his red lights and siren instantly. By the time he got up to speed, we turned right on Mooney Avenue. Pritch slid in between two parked cars, flicked off the lights and hissed at us to get down. We hit the floor and held our breaths as if we breathed the car would shake. The cop passed us hell bent for leather and disappeared.

I sat up and said, "Pritch, this is your lucky day. It must be your birthday."

He looked at me strangely, "No, my birthday is actually tomorrow, April 2nd."

I was too tired to tell him he was born one day too late. Hap had the sense to speak up and say, "Take this black coffin back to the garage before it kills us."

Back at the Governor's garage, we cleaned out the interior, got rid of the beer cans and carefully wiped the entire car for fingerprints. The sky had a slight glow and I knew I had to beat it home. Hap and I headed back to his house to pick up my car. I drove home, gliding into the driveway with the engine off so I wouldn't wake anyone.

When the car came to a stop behind the garage, I rested my head on the steering wheel and reflected on Hap and me. We were golden friends but we needed to watch out for each other in a better manner. That night we let life and other people run their course and I could see that was not often the best choice. We needed to sometimes take control of our friends and our actions. No more joy rides with fellows in stolen cars.

The Moonshine Cats (1949)

School ground slowly to a summer halt but Dick called the minute he got back in town from the Canterbury School in Connecticut. He was full of ideas, as usual. "Let's go fishing. I heard about this new lake in Kentucky and we can use a new aluminum rowboat here at Dad's dealership. Someone used the boat as a down payment on a car and just dumped it in the used car lot with no trailer."

"Sounds terrific," I said, envisioning a crystal clear lake and fish jumping out of it onto our hooks.

"Only problem is, we don't have a trailer."

I thought for a moment. "If I can borrow Dad's dirt trailer, do you think we could fasten it to the side uprights?" I asked.

"Worth a try."

The next day I had all my fishing gear and bags of clothing spread out on the bed when Mom brought in some clean laundry. "Where are you going?" she asked.

"Didn't Dad tell you? Dick and I are going to Dale Hollow Lake State Park in Kentucky."

"I've never heard of it."

"It's new. There's 28,000 acres of water and over 950 miles of shoreline. The lake is stocked with all kinds of fish." I realized I sounded like a travel ad so I just finished with, "It should be great."

Mom set down a stack of clothes and put her hands on her hips. "That sounds fine but every time you two boys get in a car there seems to be trouble in river city."

"Not this time, Mom. I promise," I pleaded, knowing she had the power to stall this outing.

"Well, all right. Be careful and make sure you check the weather."

By the time we had all the fishing equipment, worms, swimming suits, snacks, aspirin and 3.2 beer the car was jammed full. We didn't have a tent so I commandeered a brand new 15' by 15' white cotton drop cloth from Dad's paint shop. Dad helped us hook up the trailer to Dick's Ford coupe. "Looks like you are going to have a fine time," he said, examining all our supplies. He almost acted like he wanted an invitation but then I thought, no, why would he want to goof around with us?

Our first stop was the Fuller Ford used car lot on Reading Road to pick up the boat. With the help of a couple of salesmen we got it up and tied down. "It's not great but it should hold," one of them named Slim said. Charlie, the other salesman noted, "That's what we call 'riding slipshod' in the navy." Our rig looked awkward but then no one was going to grade our slipshod set-up.

We were out of there. Over the Ohio River and down into the hills of Kentucky and a few hours later on Route 27. I estimated we were about 60 miles north of the lake near Albany, Kentucky. The road rolled through the hills and was so rough every time we came out of a dip in the road the bow of the boat came down with a ping on the top of Dick's trunk lid.

We were flying along at our normal speed when Dick said, "There's a bunch of guys in a black Ford sedan right on my tail. I think they want to pass."

"Well, ease up and let them come."

"They can pass but they will have to work for it because I'm not giving those yahoos a dime." Dick was a good driver and he could hold his own, but after ten minutes the passing game became old hat.

After repeated honks of their horn they finally found a long even stretch and pulled alongside. We saw a good reason to slow down. There was some sort of official gold symbol on the side of the car and the two men in the right front and rear windows waved pistols at us to pull over.

We stopped.

"You two mutha fricking yankees is going hell bent for fire, now yo'all get out of that there automobile and face the car with your legs spread." Five deputies now surrounded us.

After checking our paperwork and frisking us, the captain

spoke up. "You boys is going in our files and we are going to let you go with a warning. One more time and you is jailbait. By the way, what you got in that cooler in the back seat?"

"Just a few beers," I said.

"You all are too young to be drinking beer. Hand it over and get out of here."

We stood in a cloud of their road dust as they spun off swigging our beer.

"Somebody ought to report those mealy mouthed cops," I said, kicking the tire.

"Forget it. You take it the rest of the way. I'll navigate into the park area," Dick said as he climbed in the passenger seat.

We finally spotted the sign for the park entrance. It was brand new but the road was a dirt lane. We drove for a couple of miles surrounded by trees. Once in a while we caught a glimpse of water but it was only a stream that wove in and out close to the road. By this time it was late afternoon and a fine drizzle began to fall. We saw no signs, no ranger station and no camp grounds.

"Are you sure this park is really open? I think we got here five years too early," I said, wondering where Dick had found out about this place. The drizzle turned into a light rain but still no campsite.

After more winding around Dick said, "Let's set up camp while we can still see." We found a high spot next to the dirt road and decided to call it home. Trying to ignore the rain we rigged the tarp over a rope tied to a couple of tree and stashed some of our gear underneath it. Then we sat down on some of the gear and stared at the raindrops. I was happy to be away from home but this stretched the idea of fun. I rummaged in a bag and pulled out a can of potatoes and a couple of ham sandwiches. Since there was no possible way to start a fire we shared the cold potatoes and inhaled the sandwiches. We forgot to bring candles but it didn't matter because the steady downpour led us into our sleeping bags to keep warm and we were out like a light.

The next morning there were no birds singing and no sunshine. We hadn't seen a living soul for the past 14 hours. It was foggy and damp and I thought I saw mold already forming on the drop cloth.

"Let's take the car and boat and do some exploring this morning. It might stop raining and we might find some terrific spot to change our campsite." Dick showed more enthusiasm as he bounded around packing things up.

"Okay with me. I don't think things can get any worse."

We lumbered down another road through the woods. It eventually started to climb. The road narrowed as we climbed higher and we contemplated a turn around spot. Too late.

As we came around a steep uphill bend in the road I spotted a thin plume of smoke rising over the trees. "Hey Dick, I

No turnaround spot for Ford and dirt trailer

think there are some more campers up here. Maybe they can tell us how to find the lake." One more bend and we found ourselves in the front yard of a cabin. I could also see a building off to one side, smoke coming from its vicinity. We hopped out of the car and a horrendous smell hit us in the face. If that building was a smokehouse I wouldn't have wanted to eat whatever was going to come out of there. I was about ready to suggest we scram when we came face to face with a local coming around the corner of the house. His most noticeable feature was a 12 gauge shotgun hanging in one hand. The rest of him was about 50, stocky, and unshaven. He spit a wad of tobacco that landed on the hood of the car.

"Hold it right thar, boys. Ye can't go no further here." The smoke increased over the shed and I wondered if the man knew something might be on fire. I looked over and spotted a tank contraption behind the building smoking up a storm.

"We are just looking for a spot to launch our rowboat," Dick said.

He peered around, scratching his head. "Ain't nobody ever launched a boat up on this here mountain. You all stupid or something? A little tetched in the head, maybe? I think you are poking your noses where they don't belong." He waved the shotgun up and down for emphasis.

I was never stupid for long. I had seen enough Ma and Pa Kettle movies to know what was going on. I never realized the manufacture of white lightening in a still created such a stench. It was just our luck to run into this sort of trouble. I wished my mother could be here to see that sometime trouble just happens to us even when we aren't looking for it.

"We are just here to fish for some bluegill, sir. I guess we made a wrong turn," I said, trying to get my eyes off the shotgun. The man started to circle around the car, whistling tunelessly between the gaps in his teeth. I gulped.

"Actually, Mister, some cops took our beer from us so we were wondering if you could recommend a place to buy any kind of hooch."

Dick looked at me like I had gone nuts.

"Booze, huh. You young fellas look like city boys. I might know where you could get something if you have enough cash on you."

I pulled out five dollars. This is all I've got." I showed him the empty wallet to prove it but didn't mention the twenty in my back pocket. "How much do you have, Dick?"

He read the urgency in my voice. "I have ten dollars." I grabbed it out of his hand and held it out. "Here you go. We'll take whatever you have."

"Yo'all just wait right thar. Don't move," our host said as he went back into the cabin.

"What's going on. What are we buying for 15 dollars?

"Shsssh, just keep quiet and go along with me. In a moment the man came back, carrying a gallon jug. He shoved it at me and said, "Now you git out of here and don't ever come back."

Dick finally caught on when he saw the jug of clear moonshine juice and we practically fell over each other to get back in the car. We sped back down that mountain like any moment an army of moonshiners would leap out of the woods to pursue us. The boat jumped and rattled behind us, making us cringe a little every time it pinged down on the trunk. We drove 50 miles to a real state campground we had passed the previous day. When we pulled in, I held up the jug and said, "At least now we will be able to start a fire."

Win a Few, Lose...

Damned if I do and damned if I don't. Whether 'twas nobler to bear the pangs of my old Chev or simply give up on it was the question. It had been a meager investment, but the repair bills were killing me, and my dates weren't happy it was so small and too cold in winter.

Mom had really been great about loaning me her '41 Chrysler if I begged on my knees, but what the heck, I wasn't tied to her apron strings and one day she gave me the bad news. "Listen, Bobby, I just want to forewarn you. Tomorrow Dad is buying me a new Chrysler and insurance won't cover you, so be happy with your car."

That solved part of the problem. I needed a better car and quick. Every time I passed a used car lot, my old mechanical brakes would bring me to an irregular squeaky halt. I hit pay dirt at Howard Hively Lincoln Mercury dealership used lot. There it was. It was like my name was plastered right on the driver's side door. A mint condition, soft green, 1940 Mercury Convertible with 32,000 miles. It had a charcoal canvas top, natural tan-colored leather seats, and had been maintained through the war by the original owner, Mrs. Todd, the classic old lady driver.

Dad gave it his stamp of approval and after a little wheeling and dealing, we got it for $1200. I was the proud and excited owner. I still had to work out the problem of finances with Dad and sell the Chev to boot.

The next day I was working as a house painter at Mrs. Eustis' ten bedroom home on Drake Road in Indian Hill. The outside grounds keeper foreman pulled up to the garage at 8:00 with a car full of garden helpers. One old coot in the back seat had trouble finding the door handle so he bailed out the rear window and landed on his back. George the foreman got out, ran around, and picked up the bearded and smelly Mr. Sanford only to realize he was drunk as a skunk. George fired him on the spot, telling him to go collect his pay.

Sanford started his hike back to Madeira when I called out to him. "Mr. Sanford, Mr. Sanford, hold up. Say I'm sorry about your job but I think this is your lucky day. How would you like to own that beautiful black Chev coupe parked down there next to the barn?

"Hashamush?"

"Pardon me?"

"Hashamush?"

I finally figured out this meant, 'how much'. "Oh, I'll give it to you for only $125.00." I knew he was good for the money because he would have to go pick up his last paycheck and I would be right there to collect my share.

"Shold," he said. I felt a few pangs as the old Chev weaved out the driveway but I was more relieved than regretful. Problem two was gone and the third was resolved with Dad when he agreed to take weekly payment from my house painting job.

It was time to give the Mercury my own special look because I knew just a few add-ons could make this car unique. Four large spinner hub caps, rear fender skirts, a pair of three dollar shackle bars to lower the rear end two inches, a little wax job, and it was ready to go. Dick, Hap and I headed for Ault Park. It was one of those rare summer nights with enough cool breeze to feel like we were someplace besides Cincinnati. I don't know what it is about summer nights but the air can go to your head and make you a little crazy. I should have been dead tired, painting houses all week, but as soon as the three of us got together the energy sparked.

At the fieldstone dance pavilion a fifteen piece band was playing. We weren't in the mood to buy a nickel dance ticket. The sounds of Glenn Miller's *Serenade in Blue* wafted through the park but we were too keyed up to pay much attention. Dick pulled out a bottle of Wagner Company soda water from a brown bag he had brought. These heavy returnable glass

Win a Few, Lose... 132

Mercury at Ault Park dance pavilion.

bottles were fitted with chrome release spigots on top and could shoot carbonated soda at least 35 feet if necessary. The pavilion was up on a grassy knoll with a half mile circular road and sidewalk surrounding it. We cruised a few times looking at the people milling about. Dick decided he would shoot a quick burst of soda on any guy who just happened not to meet his fancy at the moment.

It seemed hilarious at the time. Dick would crouch down and then pop up like a prairie dog, shooting the water and then ducking back down. When we ran out of club soda we decided it was time to leave with one small firecracker bang just as the band finished playing, "I don't want to set the world on fire."

A perfect night. For some reason we felt like we had accomplished something. After dropping off two of the three dunces I arrived home. Dad and Mother were sitting on the screened porch with their friends, Gus and Polly, having a few Scotch and sodas. Gus was one of Dad's best friends, always a faithful on the baseball field and president of the Albers Supermarket Co., a sizeable grocery chain. I stopped to say hello when the phone rang; it was 11:45 PM.

Dad picked it up, said hello and listened. Then he said, "Hold on please. Bobby, this is District Five police station in Hyde Park. They have a man there who got your license plate number when you squirted him with soda water in the park tonight. He wants to press charges. Is it true?"

Reality jolted me in the stomach. What could I say? It was time to pay the piper. I replied sadly, "Yes."

Dad was quick on his feet. "Officer, my son is right here with me and he does admit your charge. May I please speak to the other party? Thank you."

Dad spoke to him in a very kindly voice, apologized for my misbehavior and turned the conversation around. "By the way, Mr. Danzinger, where do you work?" Dad had the most amazing way with people, even over the phone. He always sounded like he really cared about anything anyone had to say. He listened for a moment and then held his hand over the receiver. "Gus, I have a favor to ask. You are not going to believe this coincidence. Bobby got into some trouble tonight, nothing serious, but he happened to squirt some water on an employee of yours. He works in your warehouse on Spring Grove Avenue."

Gus took the phone and chatted for a few moments and then said, "Look, Mr. Danzinger, you come up to my office Monday. I'd like to thank you personally. Okay? Goodbye." He hung up the phone and said, "Problem solved."

I knew the worst of my problems weren't over. Mother glared, "Bobby, this is the last time you get off the hook. Your car is going in the barn."

"I swear, Mom," I said, really meaning it, "It was a stupid thing to do and we won't get into any more trouble." At the time I really meant it.

A few weeks later Dick said, "Johnny C. just phoned and he has a brand new yellow Frazer. He wants to take it out for a trial run."

"Great, I'll be ready." I hung up, excited to ride in a Frazer convertible. After the war there was such a demand for cars, anything would sell. Henry Frazer, who made millions on ship building during the war went into business with Joseph Frazer and created an independent car company to challenge Detroit. They were poorly made cars but the younger generation liked the modern look of them.

The three of us headed to the center of Madeira with the top down. As we approached the only intersection in town we could see and hear Tag-em Willie directing traffic with his whistle. He put out his hand to hold our lane for the cross traffic to move and then waved us on. Just as we passed within three feet of him Johnny C. revved up the engine, popped the clutch and spewed dirt and gravel next to the police chief. I looked out and saw Willie's face change from small town cop to what looked like the evil avenger out of a comic book. Dick looked over at Johnny and said, "What in the hell did you do that for?"

Before Johnny could answer, Willie screamed, "Stop!" and blew his whistle loudly.

I turned back and saw him running to his cruiser. "We've got trouble. He's in his Plymouth and is going to chase us."

Johnny said calmly, "Don't worry," and floored the gas pedal, throwing us back in our seats. We picked up speed going north down Miami Road. I knew we were going to hit the railroad tracks fast so I grabbed the door handle before we jolted over them. Dick hadn't been so quick and nearly flew out the top of the car. A mile out of town in farm country we still had a decent lead but the chief was closing the gap so Johnny took an abrupt right on Kugler Mill Road into Indian Hill.

Dick shouted, "Gees, Johnny, I don't want to spend my whole vacation in jail. Get us out of this."

"I have a plan," he said. We sped over the next hill and without warning, Johnny took a neck-breaking right turn down a long driveway. I knew where we were. It was Dr. Carter's farm. We sped down the quarter mile gravel driveway. Willie was out of sight and still had not hit the top of the hill. I thought we would be in the clear if we could just get to the spruce trees near the front of the house and hide but then I glanced behind us. Clouds of dust rose from the back of the Frazer as it plowed through the dry gravel. We looked like an airplane with its tail smoking and we were sure to be spotted. We pulled up to house. I jumped out and peeked around the trees. At first Willie drove straight by the entry but the cloud of dust drew him back.

I jumped back in the car and yelled, "We have to keep going! He's coming!" We proceeded past the white farm house and into the rear barnyard area. The noise of the racing Frazer rattled some chickens who fluttered and squawked. The whole back area was fenced in. We stopped in front of a padlocked gate.

Dick laughed, "I think our goose is cooked."

J.C. replied, "No, it's too late to chicken out now," and then they both roared with laughter. I would have groaned at the poultry references but I was too worried about the police and I kept picturing my mother's face after the Ault Park incidence. I didn't know if she would let me sit in jail overnight but I didn't want to find out because at that moment Willie was bearing down on us.

"Bob, jump out and see if that gate is really locked." Johnny said.

I bolted over the side and sure enough the lock wasn't fastened. I pushed the gate open, flagged them through and then tried to wrap the chain back around. My fingers shook so much it took some time to fasten the lock. Finally I jumped on the rear of the car and climbed in the back seat just as Willie came around the house.

We sped off through tree-lined pastures, opening and closing gates behind us until we came out on a gravel road, which could take us home. Dick said, "Listen, we aren't clear yet. Old Tag-em may have recognized Bob and me from some other troubles. He probably got your license plate number. too."

"Don't sweat it," Johnny replied like we had just been out for a Sunday drive. "Let's go to Frisch's."

Dick kept on talking. "Another thing, this is probably the only yellow Frazer convertible in Cincinnati and he can spot you from two blocks away. Are you just going to avoid Madeira as long as you own this car?"

"I'm telling you, don't worry about it. That guy is more concerned about keeping up his image in town.

Willie was a good cop and worked very hard to do his job. He was right back in the intersection that afternoon, all spic and span, sharp pleated trousers, gold emblems shining, standing next to his freshly washed Plymouth.

27

Midnight Marauder

As my years in high school continued, my biggest desire was not to get all 'A's. I wanted to play one of the three major sports – football, basketball or baseball, so I could win a varsity letter that Mom could sew on my dark blue sweater. The real heroes of the school were the athletes. They swaggered around the rest of us as if they knew something we didn't. Even at an academic school like St. Xavier, sports were too important to take the chance of losing a good player to another school.

Everyone else fell into three categories. The brains could memorize anything, Greek, Latin, Shakespeare, you name it. I couldn't understand how they seemed to be able to look at a page and memorize it long enough to write it all out on a test. The nerds came in all shapes, sizes, heights and looks. Their only common bond was one minor detail about them that was different from the rest of us, either pants too short, glasses too big, or hair that stuck up in cowlicks.

Most of the rest of us fell into a big gray area of average. We were the wannabes who probably weren't gonnabes. Nevertheless, we probably tried harder to be something or someone more than we actually were. Maybe the struggle taught us something in the end but at the time I didn't enjoy being lumped with the crowd.

I carefully analyzed the potential of my physical possibilities. I was too small for football and too short for basketball. Baseball was the only option. I knew I was as coordinated and as quick as anyone but whether or not I could convince the coach was another story.

During baseball batting tryouts I slammed about ten straight slow pitches out to deep left field and by the next afternoon I was on the varsity team sheet. I couldn't get my varsity letter until I participated through the season but at least I knew it was just a matter of time.

Right near the start of our regular season we had an intersquad game among our own players. My old tennis opponent from Fort Scott camp, Jimmy, pitched for the opposing side. I had never mentioned camp or tennis to him and I was praying he would not remember that long ago competition, or at least he wouldn't remember it was me. He was still beanpole skinny but much taller now, all legs and ears held together by a baseball cap. The first time I batted, Jimmy went into his windup and threw a blazing fast ball. I swung and missed. Strike one. He threw another fast ball. This time I didn't swing and the umpire yelled, "Strike two!" The third pitch was outside, ball one. Jim walked around the mound rubbing the baseball, probably envisioning the beanie I won and he didn't. The next was a slow curve ball. I swung while it was still leisurely floating toward me and that was it. I was out.

The next time up I was determined to hit that ball but again they all flew by. During the next two innings I watched his technique. When I got in the batter's box the third time, Jim wound up and threw a curve ball. I didn't swing and the umpire yelled, "Ball one!" I was beginning to feel more confident. I knew I could hit one of these pitches. Jim threw a fast ball right down the middle of the plate. I missed it by a tiny fraction. The next pitch came in and looked like it was going to jam me so I instinctively pulled back. That ball curved around and caught the inside corner of the plate for strike two. My hands got clammy and I had a sinking feeling in my stomach. The pitch was another blazing fast ball. Strike three. It was over. I could see the coach writing stuff on his clipboard and I knew it was about me.

Back in the shower room, Coach Bonnie drew me aside and handed me my most feared death knell. "Robert, as of today, you are no longer a member of the ball club." I stood in total amazement. I didn't know whether to cry or go blind. It was my last chance to earn one of those beautiful letters. I stuttered and choked, "Why, coach?"

"You should know why. You struck out three times today."

"I know, Coach, but look who you had pitching at me, probably our best pitcher."

"Look here, Bob, anybody that can't hit off Jim Bunning doesn't belong on my team." There was nothing left to say. I slunk out of the locker room trying not to cry. I resigned myself to being just one of the crowd again.

The next day, Mr. Robinson, the algebra teacher called me up after class. He had just given me a conditional failing grade of 69 on my third quarter report card. It was my only low grade but it was enough to mean summer school unless I could raise it and the thought of summer school was downright frightening.

I thought I would get a lecture about not living up to my potential but instead he said, "Bob, you know I'm the school tennis coach and some of my players tell me you are one of the best. If that's true I'll put you on the varsity. How about coming out tomorrow? We have this big match with Walnut Hills High and they have one of the best teams in the state and one of the best players. Have you heard of Tony Trabert?" I had. I thought fast. I hadn't even considered getting a letter from the tennis team.

Mr. Robinson said, "We really need you. What do you say?"

I felt the rush of pure power. "That's impossible," I said.

He stared at me. Turning down a varsity spot was unheard of. "Why?"

"Because of the 69 I got. I need to spend every afternoon until June studying algebra so I will pass. I don't want to go to summer school."

He sat quietly, tapping his pen on his desk and then glared at me. "I get your point, smart guy. O.K. it's a deal. But if you don't produce on the clay court, you better figure out a way to do better on your algebra tests." Two months later I finally got that letter and knew I had learned something powerful about the art of negotiating.

By senior year the studying went smoothly but I wanted to get on with real life. I already had decided to go into Dad's interior design business and the study of Latin didn't appear to be pertinent. St. X had one social fraternity – Omicron Phi Alpha – not part of the school curriculum but a good excuse for something to think about besides studying. We met on

Sunday afternoons, usually at a member's home who just happened to live near a house where our favorite girls' sorority meeting was being held at the same time

I hadn't been able to avoid total responsibility for the group. During the spring of junior year I had given a couple of seniors a ride home and we had a real discussion about the direction and purpose of our fraternal organization, without mentioning the girl factor. After I treated them to a half-hour lecture on how our group could operate better they got the idea I should put my soul where my mouth was. They nominated and elected me president for my senior year.

The fraternity didn't take much time to run because our only big events were three dances a year. It was a gamble each year to see if we could hold a fling successful enough to pay off all the money we committed up front.

For the first dance, I called Charlie Kehrer's agent to line up his 18-man big band. Each band member cost $15 apiece but I didn't want to skimp. Our formal 'Fall Fantasy' was expected to be a huge success so I booked the largest room downtown at the Gibson Hotel. Their L-shaped roof garden room could hold 600 so we booked it in June for an October fling. The hotel agreed to operate at least five bars selling chips, pretzels, soft drinks and 3.2 beer. I hoped this dance would live up to everyone's expectation.

I had arranged to pick up my date, Sudie, in Northern Kentucky early because I knew I would have to follow the drill of sitting and watching television with her parents in the living room for a few minutes while Sue waited to make an entrance. Cincinnati TV station WLW-T had broadcast the very first television show over the local air waves 18 months earlier, so I looked forward to watching Jack Benny play the violin badly.

Sitting in their living room, I was starting to sweat the time because I wanted to check on the set-up at the hotel. Sudie finally came down, looking so great it made it worth the wait, but I was in such a hurry to get going, it was tough to get the gardenia corsage pinned on without poking her. I jogged her out to the car and helped her in, trying to push the skirt in far enough to close the door. Her dress almost filled up the entire front seat. The pink crinoline skirt frothed and foamed like a small ocean and I had to keep pushing it aside so I wouldn't put my foot down on it.

At the Gibson Hotel we arrived just early enough to check out the ticket takers, bouncers, security officer, and the bars. Everything looked okay but I was still nervous, waiting for the first arrivals. After a few hours, though, it was clear it was a sellout. At $3.00 a couple I knew we would make enough to pay off the bills. Everyone else danced the night away doing the Bunny Hop, the hand jive, the Moxie, and the Bop. I was too worried about things running smoothly to totally enjoy it but everyone else's feet smoked.

Sudie, Bob, Jane, Casty, Maddie, Paul

The last dances slowed down. The band played Artie Shaw's *Dancing in the Dark* and the cigarette smoke, accumulated over the evening, gave a nice romantic misty feel to the room. I finally relaxed enough to savor the last dance but all too soon it ended.

When I had taken Sudie out before we always ended up blissfully parked in front of her house kissing. That night we parked and in five minutes we were eyeball to eyeball and lip to lip. The windows steamed up in the cool October air.

Suddenly, without any noise or warning, the driver's side door burst open and a huge hand grabbed me around my neck. I was facing Sue and she screamed as if she had seen that living legend, the urban monster with a hook for a hand who preyed on kids in parked cars. In a flash I realized I was not going to die at the hands of a demon but maybe at the hands of Sudie's father.

The hand yanked me out of the car and threw me down on the street on my back. It was so dark I could only make out a huge looming shape, pausing before stomping me. The shape bent down and peered into the car and then I heard his voice, "I'm sorry, I live next door and I thought you were out here with my daughter."

Testing the Limits

I was leading a steady, calm life when Dick came home for Thanksgiving. He called and I had already planned our weekend. "My girlfriend, Sudie, is playing hostess to a covey of birds at a sorority slumber party. My sister, Madge, and her friend Kay are going so I thought we could crash the party and join the festivities."

"Where's it at?" he asked and I could tell he was interested.

"It's at Sudie's parents lake cottage in Ryland, Kentucky."
"I'll drive. I can borrow a '47 four door Pontiac from Dad's used car lot." Dick didn't get a chance to drive at school so he was always raring to get behind the wheel when he came home. We picked up our friend Mitch and drove south of Newport, Kentucky, down to Ryland. A small cavalcade of four cars followed us. News of the slumber party had been broadcast throughout the airwaves of the teenage wireless system and it was too good an opportunity to miss. By 9:00 it was dark and I thought we would have the best chance to sneak up to the cottage without being noticed. The lake community only had one road going in it so we decided to drive part way, park, and hoof it the last 100 yards. We pulled up to the main entrance. A man stepped out in front of our car and held up his hand. Dick stopped. "Who's that? Do they have a security guard here?"

"Worse. We're out of luck. That's Sudie's father." Her dad and I were good pals. He was a very friendly guy, always smiling and he wanted me to call him by his first name, Louie.

However benign he appeared, I knew he could be as stern as he was in the courtroom he presided over in Fort Thomas, Kentucky.

Louie walked over to the car. "Hello, Bob. Hello, boys. What are you up to tonight?"

"Oh, just driving around. It's nice to see you." I smiled and he smiled back, his hand on the top of the car. We were all being so polite it was unreal.

"Nice of you to stop by, boys. We will see you again sometime. Enjoy your drive." He gave the car a push as if to remind us who was in charge. We backed out, meekly. I always forgot fathers had once been teenage boys too, and Sudie's father was smart enough to prepare in advance for any onslaught we might make.

"Let's go to Marshall's out on Dixie Highway for a few beers," Dick suggested. The road back to Newport ran fairly straight but it had a few dips that followed the hills in the lake country. Normally I wouldn't have noticed them but when Dick started hitting them at 70 miles per hour, I felt the jolts in my back teeth. Dick always drove fast. Because of his driving habits, he was the type who watched the road far ahead but spent as much time checking the rear view mirror for police cars. True to form, after a few miles he announced, "We got the fuzz on our tail and he's going to play heck to catch me."

Mitch and I knew we had little influence on Dick so we stayed silent. I wasn't looking forward to a police chase. I kept my eyes glued on the roadway ahead praying we wouldn't rear end someone out for a leisurely drive. I glanced at the speedometer. The needle crept up on 100 mph.

We approached the outskirts of Covington sooner than I expected. Far ahead I caught sight of a yellow left turn sign and told Dick to hit the brakes hard. His reaction was typically quick. He laid a streak of rubber from all four tires. With the extra weight of the engine up front, the car had a natural tendency to understeer and the rear wheels lost adhesion. We skidded sideways at 60 miles per hour and I knew disaster was upon us. I yelled to Mitch, "Lock all your doors and Dick's too because we're going to turn turtle."

At once, the two right wheels grabbed the pavement, the car flipped over in mid air, landed upside down and crushed the top. The entire windshield shattered and hundreds of glass splinters felt like a sandstorm in my face. The steel top scraped down against the roadway, creating long flashing sparks in the darkness that raced through the car as if lightning had hit it. We flipped two more times, tumbling around in the car with no seat belts. When the Pontiac finally came to rest right side up, the two rear wheels perched on top of a two-foot high guardrail.

My first thought was fire because I could smell the gasoline. I yelled at Mitch and Dick to get out as I opened my door. I could hear Mitch trying to get out from under the seats which had become dislodged. After pulling the seats off him, I raced around to the front driver's door and gave it a few yanks. At first it wouldn't open because it was crushed, but after a few more tugs it opened. I thought Dick wasn't getting out because he was hurt but when I peered in I saw him sitting quietly, staring straight ahead, both hands on the wheel in a vise grip. I asked him to hurry and get out but he just sat as if he didn't hear me. He was transfixed. I peeled his fingers off the wheel and dragged him out where he could sit down.

Seconds later the sheriff's car showed up with his red spotlight blazing and siren blaring. He got out and walked over to Mitch.

Pontiac totaled in Newport

"What happened here?"

"I don't know. I just got here," Mitch replied. The deputy walked back down the road to check the skid marks, came back and said, "Who was the driver of the wrecked vehicle? We didn't say anything but we couldn't help looking at Dick, who sat in the grass as if he were Mahatma Gandi contemplating the meaning of life. The sheriff walked over to him and asked, "You were exceeding the speed limit," and wrote him a ticket on the spot.

By the time a tow truck arrived, Dick was back to normal but I still shook when I thought about the car turning over and us tumbling about like marbles in a dryer. It was the most horrendous experience of my life and the nightmares of the event made me less erratic. I didn't want to end up dead so soon, killed before I had a chance to see more of life.

I spent the remaining weeks before Christmas hitting the books, determined to approach life more seriously but four weeks of seriousness at that age was all I could take. Dick came home for Christmas vacation and called, "Moonbeam just phoned and wants us to go for a ride in a Mercury station wagon he just bought from my dad's car lot." I don't know why I didn't let my memories of all our previous drives deter me, but I was ready and waiting when they pulled up. Moonbeam was an acquaintance from grade school whom I rarely saw. He had a round white face and had been called Moonbeam forever.

When they pulled in the driveway I was so busy admiring the wood paneling on the sides of the wagon that I didn't notice they had an extra passenger until I opened the car door. It was another character from grade school, Neil. I knew he was bad news. Here I was trying to straighten up my life, and Neil, who had a reputation for being crazy as a loon was sitting in my driveway. He had a reputation for being a junior achiever in pyrotechnics, and he supposedly didn't care what he blew up, as long as it made a big bang.

I hesitated for a moment, and then thought, what the heck, how much trouble can he be on a cold Saturday afternoon. I hopped in and said, "I can't stay out long, where are we going?"

"Lunken airport. There is a lake down there on the playfield. We thought we would go see if anybody we know is ice skating." I knew they meant any girls we knew, which was fine with me.

When we arrived, the scene looked like a Christmas card come to life. New snow on the ground, pine trees tipped with white and pretty girls in skirts and long stocking hats going round and round. We sat in the car for a minute admiring the sights and then Neil reached down on the floor and picked up a brown paper bag. I got an immediate chill. Those skaters could be skating on thin ice with Neil around.

"Neil, what's in the bag?" He didn't answer but he pulled out an old paint can and pried off the lid. We all watched him. He reached in and pulled out a silvery claylike substance. I was getting more and more nervous. "What is that?"
He grinned, "I don't know its exact name, it's some kind of sodium stuff."

I wished I had paid more attention in chemistry. I knew he

wasn't talking about salt, but beyond that it could have been anything.

He got out a pocketknife and cut a hunk of it the size of a Baby Ruth bar and then climbed out of the wagon. He called back to us as he walked to the pond, "Keep the car running, I'll be right back."

Dick was looking a little nervous, too. He said, "Hey, Moonbeam, what's going on?"

Moonbeam smiled and said, "Just watch."

We got out to get a closer look, drawn like passengers to the rails of the Titanic. Neil stood at the edge of the pond, casually like he was looking for someone he knew, and then he reached down and slid that chunk of sodium smoothly across the ice. It skimmed unnoticed, the grayness blending into the color of the ice. It came to rest quietly, near the center, like a small bomb in waiting. I knew something bad was going to happen and my shoulders tensed up.

A hole appeared underneath the chunk as the ice started to melt away and then it fell through into the water and disappeared. Immediately a one-foot blue flame shot out of the water followed by a long subterranean rumble and then Baarrooommmb. The air around the lake filled with pieces of ice, sprays of water, and I think a couple of flying carp. The skaters scrambled to get away. I held my breath until it was clear no one was going to fall through the ice. We went back to the car, Moon still smiling, and Dick and I feeling jumpy waiting for somebody to figure out who caused the trouble. "You don't have anything else in that bag, do you, Neil?" I asked, dreading the answer.

"Just a couple of sticks of dynamite."

Things weren't looking good, I decided.

Moon made that station wagon fly out of there. He said, casually, "We've got one more stop before we go home."

When Mooney got in his Barney Oldfield speedster mode nothing would stop him. Trying to slow him down was like trying to stop a bullet with a banana cream pie.

We pulled up to a dilapidated, isolated farmhouse in Indian Hill. It looked empty and I prayed it was. We all got out, Kelly with the brown bag. "Wait here, he said and disappeared into the old house. After a few minutes, he waved from an upstairs window. It was quiet for awhile. When a branch cracked under the weight of the snow covering it, I nearly jumped out of my boots but then silence fell again.

Suddenly Neil came running out of the house with a wild-eyed look of a horse about to spook. He said nothing as he jumped in the car. We turned to join him when a huge explosion knocked us half off our feet. I glanced around just in time to see an upstairs window disintegrating as an old claw-footed bathtub shot through it. The bathtub rose slightly in the air and then came straight down, hitting the snow and burying itself part way up. Luckily, Neil had retained enough sense to pick a room slightly off to the side of the station wagon. Otherwise Moon would have had a new kind of luggage holder riding on top of his wagon.

I stood looking at that tub and knew one of those life-defining moments had arrived. This was not the way I wanted to spend my free time. I did not want to measure my successes in terms of the amount of noise my friends and I could make.

We jumped back in the car once more. "Moon, I need to go home, now."

Dick joined in. "I'll get out at Bob's place, too."

When we pulled into the driveway, I said, "Thanks guys, we had a real bang-up time, a real blast, don't call us again. We'll call you."

I stopped Dick before we went inside. "Let's make a pact, we already got rid of our firecrackers. Now let's get rid of some of our so called friends, especially those two clowns."

Blazing a Trail in the Park (1950)

The end of high school approached rapidly. After a lot of talk with Dad, we decided I would go to the Parson's School of Design in New York City for college. Dad thought it was the best school for interior design in the United States and I was both excited and scared about living in the Big Apple. I tried to ignore the last high school trial awaiting me but couldn't. Seniors had to pass a final exam in every subject with a minimum score of 70 to get a diploma and avoid the indignity of summer school. I worried Advanced Algebra would do me in. After I received my test scores I felt a huge instant relief. I could kiss off Latin and all that other memory work, the long hours of daily homework, and no more classes in a rundown, sooty building.

At graduation a white-bearded Jesuit missionary tried to inspire our loyalty by telling us "What you did at St. Xavier will follow you all the rest of your life."

I hoped that would not be true.

The newly graduate male high school student looks forward to rewarding himself with one special thing before he embarks on a summer job. My prize was an invitation from Hap, for Dick and me to spend a few days at his family's cottage at Castle Park resort on Lake Michigan, near of the town of Holland.

Dick and I drove up in Dick's red convertible. The Castle Park Clubhouse Inn was a reminder of elegant times gone by. The building was a story and a half, a high pitched roof, and dormer windows for the few upstairs guestrooms. The front of the roof swept down and then out to cover an open porch the full length of the Inn. The porch was full of old ladies crocheting. The old wooden resort building had been housing guests for over 100 years. Hap's folks had a three-bedroom cottage on the property set high on a bluff with a great view of the sunset over Lake Michigan, perfect for a summer weekend. We spent two days and nights swimming, boating, playing tennis and having two great beach parties with a few gals on the Inn staff.

Hap, Dick and Bob at Castle Park on Lake Michigan

On Sunday morning Dick and I went in to the town of Holland to purchase supplies and fill up with gas for the trip home. When we arrived back at the park entrance we saw Hap talking to an old grade school acquaintance named Clive. He was one of the brightest kids in class but always seemed a little erratic and too quick on the trigger. He reminded me of Kelly, which should have switched on a light in my head. We pulled up and stopped to chat in the large circular driveway that wound around up to the main clubhouse and back to the entrance.

Hap suggested to Dick, "Why don't you back up and turn your car around so we can go back to the cottage to load your luggage?" Dick restarted the Ford, put it in reverse and immediately crunched into a guard rail support behind him. Unfortunately the bumper was higher than the rail and the point on the end post punctured the gas tank. I smelled fuel before I saw it but it quickly began leaking out profusely.

We had no way of knowing how fast a whole tankful would spill on the gravel and wood chip road and the four of us got a little frantic. Since it was Dick's car, we listened as he called the shots. "I don't want to just sit here and create an 18-gallon puddle of gas, that's way too dangerous. I'm going to drive it around so the gas will spread out." I couldn't think of a better idea so I didn't say a word. He hopped in and drove slowly around the circular drive. After one complete circle he coasted back to us, dry. "The gauge is on empty," he said.

Hap, Dick and I took turns examining the puncture, trying to come up with a plan. I looked up to see Clive walking over to the guardrail. He pulled out a pack of matches and lit one. It was like a bad dream where I wanted to shout 'Stop!' but nothing came out of my mouth. He bent down and lit the wet driveway. It caught and blazed a trail of flame that danced up the road to the Inn. As the fire raced past the front porch all hell broke loose. The old ladies scattered like a startled flock of sparrows. Some ran inside to sound the alarm and some just hopped around helplessly. Five gals in a gazebo in the center of the circle became frantic when they realized they were encircled inside a ring of fire.

Their problems dimmed as we watched the fire race around back towards Dick's car. We ran behind the car and kicked away the soaked gravel and chips just in time. The fire halted about four feet from the car, fading out as it burned the last of the gasoline. Meanwhile the manager and three of his helpers ran out and shot foam out of fire extinguishers, stomping on bits of remaining fire near the Inn. Finally the whole thing was out, smoke drifting up like the aftermath of a huge cookout.

The manager roared over to us and screamed, "Why did you set that gasoline on fire?"

Clive answered, "We couldn't just let it sit there in a pool and blow up the car." I didn't think his logic would hold up but the manager was too upset to discuss the situation.

Blazing a Trail in the Park

The manager yelled and shouted more at us but we were left standing speechless. After his tirade, the three of us went back to Hap's cottage and got some bubble gum from Hap's sister to make a temporary repair on the tank. Fortunately, Hap's mother knew nothing of the incident and we hoped to get out of there still in her good graces. After we put our suitcases in the car, we went out on the porch to see our gracious hostess. I said, "Thanks a million for everything. We had a great time."

Hap's mom replied, "I'm glad you enjoyed yourself and everything went so well."

Dick said, "Huh well, there is one problem."

"What's that?" she asked, puzzled.

Dick twitched and said, "Bob and I have been banned from Castle Park for life."

Big Apple Apocalypse

I had been interested in design even before I knew exactly what it was. Line and color always caught my eye, whether looking at clothes, the latest shape of a Ford or the way my father redecorated our living room every five years.

I drove to New York thinking I was ready to get away from home but as I drove through the Lincoln Tunnel under the Hudson River, I worried about what lay ahead. Dad had arranged a room at the New York Athletic Club on 59th Street, which overlooked Central Park to the north. My room on the fourteenth floor, measured 9' by 15', had a private bath, a good mattress and a spectacular view of the park, all for $3.00 a day.

I couldn't understand why the auto horns blasted all day and night. At home there was always a peaceful hush, broken occasionally by a train whistle in the distance. As soon as I arrived I knew my heart was back home and I belonged there. After dropping my suitcases and taking off my coat, the physical and mental exhaustion took over and I was too tired to unpack. I flopped face down on the cotton bedspread and tried to relax but my mind kept churning. What in the world was I doing here in the middle of a strange city with no friends?

It felt completely foreign. I was 18 and knew I belonged somewhere. I didn't know where but I knew it wasn't there. My heart started to throb, my head seemed to fill up with pressure, my body quivered and I started to sob into the long night.

By Monday morning I was in a better mood and the anticipation of college in a new land challenged me. It was raining outside and there was something strange in the air. The whole city smelled of roasted coffee beans and exhaust fumes. Every block had one or two delis selling coffee and an 'English' to throngs on the run. I went down into the 57th Street subway to get to Long Island where the first year Parson's classes were held. When I came above ground at my destination station I looked left, and right, and up, and down and didn't see anything that resembled a campus. Scattered factories, warehouses and condemned vacant buildings filled the streets. I finally found my school in a five-story commercial building and met the head of the department, Mr. Castle, who introduced me to his assistant, Mr. Woody. While I spoke to Woody, his beady little brown eyes didn't focus on me for long but darted all around the room like he had just arrived at a smorgasbord and didn't know which new item to select. When he did stop to look at me, I felt pinned down.

Woody said, "Grab a stool and drafting board. We'll talk more later when I have time." I found a good seat by the window, next to a couple of 26-year-old belles from the South who told me their names were Wheezie and Nancy.

Eventually the studio filled up with about a hundred aspiring interior design students, ranging in age from 17 to the early 40s. There were quite a few men in their late 20s and some looked like vets but since the war ended five years ago, I wondered what they had been doing in the meantime.

Most of the girls looked reasonably collegiate, wearing the normal long slim skirts with fitted blouses or twin sweater ensembles. Half the men also looked preppy or businesslike in pressed slacks, shirts and loafers. The rest were making an artistic dress statement that would have shot my mother right down the laundry chute. Some wore Hawaiian floral luau shirts, unbuttoned to expose their dyed orange chest hair, which coordinated with the orange hair on their head. In the Midwest I had never seen anyone with neon hair. Neon was reserved for drive-ins and diners. I wondered why orange was the color of choice. Another bunch wore threadbare jeans and beaded Indian headbands. And finally there were the pale people with gaunt model faces of indeterminate sex, creatures who have inhabited New York since the first speakeasy opened. I studied them like they were characters in a play and then I noticed one guy eyeing my feet with a smirking look. Who did the creep think he was? I saw nothing strange with my pegged houndstooth pants and my terrific fake alligator saddle shoes.

I didn't expect to figure in any great New York City dramas but it quickly became clear that every day was going to be one long epic struggle between baby-faced cornfed Bob and the con artists who lurked around downtown waiting for an innocent like me. I thought it would be easy to go out to dinner, find a nice small inexpensive Mom and Pop place. I was wrong. I couldn't find anything nearby like that. In order to keep my budget balanced, I ended up at the Horn and Hardart Automat on 57th street. The dining room had 20-foot ceilings, cool white fluorescent lights, no dividers. The lower part of the walls and the floor were covered with beige tiles. With no fabric on the windows or the chairs, the din from the clatter of plates, dishes and falling trays overwhelmed me.

Every kid had heard of automats and I was excited to be able to actually eat at one. Two of the four walls of the restaurant were covered with miniature glass doors. After you inserted a coin next to the little glass door, you could open the hatch and pull out the chicken potpie. By some trick of glass distortion everything looked much smaller out in the light. I added vegetable soup and custard pie to my tray and sat down at an empty table. The soup was so bad Kydoo would not have eaten it, so I switched directly to the pie to kill the taste.

While I ate I looked around trying to place people. I thought some looked like out of work actors and others like bookies, though how I knew this was unclear because I had never met an out of work actor, much less a bookie. At least I could recognize some definite hookers and a few bums. None of the smart New Yorkers who inhabited the magazines were here having a pre-theater meal while talking happily with their friends.

I sat searching for a few pieces of real chicken in the potpie when an unshaven man sat down right next to me. He looked about 35 and seemed okay but when I looked around I noticed there were a dozen empty tables surrounding us. He started stuffing his face with macaroni and cheese and then muttered something I couldn't understand.

I said, "Pardon me, are you speaking to me?" in a polite voice. He mumbled some more, still not looking at me. I wondered if he was carrying on a conversation with the macaroni. I decided to sacrifice the rest of the potpie and get out of there. I pushed my chair back and stood up. He grabbed my sleeve with a death grip. "What the hell are you doing?" I said, trying to get away.

At that moment he managed to speak clearly and slowly. He said, "How about going over to my place?"

I was sure everyone in the place had heard him. I said, "No thanks, bud. That potpie already made me feel sick and if you don't lay off I'll decorate your shirt with creamed chicken."

When I made it out to the sidewalk, I walked as fast as I could back to my room. I was having the big city experience but couldn't take another minute of it.

The next morning I was still trying to figure out why the guy had come on to a kid like me. Since I was eating dinner with my raincoat on, it couldn't have been my body, so maybe it was the blond hair. I couldn't decide if it was just something different or typical of New York.

One day I needed art supplies so I headed out for a craft store a few blocks away on 57th street. In the shop I wandered around picking up lots of items when I noticed a man following me around the aisles. He didn't work there and I didn't think he was admiring my old raincoat. Not again? I told myself I was getting paranoid. Maybe the guy needed the same supplies I did. I paid for my stuff, left the store and headed west for 5th Avenue. The man continued to trail me and I started to sweat. I walked two blocks and he was still behind me. I became convinced he would chase me around the city until I dropped with exhaustion.

As he drew closer I walked faster. When I reached 5th Avenue the crosswalk light had already turned red but I didn't care. I made a quick dash across Fifth Avenue passing within an arm's length of a traffic cop. My pursuer started to follow but the policeman blew the stop whistle on him. I watched him go back to the curb and look at me with an intense stare. I took off jogging. I didn't understand it. Why couldn't I have women chasing me?

I decided something would have to change or I would be

afraid to leave my room. Somehow I would have to look older and more street smart. I needed a hat. With the right hat I could look like a tough New York City detective and no one would bother me. Well, okay, I would look like a short, exceptionally young detective, but I could also wear my raincoat all the time, turn up my collar and maybe no one would be able to tell I was straight off the farm. I found a hat shop and bought a brown felt hat that looked like one of Dad's. When I put it on my head I felt such a surge of confidence that I stopped at a tiny photomat on Times Square and got a 25¢ picture of my new fedora.

The crooks and weirdos have better be on guard now; Mr. Bob had a hat.

Bob and his new hat.

The Gotham Shuffle

Even though I kept busy with classes I missed my friends. When I found out there was a guy from Ohio in my class, I hoped he and I would have something in common. Bogey was a 34-year-old Italian-American from Youngstown. Youngstown had a reputation as a gangster-riddled steel town but I figured a guy in interior design couldn't fit that stereotype – even though he looked the part.

After we talked a couple times he invited me to go to a football game in New Jersey with some of his friends. "I got a couple of buddies, good Catholic guys, army vets, ya know," he told me. Football sounded like a virile pastime so I was excited when we drove out of the city that Saturday morning in a 1949 Buick convertible on one of those perfect fall days. We could have been picture book college students except for our companions. The other two were from Youngstown too but didn't resemble any good Catholic boys I had ever seen.

Sammy, the driver, had long black ducktails and wore his collar up to support them. He had on a black leather jacket and boots to match and I was afraid he looked so much like a hood they wouldn't let him into the Princeton football game. The other guy, Tony, was the toughest looking runt I had ever seen. He had a burr haircut and biceps that were as big as his head. Bogey told me Tony had just come off two good wins at Madison Square Garden in the light-middleweight division and looked tough enough to take on a heavyweight. After two minutes these Ohio boys were making my ears burn. Sammy knew more four-letter words than I knew existed. Tony's vocabulary was better than Sam's but much more limited and consisted of descriptions of 'broads' all through New Jersey. Later when they dropped me back off at the Athletic Club I decided even though we didn't have a lot in common, I was at least expanding my horizons.

Another new friend, Crew, could not have been more different from Bogey even though he too was a WWII vet. He had red hair with lots of charm and sophistication, like someone right out of a F. Scott Fitzgerald novel. I thought I would get a taste of sophisticated New York society when Crew invited me to go out with him and his girlfriend to show me the bars. She was a 5'7" knockout brunette, Robin, president of her college sorority up at University of Connecticut.

We stopped in at the Taft Hotel on 49th street for whiskey sours and listened to the piano player bang out some of his original tunes, overpowering our conversation. His lyrics were utterly filthy and pointless: 'He's got the cutest little dinghy in the Navy' and 'I loved to nibble on her cupcakes' were the cleanest songs. I bought three of his 78s and envisioned the start of a fine music collection. Crew didn't seem too interested in his date but I was too shy to make points with her.

Crew had so many friends, it was tough to arrange time to socialize with him. My best hope for a new buddy was a tall skinny guy from Connecticut named Bates. He was a 26-year-old army vet, friendly, quick to smile, and lived on a tight budget, spending a dollar a day to live in the deserted Army Barracks on Roosevelt Island in the middle of the East River. His nickname was 'Budget Bates' and he was rumored to know every cheapo place to eat around school. Bates and I discovered we had a common dislike for crowds, dirt, and noise in the city, plus we both liked athletics. He and his New England friends grew up on skis and he couldn't wait to hit the slopes. Snow skiing in Ohio was non-existent but I was ready to give it a try. I thought I was probably athletic enough so it wouldn't be a problem to learn, plus I would meet some more potential friends.

At Macy's department store I bought equipment. One pair of skis, seven and one-half feet long, poles, and boots, all for $50. The gear was the most modern available. The skis were made of ash, lined with steel edges. I worried the ash needed

Bob, Crew and Robin

to be protected and the edges could rust, so I decided to coat the bottoms with red lacquer and wax. The boots were lace-up leather and I figured out the ski cable wrapped around behind the boot to keep it in the toe slot. The baggy pants, jacket, hat, and gloves were hand-me-downs from my brother but I still thought I looked sharp and couldn't wait to murder the mountain.

Bates and I drove to his parents' house in Torrington on a Friday in January after school. We had barely gone to bed when he woke me at 3:30. "Come on, Bob, our ride will be here soon." I stumbled out of bed and into the cold night, my breath freezing on my face. At 4:00 AM a Ford convertible with a ski rack rigged to the rag top pulled up for us. All the way to Stowe, the conversation was almost in a different language about extreme ski trails in places of which I had never heard. After six hours we arrived at Stowe, Vermont. Other cars full of Bates' friends met us in the parking lot. When everyone was assembled I looked them over and thought my skis and outfit held up well in comparison. Everyone else headed for the chairlifts but Bates grabbed my arm and pulled me aside. "I think you should try the bunny slope first, Bob, to get the feel of your skis."

I managed to figure out how to shuffle over to the rope tow. The worst part of the darn skis was they were so long the tips kept crossing over each other,

Bates, Bob and Bogey

Bob and Jane ready for the slopes

scuffing up the new finish and nearly toppling me. By the time I grabbed hold of the rope, my legs were already shaking with fatigue.

After a long day and many, many falls I was ready for a rest. Instead of me murdering the mountain the bunny was killing me. I slumped against the car, waiting for the rest of the group. Bates finally showed up looking grim. "What happened?" I asked.

"Susan and Jeanine both broke their ankles and are at the hospital having brass pins installed. It is really icy up there." I was a little more thankful for the bunny slope.

We stayed at a Bed and Breakfast tourist home. The rooms had two sets of bunk beds and a tight price to go with the close quarters, at $1.50 a night. I was famished the next morning and ate enough scrambled eggs, bacon and toast to hold me through my upcoming ordeal. I was determined to make it off the bunny slope.

Bates just assumed I learned all I needed the previous day and suggested I buy an all day lift ticket for $5.00. Skis on, we shuffled forward in the line waiting for that great moment to be whisked away. I noticed an employee handing out blankets as each person got on the chair lift. I joked, "Just how long is this ride anyway? I've never heard of blankets for a ski lift."

"You have never been on top of this mountain and you are going to need it. You get on first and I'll be right behind. When you get off, sit on the edge of your seat and use your hand to push off your seat. Got it?"

Our turn was coming too fast to ask more questions. I slid onto the chair lift and the attendant threw the blanket over me. We sailed up over the trees and I felt the wind cut through the blanket. My face turned raw. At the top Bates yelled, "Now, Bob." I wasn't sure what I was supposed to do with the blanket so I tried to toss it to the attendant as I slid off. That unbalanced me and I tumbled down right at the feet of two girls who smiled at me like I was a cute dumb kid.

We took off down a run called the Goat which was a narrow trail cut through the woods about 20 feet wide. I was scared by the steepness and the fast skiers speeding around me, but every time I tried to edge over to the side, I hit the rocks protruding out of the snow. I tumbled down but my skis wouldn't release. My ankles felt like they had stretched to a breaking point and I was still in sight of the top of the lift.

It was probably a good thing my skis wouldn't release because I was too cold to move my fingers. By the time I reached the bottom, the rest of the group was already loading up for their third run. I thought longingly of a warm drink, warm toes, and a warm building but Bates urged me on. "One more time, Bob," he kept urging as if I were a dog reluctant to do a trick.

One by one the group took off from the top. As I stood, nearly frozen stiff, Bates skied up to me, anxious to catch up with the rest of the group. "Why aren't you going down the mountain?"

"I would if you could somehow manage to get me back on a return chair." Bates looked at me with pity and I knew I wasn't going to be an equal member of the ski crowd anytime soon.

My knees were still stiff four days later when Crew invited me for a party at his parents' house in New Jersey. I expected a huge mansion to go with his smooth look. An hour before I was ready to leave I got a call.

"Bob, it's Walt. Remember me? I went to school with Hap and Pritch. Hap gave me your number and I'm in the City for the weekend. You want to go down to the Village with me to hear some jazz tonight?"

I didn't remember much about the guy but I thought I should be polite. "I'm going to a party in New Jersey. Do you want to come with me?"

He agreed and we took off for New Jersey in my Olds. Crew's parents were gone for the weekend but I figured the servants would still be there. Not so. We pulled up in front of a

1920s style small bungalow. Two bedrooms on the first floor plus a guest room in the attic. It cost us $3.00 at the door for beer and chips and no butler to hang our coats. We walked in and Walt stopped so suddenly I bumped into him. A few of the guys were dancing with each other, kissing and embracing. I was used to it by now and didn't think twice about it but Walt must have been leading a sheltered life at Colgate. "What kind of party is this, Bob?"

"Don't worry about it, there will be plenty of straight girls here." I hoped he wouldn't notice a guy over in a corner dancing with a beautiful, blond, long-haired dog. The party got so crowded I lost sight of Walt, but I wasn't worried. If he was a friend of Brit's he should be able to handle himself but by 1:00 AM I decided it was time to head back across the Hudson. The party had not slowed down and I needed to wend my way around looking for Walt. For such a small house I couldn't believe I had misplaced him. I decided to check the bedrooms. Maybe Walt had gotten really lucky. In the first room I disturbed a couple, neither of whom resembled him in the slightest. "Sorry," I mumbled, but they didn't even notice.

The next bedroom was crowded with a bunch of people sitting around on the floor listening to someone playing the guitar. But no Walt. After checking the basement, I headed up to an attic bedroom. There he was, completely intoxicated and relaxed to the point of being unconscious, lying prone on his back. Another male figure was crouching in the shadows next to Walt's bed like a famished cannibal, ready to devour a morsel of human prey. Poor Walt was about to have sex and he didn't even know it.

I cleared my throat. "Sorry, but Walt needs a ride back to the city with me and I need to leave now."

The guy turned and looked up. It was Mr. Woody, my esteemed teacher.

A Normal Mess (1951)

My next strategy to cope with homesickness was to visit some old friends. Mitch invited me up for a weekend at Yale so one Friday I went to Columbus Circle to pick up my car. The auto garage was four stories high but only 40 feet wide, with cars arranged like stacked sardines in a can. When my car finally got pried out of the tier, I hopped in and headed up Amsterdam Avenue, speeding along, anxious to get to Connecticut.

After a few blocks I noticed a yellow Checker cab coming up on the inside lane but I was in no mood to let him pass. I knew the first commandment of driving in the city – 'Thou shalt not ever cut off a local cabbie.' He came up along side me and glared. We kept parallel to each other, neither one willing to back off. Up ahead I spotted a car illegally parked in his lane. Fifty yards from the rear of that auto, he squealed in behind me shaking his fist. The light in front of me turned yellow, then red, so I slowed to a stop like the good driver I was. This racing incident enraged the cabbie and after he jerked to a halt next to me, he jumped out and ran over to a loitering traffic cop.

I started to worry. The cop and the cabbie walked over to me. I thought, now I'm in trouble. The cop leaned in the window and said, "This man wants me to arrest you for speeding, improper vehicle operation, and attempting to create an accident. Let's see your driver's license."

I pulled out my Ohio license, giving him my best 'new to the city' grin I could manage. He studied it and turned to the cabbie. "Now, let me get this straight. You're trying to tell me this 18-year-old kid, straight out of the farm belt, has created road havoc for a New York City taxi driver? Don't waste my time. Move it, both of you." Before the cabbie could get back in his car, I was off. I decided the next week I would paint a little three-inch yellow 'Checker Cab' on the side on my car like the war pilots when they shot down an enemy plane.

Mitch at Yale

When I got to New Haven on a tour of the local watering holes, I learned eggheads could drink as much as the rest of us. Back at campus we walked around the commons and I admired the ivy-covered college. No ivy grew on New York City buildings; the pollution would have choked it. The dorms were mostly three stories with high peaked gabled slate roofs and looked like they should be full of serious students.

Most undergraduates lived in small suites that held five or six. These units contained two or three bedrooms and a living room with a wood-burning fireplace. It all felt very English-Henry the VIII, heavy dark walnut woodwork, cream-textured walls, Jacobean furniture and leaded-glass windows. All it lacked was a cute serving wench with tankards. We spent the afternoon with about 25 guys crowded in a living room filled with heavy cigarette smoke and heated to the boiling point from the blazing fireplace. When there was no more firewood, someone had the brilliant idea to use the furniture to keep it going. I watched in amazement as first the chairs, then the small tables and finally a bed frame went into the fire. I decided these guys might be starting to crack from too much studying. It was time to take a walk. Mitch followed me out and we ambled around the grounds.

"Nice bunch of guys, Mitch," I said. "Pretty smart of them to think up a way to keep the fire going."

"Yeah, they are a bright group of fellows. We have a problem though."

"What?"

"That bed frame was where you were going to sleep tonight."

My room at the Athletic Club became a weekend underground railroad stop for all my unfortunate Cincinnati friends who thought they had to escape from the boredom and isolation of their Ivy League campuses. Hap arrived one afternoon in November from Brown ready to sample the big city. I tried to get him into my room unnoticed because the Irish maids were instructed to report and charge any unregistered guests. When we left the room at 6:00 PM, I looked up and down the halls only to be nabbed by the Irish Gestapo at the elevator.

We paid for his stay at the front desk and took the subway to Washington Square in the heart of Greenwich Village to hit the jazz joints. I had dressed in my new checkered sport coat and decided I looked like one cool cat. Around 11:30 we were listening to Maynard Ferguson at the Blue Note Jazz Club and finishing our beers, when a man at the next table leaned over the six-inch space and said, "Hey, fellows, if you are tired of listening to music, I know something else that might interest you." He sat back, waiting to hook us. "I can take you to a private girlie show that is so exclusive, it's by invitation only. I'll only take you as friends and if you don't want to go, it's okay." He picked up his cigarettes, got up and left.

"Should we go?" Hap asked.

"I don't know. What do you think?" I was almost ready to leave anyway. While the jazz was fabulous, the smoke in the room was accumulating to such a point I could barely see Hap, sitting right next to me, much less the musicians.

"I don't know." Hap replied, draining his drink.

Since nothing happens if you don't take a chance, I stood up and headed to the door. Hap came after me and we found the fellow waiting for us outside. He beckoned us to follow so we trailed him down a long side street and stopped at an alley. He pointed to the back of a brownstone at the end of the alley with a red light in the window and said, "There it is. It's $5.00 apiece. I'll take the money up and ring the doorbell. I need to vouch for you so stay here and come quick when I call."

We forked over the money and waited, my imagination full of visions of scantily clad dancing girls. Our new friend walked up to the black door, did a soldier-like pivot to the right and took off running out the opposite end of the alley. Hap and I looked at each other with open mouths and then chased after him, quickly losing him in the maze of back streets. It was as if we had flashing neon arrows pointing at our heads with signs that read: 'SUCKER'.

33

Switcharoo

    The war in Korea made all my efforts in New York unimportant. When the conflict first began, everyone thought it was just a skirmish, and the mighty U.S. army would quickly settle the problem. After all, we had taken on the power of Japan and Germany. How could one small Asian country be a match for that? Before school started in September, I had received a 3A classification for the draft, basically meaning they didn't want me immediately as long as the war ended soon.

    After the Chinese entered the war and the North Koreans occupied Seoul, my army reclassification of 2A arrived in the mail, making me cannon fodder in the near future unless I did something fast. I knew the only way out of the draft was to join Reserve Officer Training or the Air Force Reserve but unfortunately Parsons had neither. The uniforms just weren't stylish enough. After some telephone conversations with Dad, I decided to finish out the first year at Parsons then go back to the University of Cincinnati to join the Air Force Reserve. If the war situation didn't get any worse I would at least be able to finish my degree before serving two years of Air Force duty.

    By April the war had turned in our favor but I decided not to take a chance on it swinging back. I spent my last few weeks of spare time walking around the city soaking up the sights and the museums. Meanwhile, President Truman had his disagreement with General MacArthur and dismissed the popular officer. But since public sentiment was with the old soldier, New York scheduled a ticker tape parade for him and his wife. I grabbed my camera and headed to the corner of 7th Avenue and 57th Street to watch. The crowd stood ten deep and a good photo was almost impossible to get. As he passed, I got goosebumps looking at such a renowned person. Then I noticed the car in which he was riding – a 1941 grey Chrysler convertible. A man of his stature deserved a Cadillac or Lincoln stretch limo of more recent vintage. I wondered if Harry had ordered it for him.

MacArthur waving to crowds

In my short time in the big city I felt like I had crammed in years of new experiences. For one last New York moment I decided to go to Parsons' annual Beaux Arts Ball. Everyone at school had been so excited about the dance I just had to see what it was about. Design work in classes had slowed to a snail's pace as groups of students whispered about their costumes. I had been too busy trying to keep up with the work to pay much attention. Three days before the ball, my date told me she was going as a rabbit so I thought I had better come up with something fast. I didn't want to be a companion rabbit and I thought going as a big apple would be appropriate.

Nancy, the bunny, and I walked into a scene out of the Arabian Nights. We ducked into the ballroom through fake tent doors and found ourselves surrounded by potted palms and twinkling lights placed to resemble the stars above the Sahara. Knowing some of my classmates, I peered around to make sure they hadn't included camels for realism. No camels, but the ball gowns and costumes so unreal, the students looked like exotic new creatures, covered with acres of tulle, satin, and chiffon in a whole spectrum of colors. Someone in a red crepe dress beaded with silver sparkly things and wearing a matching headdress tottered towards us on high heels. Whoever it was had been drinking too much desert nectar. I couldn't make out the face in the dim light but then I heard Crew's voice. "Bob, you made it. Fabulous," he said as he adjusted the feather boa around his neck. I was underdressed. A mere good looking young woman in rabbit ears and fur could not compete with the array of male peacocks twirling through the ballroom, their skirts whirling around like tiny tornadoes of color. I thought of the nuns at my grade school shrieking and running for cover. I had come a long way from that concrete playground.

I knew I wouldn't see much of my New York friends in the future so I wanted to make sure I said my goodbyes. When Bogey heard I wasn't coming back, he came up to me in class as I was putting the finishing touches on a colored rendering of a contemporary living room. "Hey, Bob, you know my buddy, Tony? Well, he's winning lots of fights and he's gonna have this big party at his new digs on Fifth Avenue, Saturday night. His place overlooks Central Park and the chicks just go wild when they see it. Why don't you come along? We had a party last weekend and by midnight we were all drunk and naked. It was howling." I thought for a moment. Bogey kept talking, "Look, Tony likes you and wants you to come."

I kept thinking. So Tony and Bogey want me to come. Fancy apartment, lots of girls, potentially naked. I chickened out. I still worried about my mother killing me, even long distance. I was sure with my luck her omniscient ability to know when Bob was getting in trouble would lead her to find out about a decadent party 700 miles away from Cincinnati. I knew I would be living at home soon and wanted to keep the peace.

Bates asked me to join him for a last lunch at a local Greek restaurant about two blocks west of the school factory. We feasted on goulash, vegetables, and bread all for 35 cents. He told me his news, he was engaged to Jane, the girl from Torrington who had been on our ski trip. I knew she was just what he needed. She had the one trait 'Budget Bates' most admired: oodles of jack.

Crew was a different story. He was now part of the orange hair contingent, which I finally understood was a creative way to proclaim interest in dating both sexes. I asked him, "What are you doing this summer?" as we packed up our supplies. "I got a job singing in a gay bar down in the Village". I thought of his beautiful former girlfriend. "Why the big change in your dating habits, Crew? Robin was spectacular looking."
He punched my arm. "It sure increases the possibilities for getting dates on Saturday night."

My last day in New York I parked the Olds at the rear door of the Athletic Club to load up. I had nine months and whole room full of stuff to fit in. My suitcases filled up the trunk, half the back seat, and I still had to find spots for the pieces of my drafting board, a basketball, three fishing tackle boxes full of art supplies, a gift of four bags of dirty laundry for my mother and one pair of snow skies, red lacquer bottoms, slightly scuffed.

As I passed through the Lincoln Tunnel the round light of the tunnel entrance finally turned black in my rear view mirror. The loud humming noise of the tunnel pipeline would be my last New York City experience for some time. I decided that in the future if I was married and lived in the middle of Manhattan I would send my children to school in Ohio.

Loading the Olds on 58th Street.

Under Suspicion

As soon as I got back home I enrolled at the University of Cincinnati for the fall term and joined the Air Force Reserve. U.C. had a five-year design program, splitting the terms between seven weeks of classes and seven weeks of co-op work. After each session of classes we were supposed to work in the industry related to our field to get some real life experience.

It was easy to decide which fraternity to join. Dick and some other acquaintances had joined Sigma Chi the previous fall and they convinced me it was the best group. The Sigma Chi house sat right on the edge of campus on a half-acre lot directly adjacent to a huge parking field. There were 70 active members and 32 members of the pledge class. The rules of the house were simple. No firearms, no beer or whiskey and no females, ever, on the second or third floor of the house. The enforcer and director of moral standards was the live-in, 75-year-old housemother, Mrs. Albert, or Lady 'A' as she was known in fraternal circles.

I quickly learned many new things at college. I discovered something that waits tables, washes dishes, scrubs floors and cleans toilet rooms is called a pledge. For five months the active Sigma Chi members had the power of discipline over the pledges, supposedly to develop character. I didn't enjoy it.

I must have shot my mouth off too much because my pledge brothers elected me president of the pledge class. Just like in high school it was time to put up or shut up. Along with the actives' weekly dinner and secret basement chapter conclave on Tuesday nights, we had our meeting upstairs in the dining room. Red Dog, our active pledge trainer, started each of our meetings with a 20-minute exam of questions taken from our Pledge Manual. After that we were on our own to meet. Our first project was to design, construct and operate a float for the upcoming football game between our U.C. Bearcats and the East Texas Miners. Being the pledge president automatically made me float chairman.

I never liked to enter competitive events for fun and always liked to participate with the firm belief that I at least had a good chance to win. The campus trophy for the best float stood before me as a challenge. Every other fraternity delegated their older, most knowledgeable and talented architecture and design student members to this project to make sure their groups stood a good chance of taking first place. I stood in front of the entire chapter one night and made a short speech. "Sigma Chi needed more unity and member co-operation if we are to win the float award. We hope the actives contribute to the design and float building process."

Ed King, the chapter president, answered, "Bob, you will learn to stop complaining and trying to shirk your pledge responsibilities. Every other Sigma Chi pledge class has managed to build a float without the actives' help." With that put-down I promised myself we would win, somehow, someway. We immediately found problems. Just for starters, no one told us everyone used old World War II army jeeps as the base for the float. A jeep would have been the smallest, lowest most compact vehicle that could have given us the flexibility of design. Unfortunately, no one enlightened us.

The only truck we could find was one of Dad's 1949 White Company two-ton flat-bed paint delivery trucks. We worked two weeks on preliminary construction details, then collected all the materials in the rear yard of Dad's business. The area was walled in on all sides, held only seven cars and was accessed by one alley. There we spent night after night working on the float, neglecting our classes, determined to win.

On the Friday night before the big game, our entire pledge team was there to do the final assembly of our float. Everything was going along smoothly. As I walked over to the alleyway to pick up a hammer, I noticed out of the corner of my eye a familiar ugly plum-colored 1947 Dodge creeping up the driveway. It was none other than active member Ace, checking on us.

Now Ace wasn't a real bad guy and maybe he deserved better but my mind raced to come up with retaliation for the actives' bad attitude. I looked around the yard and spotted Irish, the biggest and strongest kid in our group. I said, "Irish, quick, listen. Ace is coming up the alley and will get out to talk with us. Pass the word to all the pledges to grab him, but not until I drop this hammer."

Ace parked, got out, sauntered up to Curley and me and said, "Sure doesn't look like you pussies are going to finish this wreck by tomorrow's parade."

I stood there waiting and tossing the hammer confidently into the air and catching it again. By this time, all eyes were on the tool. "Oh, we'll by fine by tomorrow, Ace. Don't you be a-worrying." I could see all the pieces were in place. I let the hammer sail up into the air for its final flight.

As it fell from the sky, I put both hands in my pockets and looked at Ace square in the eye. Before it even hit the ground, a mob grabbed Ace, tied him up and stood him for trial for interfering with the pledges work detail. Ace broke out in a sweat. Even though no one disliked Ace, he was a wiener, and something about him grated on my nerves. He looked like Bugs Bunny after Elmer Fudd had caught him and was ready to boil him in a pot.

I don't know who started it but soon, "Take him for a ride! Take him for a ride!" filled the air like some sort of primitive religious chant. Irish found an old rag and blindfolded him and then five of us tossed him in a car with a few liquid libations to keep us going. We took off for Clermont County and eventually dumped Ace with no money on some deserted pitch black road out in no man's land, ten miles from the city limits.

The capture and ride exhilarated us but leaving the float project unsupervised for two hours was a blunder that required a few of us to work through the night until the parade started. We got the float to the fraternity house by 11:00 A.M. to put on the finishing touches of crepe paper. The school band warmed up in the parking lot right beside us and when I stepped back to admire the finished masterpiece, I felt like they were saluting our object d'art. We had successfully created a coal tunnel, a cave, a Bearcat coal car on tracks outside the cave, and a ten-foot high West Virginia Miner football player. Curley stood next to him, dressed as a Bearcat with a jumbo mallet in his hands. The sign on the cave read, 'Knock the Pants off the Miners.' We had a surprise in store for the crowd at the stadium.

We were ready to go. The chairman of the University Parade Committee waved us into the 26th spot in the parade, behind the Tri Delt float. Sirens wailed as I put the White truck into first gear and slowly let out the clutch. The crepe paper covered the entire hood except for two peepholes for me to see.

When we made our way into the stadium to the judging stand on the 50-yard line, I gave Irish and Curley a double whistle, our signal. Curley went first. He lifted the mallet and bonked the miner football player on his helmet. Irish was under the float, lying prone, manning the ropes. When he heard the clank of the mallet, he pulled the strings. Down came the player's pants to his ankles exposing a tiny tan G-string.

I couldn't see the fans through the peepholes but I knew I would be hear the crowd's reaction as they watched the Miner football player drop his pants. But instead of the expected applause, there was stunned silence. Then the crowd burst

Sigma Chi float

forth with screams and laughter. Confused, we pulled out of the stadium and parked. As I climbed out of the truck, the Dean of Men, who must have followed us out of the stadium, grabbed my arm. He spun me around and pointed at the football player with his pants in a down position. "How could you design such an obscene float?"

I was startled. I looked back at the float and then realized the G-string in the bright sunlight didn't resemble underwear at all. We had created the first pornographic float sculpture in the University's history.

Clan Uprising (1952)

Even though we hadn't won the float contest, I thought our efforts should have been appreciated. The active members of the fraternity had a different view and they also frowned on our treatment of Ace. In all the excitement I had completely forgotten about him. When we got back to the fraternity house he was there, glowering like a geyser about to blow.

The next day the President of Sigma Chi, Ed King, called a general meeting for all actives and pledges to attend in the living room of the fraternity house. Ed was a World War II vet who seemed more like an uncle than a fellow college student. The pledges sat in the middle of the floor while the actives sat and stood against the walls. When Ed spoke everyone listened. "In the history of this chapter or at least as long as I've been around, I have never seen a more undisciplined bunch of roustabouts as I see sitting before me. You pledges just hit thin ice and are up to your wazzoos in cold water. I can guarantee you will find out it is worse than being in hot water. For starters, all the pledges' work detail and time for chores will be doubled until further notice. We'll see how that goes and then decide if the punishment needs to be increased."

I was sitting on the floor in front and my tail end started bouncing up and down like a baby jackhammer because I was so upset over the penalty. Ed noticed me and said, "Bob, stand up and tell me, what is your problem?"

I tried to sound dignified, "Mr. President, you and this active chapter charged this pledge class to build that float, with no help from the actives, and we took up the challenge.

Then, as we were trying to get the work done we took a lot of grief from some active members. We deserve more respect and no punishment."

Somebody yelled out from the back, "Who are you going to try to dump next, Bob? Think you are going to get the better of us again?"

Ed raised his hand for silence. "All right, be quiet everyone. Bob, that's enough. Remember who you are. You are only a pledge. The active members will discuss this further without the pledges present."

Little did they realize another active had thrown out a challenge and we were up to it. Roy Rogers, an active from North Carolina, decided to join my pledge brother, Curley, for a few beers the next Saturday night. Roy lived in the house and had such a southern accent I had a tough time understanding him. Irish and I got wind of the plan and started to put the wheels in motion. The two of us went outside, got in my Olds and waited for Curley and Roy. I didn't have anything against Roy personally; he was just the first to fall into the trap. When they appeared, Irish asked, "You guys going down to Ships for a beer?"

"Yeah," Roy said.

I took over, "Hop in and we'll join you." We hit two neighborhood bars, then headed for the smorgasbord of Northern Kentucky bars. We were careful to limit our consumption while buying Roy most of his brews. After five bars Roy was three sheets to the wind. It was time to ride him out of town. We headed down Route 27 to Cynthiana, Kentucky for the drop. After about 30 miles I got tired of driving and said, "Look guys, he's out of it, lets just put him here on the side of the road and let him sleep it off." All agreed.

Roy came out of his stupor enough to babble, "Now, for crissakes, help me out of this car. I'm going to be sick."

Curley said, "Put your arm out and I'll help you."

Roy answered, "It ain't that long, what do you think I am, a monkey? Irish, this pledge animal thinks I'm a monkey." He stumbled out of the car. "Come here, put up your fists, look out I'm takin a swing." He punched at the air and nearly fell down. "Hey, maybe that last beer in Covington was spiked, you think I'm drunk, eh? Kiss off, you little shrimps. I'll never buy you bunch of baby cakes any more drinks." With the end of his soliloquy, his rubbery and boneless body collapsed in a roadside ditch amidst the ragweed.

Roy's little speech got on my nerves and I was glad he was out of the car. But as he lay there conked out in the dew wet grass, this sorry situation looked like a scenario we had not thought through. Roy was all shot to hell and couldn't move. It was a depressing sight just to see that poor guy sprawled out in the middle of nowhere. My conscience kicked in and I said, "This isn't going to work. We can't just leave him here." While we stood around trying to figure out our next move, a set of headlights appeared on the dark horizon. As they approached, we assumed a casual stance that might suggest an unplanned stop to take a quick whiz. At 75 yards we could see there were two cars and they were slowing down, approaching from the north.

Irish said, "If there's one thing I don't want is to have a few soft shell guys like us tangle with a bunch of hillbilly busters out here at midnight." He was right. You never knew who would turn up on a country road in the dark of the night and feel the urge to fight.

The two vehicles both pulled up and parked behind my car. I detected unlit spotlights on top of the two cars. As the one in back swung his door open I could make out the words, 'Kentucky State Police'. I was both glad and sorry. At least we weren't going to be beat up but we still had to deal with troopers. The first cop put his hat on top of his very tall frame, gave a spit of tobacco and asked in a very civil tongue, "What's going on here, boys?"

I answered, "I'm not sure, Officer."

The other trooper walked over and spotted Roy. "What is that boy doing in the ditch?"

We all looked over as if we had no idea. I said, "Beats me. We were driving by when we thought we saw somebody so we stopped." I hoped they wouldn't notice it would be tough to spot someone in a ditch in the pitch-black night. "I think he is drunk." This would be believable because beer fumes surrounded us like an evening mist.

The two officers went over to examine Roy and came to the same conclusion. "This young fella smells like a pickled herring, Elmer," one cop said to the other. "Let's get him in my cruiser."

"Who is this kid?" Elmer asked. Everyone shrugged their shoulders.

The other cop looked through his pockets. "Dunno. Ain't got no I.D. on him. I'd get on home, boys. It's getting late." They slid Roy horizontally into the back of the state wagon and drove away. Even though we had gotten Roy into his stupor, we still felt much better knowing he was safe and in good hands.

The following day Ike and I were doing our weekly Sigma Chi house jobs when the phone in the hall rang. Ike answered it. He was one of the pledges I had quickly become friends with. His parents were from Greece; he grew up in a poor section downtown on the riverfront and was making his way through college on a five-year sports scholarship playing baseball at U.C.

"Hello, he's in what? Where? Just a minute." Ike yelled up the stairs, "Ed King, get the telephone."

Ed came clanking down the stairs and picked up the receiver. "Yes, who is this? Where are you calling from? He's in a what? Yes, I'll take full responsibility. Put him on a bus. O.K. Thanks." Most of us were in the dining room, trying to listen while we cleaned and polished when Ed came in and demanded, "Who's going to tell me how in the hell Roy Rodgers ended up in the Cynthia, Kentucky jail house all night?"

I knew we had to admit it. Even if Roy had an alcoholic memory loss he would still remember starting out the night with us. The fun was over. In every revolution there comes that bitter time when the action and the flag waving has to stop. In the end, a few of the more aggressive revolutionaries find themselves hauled off to the guillotine. Since I was perceived as the leader of the pledge pack, it was going to be my neck and the actives found the perfect venue: Hell Week.

One week of fraternal Hell Week is similar to six weeks of army boot camp. There is constant harassing by one's elders to teach one discipline and to gain more appreciation for the final initiation into the elite ranks of membership.

They had been frothing at the mouth for six months to get their paws on my skin in retribution for the grief we had given them. It started on a Monday night with a triple work detail and by Thursday midnight I was worn out. All the pledges had to live at the house for the week and we were crammed in sleeping quarters up to the rafters. The campus intrafraternity council had banned excessive tortures that drew blood so

Fellow art student Tom Wesselmann and Ike involved in one example of senseless Hell Week stunts — lying in the Sigma Chi frontyard eating watermelon.

most of the time it was more mental than physical degradation. I had to be respectful and polite to every single active member who wanted to order me around and they did. I badly wanted the Sigma Chi White Cross badge so I put up with everything, cleaning anything anyone asked me to.

By Friday night we were half dazed with the pace of the week when the actives blindfolded us and led us outside to waiting cars. Through the twists and turns I became even more confused at the anticipation of things to follow. It was a long bleak ride before we found ourselves stumbling along a rocky slope. Not a sound or a voice could be heard except for a lone train whistle far away. I had no idea where we were. A cold wind blew and it seemed like we were on a very tall hill but I couldn't figure out where. An active stood behind me and directed every small movement with his two hands firmly grasping my arms. We stopped and were turned 45 degrees. Still silence.

A hollow, very deep, liturgical voice started to tell a story of young people like us, what they experienced, what they saw and how this had changed their lives forever. All of a sudden, a strange crackling noise could be heard and then a wave of warmth hit me. My blindfold was quickly removed. There before us was a 15-foot high white Sigma Chi cross full ablaze in the black night. The flames shone pure yellow against the black sky. Behind the cross stood a group of about 25 figures in fully hooded white robes with two small holes for vision. I knew in my brain they were the active members, even though in the wavering light they looked eerie enough to be apparitions. The blindfolds were quickly secured again to our heads while the image of the cross still burned in my eyes. We started to trudge back down the hill when I heard police sirens. They came closer and closer and then I knew they must be coming up a road toward us.

The sirens stopped. I lifted a corner of my blindfold and saw two police cars. The lead cop jumped out. He shouted, "Who is responsible for burning that cross?"

I heard a low voice talking to the policeman and I figured it must be Ed King. Whatever he was saying didn't have an effect because the policeman barked out, "I don't care. Someone put out that goddurn fire right now before we get any panic down in the valley. Do you boys have any idea of the trouble and excitement you caused in the Negro neighborhoods that can see this hill? They think the Klu Klux Klan is burning a cross. Didn't any of you think about that?"

Ugly People

As an active member of the fraternity I thought I would be able to concentrate more on school but the classes just moved too slowly for me. I was impatient to learn the practical aspects of what I needed and time in class dragged. It was the extracurricular activities of school that kept me going.

We hadn't managed to wow the campus with our homecoming float but my friends and I were determined to win something. We decided our next best chance would be in the annual campus 'Ugly Man Contest'. It was clear Irish was the man to go for the trophy. At 6'3" he had a pair of Mack Truck arms and shoulders that could have put Charles Atlas to shame. He wasn't ugly but he had a schnozz that just wouldn't quit. His nose had a drop on it that made him look like he was eating a banana, and we thought if we doctored him up, we could make him good and gruesome.

We weren't sure what people did to win but were sure we could come up with something creative. The day of the competition, I helped Irish with the makeup and Billy Hadley, the new pledge who was my fraternal little brother, drove us to the auditorium. Irish had a brown paper bag with him. "What's in the bag?" I asked.

"Just a little extra surprise," he answered, refusing to let us in on the secret. We dropped him off, parked the car off campus and ran back to get a good seat. Wilson Auditorium was packed with girls anxious to voice their opinions. It wasn't often the females got to do the whistles and catcalls so they were determined to make the most of it.

The Master of Ceremonies, the Dean of Men, opened the show with an announcement, "The contestants will appear front and center individually and then line up on stage to be viewed and compared together. They will parade down the right aisle, through the rear lobby and back up the left aisle to the stage. A committee of seven art teachers will select the three finalists and the audience applause will determine the final winner."

The curtain opened and the boys of horror came out and strutted their stuff. I whispered to Bill, "This wasn't at all what I expected." They were all of average build, dressed in old clothes, silly hats and ugly makeup. They looked like bums. All except Irish. After everyone was already on stage, he strode out and a silence fell over the audience. He walked to the center front of the stage and posed with one hand tucked in his jacket. In his natty black tuxedo, he looked like a giant Phantom of the Opera with every thread in place below the neck. Above his Adam's apple he was grotesque, like a bloody, mangled Bull Rhino. No one but Bill and I noticed the paper bag, now showing a wet mark like some sort of liquid was seeping through.

The Dean did a double take when he saw Irish but he recovered and said, "The contestants will now parade through the theater to give you a closer look." The lights came up and they stepped down off the stage. As Irish passed, murmurs of disgust rose from the girls. All the contestants left the auditorium to come back up the other side and onto the stage. They all reentered except Irish. Everyone craned their necks around waiting for him to make his entrance. Finally, he walked in and moved

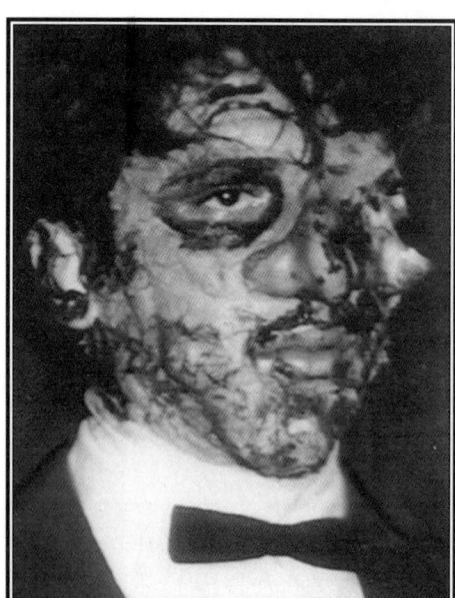

Irish as Mr. Ugly Man

with stately grace down the left aisle. Halfway down he stopped, reached in the bag and pulled out a handful of raw chitterlings. He lobbed them at the girls as if he were tossing them roses. Pig intestines look remarkably like human intestines and the girls' screams were deafening. The Dean quickly awarded the trophy to Irish, presumably so he could escape from the commotion.

After Irish's triumph, we couldn't settle for a regular Friday night. Curley and I were hanging around the front door with two others, Hank and Fred, when Irish came out, no longer horrifying. "Want to drink some beers at Ships?" Curley asked.
"No," Hank said. "I'm tired of Ships." Hank was a bruiser of a guy and no one argued.
"How about a movie?" Irish suggested.
"Nah," we all answered in a chorus.
"Let's go down on the river, have dinner and see the Delta Queen in dock." This was my idea.
"No, but the river gives me an idea," Fred said. "Let's cross it and get some girls in Kentucky." It was unanimous. The five of us struck out from the fraternity house in my car at 8:00 PM. I wasn't surprised Fred had made the suggestion. He was a little guy, rather quiet and I was never sure what he was thinking. He had that wise smile on his face that suggested he knew more than I thought.
We headed south over the bridge. First we went to some bars in Covington to work up our nerve, then we drove on to Newport. I stopped next to a bored-looking cabby parked on York Street and Hank asked out the back window, "Where is a good place to get some poontang around here?"
The cabby waved his hand to the left, "Go north about three blocks and you'll see the Hi-D-Ho Club right in the middle of a big parking lot." He stared at us for a moment. "You sure you boys are old enough?"
We didn't bother to answer and took off in the right direction. I followed the cabby's directions and watched for the sign. We drove past signs for Tony's chili parlor, Ted's Newsstand, Charlie's Pool Hall, and one that said 'Steamboat and Rail Rooms For Rent-Deck Hands Welcomed'. Each place was more progressively rundown than the one before. "I think we are getting close." I said, because we were about to run

into the river.

I finally saw the place and it looked like an old wooden apartment building whose tenants had jumped ship long ago. Some of the windows on the lower floors were broken and a single light bulb shown outside the front door. But this was not a night to consider aesthetics so I parked and we climbed the steps to the second floor club. The sign read, 'Rita's Hi-D-Ho Club.' No one was outside. I was surprised; I either expected other people to be there or maybe a bouncer at the door, checking ages.

At the top of the stairs Fred peered at the small print on another sign. "The sign says you must be 21 years old to enter the club and....I'm only 18," Fred announced.

"Don't worry. We can fool them. I'll run interference for all of us," Hank assured him. I was glad he was confident because I was not.

Rita herself met us at the doorway. I didn't know what a madam was supposed to look like but I didn't expect an anchor tattoo on her wobbly upper arm. Rita's girls reclined in various relaxed positions in skimpy outfits throughout a large red-flocked living room with overstuffed sofas. Rita told us to make ourselves at home and made it clear we were supposed to quickly select a girl. I think she had seen too many college boys chicken out to let them spend time thinking or ogling. The problem was the pink lights were so dim it was tough to see much detail about any of the so-called girls. Anyone of them could have been our 75-year-old housemother with a wig and a little makeup.

Hank moved fast, took his pick — a skinny redhead — and disappeared into a back room. To my surprise, little Freddy pointed at the biggest blond but before she could get up, Rita tapped Fred on the shoulder and beckoned him to follow her down the hall.

Irish, Curley and I milled around uncomfortably. Our minds were made up before we came in the door we were not going to purchase the merchandise. Rita and Fred reappeared back on the scene in two shakes. She must have known from experience that we did not have that buyer look. "You nice boys are going to leave now," she said, herding us to the door.

We didn't argue. The four of us went back down the stairs, out to the parking lot and waited for Hank. To our amazement, Hank came out the front door within ten minutes. I could tell he was madder than a hornet. He climbed in the front seat, slammed the door, and says, "You won't believe it. That broad ate snacks the whole time. It cost me 25 bucks for five minutes with her just to watch her eat those damn crackers."

Hank glared at Fred. "And what happened to you, Pal? I thought you were all gung-ho when we went in. You said you were going to follow my lead."

Fred said, "I was, but the old lady pulled me aside. She took me down the hall and asked me how old I was. I told her 21 but she didn't believe me. She asked me to do an exposé of my 'fruit of the loom' drillies and told me I was only 18. When I asked her how she knew, she only laughed and told me she heard me tell you guys when we came up the front steps."

Grasshopper Bait (1953)

When school was over for the summer, I went back happily to life at home. I was looking forward to some traditional summertime activities so, when Dick suggested a fishing trip in Indiana, I was game. We thought we would have much better luck than our ill-fated fishing expedition to Kentucky because we had seen an ad in the *Cincinnati Enquirer:* Spike's Fishing Lake, beautiful waters teeming with fish, in the wooded countryside of Indiana, etc...

Dick and I left early in my Olds and reached the lake at 9:00 AM with my boat. Neither of us were serious fishermen but we both just wanted to be outside doing something. When we turned in the gravel drive marked 'Spike's Fishing Lake' the entire area looked better suited for an airport – completely flat cornfields everywhere.

Spike came out of a shed to greet us. His mustache cast a shadow on his protruding lower gums and that was about the extent of the shade around the lake. "Howdy, fellows. I see you need some good bait. We have some nice lures for five dollars a bucket." I couldn't believe it; five dollars should have bought the lake. He had us though, we didn't want to drive all the way back to Cincinnati without fishing. We had to fill out a lengthy form listing our names, addresses and other vital information to be allowed to launch our boat.

Dick rowed out about 30 yards while I assembled my gear to test the water. I put a heavy weight on my line and cast out. The weight dropped all of six feet to the bottom. Dick rowed out another 30 yards and I tried again. This time the weight sunk 12 feet before hitting the mud. Obviously we weren't going to be catching any large bass in this big puddle. I threw out the anchor even though the absolute lack of breeze told me we wouldn't be moving anywhere very fast. We sat for an hour baiting live worms and grasshoppers without a nibble. The heat and humidity built up until I imagined I saw tiny bubbles popping all over the surface as if the lake had reached its boiling point.

Dick decided to entertain himself by complaining. He started with the misleading advertisement, then moved on to the lake, the bait, the fishing tackle, the heat and Spike himself. As it drew close to noon he added hunger to his litany. Finally he threw down his pole, stood up and announced to the world, "This place is the pits. Even if there ever were any fish in this cesspool they long ago got boiled or died from mud inhalation."

"Sit down before you fall out. I've about had it too. Let's go back to shore and have a beer before we head back."

We beached the boat a few hundred yards from the dock. Spike was no where in sight.

Dick and Bob with the boat

Our choices of shade were extremely limited. The only possibility was an old maple tree partway split down the middle from lightning that was still trying to grow a few leaves with an ancient flatbed truck parked under it.

"Let's sit in the truck to drink our beers," I suggested. "It has to be cooler than our car." My green Oldsmobile had been boiling in the sun so long it looked like a hot, mossy olive-colored giant grasshopper from our bait bucket. We climbed in the junker and were nearly overpowered by the smell of old car: cracked vinyl, musty seat cushion stuffing spilling out and mouldy headliner torn and falling down on our heads.

We popped the tops of the beers but Dick just couldn't

relax; he had the familiar twitchy irritable look I saw when we had the Bart poinsettia incident. The truck cab was full of bits of wire, rusted tools and other miscellaneous junk. Dick rummaged around until he found an old fan belt. He held it in his hands and contemplated it, whistling between his teeth. I sipped my beer wondering what he was thinking. After a moment he stretched the belt over the steering wheel, pulled it back over the steering column and then stretched it down and pulled it over the brake pedal.

"Okay, Bob, I'm ready to go," he said, smiling for the first time that day.

Two days later I got a call from Spike. He spoke fast, "The Indiana State Troopers are interested to know why you fellows rigged my truck. I nearly drove it through the wall of my shed while my wife was inside. I want both of you up here Saturday to talk about this. If I don't see you, you'll see the police at your door." He hung up and I wished we had never gone fishing.

The next Saturday we made the two-hour drive back to the fishing hole from hell. Spike was waiting for us. As soon as we got out of the car he said, "I'll get to the point quick. You and I both know what you did to my truck and its going to cost you $5000 each. I did some checking and I'm sure your parents can pay. I'll give you seven days. Otherwise it's prison, boys."

My head was hot and ready to explode like I had swallowed a steam iron. We had seen trouble before but not like this. The idea of parental financial involvement was no longer an option I wanted to contemplate, but I couldn't think of a way out.

Dick answered, "Okay, we'll pay you next week." I looked at him in total disbelief. There was no way our fathers would give us the money. "I'm not sure how we will do it but you have to promise to give us a few extra days if we need it." Dick emphasized the word 'promise' and that gave me an idea.

"Look here, Spike. You say $5000 each today, but some time in the future you could call us up and ask for another $5000. How do we know you won't do that?" I tried to sound tough and smart if that was possible after our stupid trick.

"You can trust me."

"No, we are not going to fork over $10,000 unless you can assure us you won't put the screws to us over and over."

Spike was speechless. I don't think he had planned on negotiations. He looked at me as if he expected us to come up with a solution. I knew we had him. "If each of us sign a mutual agreement saying we pay once and no more, then we will pay the $10,000."

He darted inside to get pen and paper before we would back out. I knew he was already counting the dollars in his head. We set up office on my fender. I wrote out identical statements on three sheets:

> Sam Johnston demands and Dick Fuller and Bob Greiwe agree to pay a total of $10,000 for possible damage that could have resulted to him and his truck. The payment assures Dick and Bob that this incident will not be reported to any police and that this payment will be final.

We all signed each copy. With business done I was ready to get out of there. I could tell by the smirk on Spike's face he didn't suspect anything could be fishy about this deal.

We drove away as fast as we could. When we pulled onto the main road I said, "At the next town let's stop and see if they have a Cincinnati phone book. I'm going to call Lynch Smith and find out if we can see him this afternoon." Lynch was a Cincinnati Sigma Chi from Alabama who had set up a new law practice and he would appreciate the business.

Two hours later we arrived at Lynch's small downtown office. He had graduated from law school the year before and was still young enough to appreciate our predicament. I had not been able to explain everything on the phone but he knew we were in serious trouble. He took an official tone, "Just for your protection and my record keeping I'm sure you have no objection to my recording this conversation. All of your responses must be oral so I can record them. OK?" He pushed the button on the tape recorder. "What lake did you go to?"

Dick deadpanned, "Oral."

Lynch pushed the stop button. "Now quit fooling around, you guys. You sounded on the phone like you were about to be arrested." He started the tape again and we went through the whole story. When we finished, I pulled out our two signed statements and laid them on his desk. After he read them he smiled his familiar grin and reached for the phone.

"Mr. Samuel 'Spike' Johnston? This is Lynch Smith. I am legal advisor for Mr. Fuller and Mr. Greiwe who are here in my office. I have two documents in hand you all signed today. Do you recall which ones I am talking about? I'm glad you do. I want you to clearly understand the blackmail charges my clients are bringing against you. These charges carry a jail sentence of 10 to 25 years. Do you fully understand the seriousness and ramifications of your crime?"

Spike's answer was so loud that Lynch held the phone away from his ear. Lynch hung up and said, "I think you two gentlemen are off the hook."

I went home relieved to be out of trouble once again. It didn't seem fair that none of my siblings ever got in trouble. I wished one of them would do something wrong enough to improve my reputation in comparison. I thought my chance had come when Dad laid down the law about my sister Madge's boyfriend. At 16 she was going steady with Eddie, who just happened to be a first cousin to my good friend Happy on one side and also first cousin to Maddie, Kay and Billy Hadley on the other. The Little King didn't care who Eddie was related to. He could have been Eisenhower's son and Dad still would have been suspicious.

I overheard the discussion in the living room, "Look here, Madge, your mother and I have discussed you going steady with Ed and we don't want it getting too serious so we want you to date other boys," Dad said in a fatherly tone. Madge was the oldest of my three sisters and from the day she was born she was Miss Goodie. She was a wonderful little girl, but when big mama or the Little King said jump she went through that hoop faster than a circus tiger on fire, and she did it with a smile on her face.

I waited to see if Madge would finally break out of the mold and refuse to stop dating Eddie. There was silence for a few moments and then I heard her say softly, "O.K." Word of Madge's availability spread to her clique of friends but unfortunately for Madge, there was no one too interesting on the horizon.

The only possibility appeared when Dad hired a landscape company to clean up and trim trees after a bad windstorm. The crew chief brought two helpers and his son. The kid was about 18 years old, stood about six foot three and was so skinny his legs looked unable to support his body. When he walked, his chin thrust to and fro and he took high steps like he was tripping through tall grass. He looked exactly like a grasshopper.

That same day Madge made an announcement at dinner. "Daddy, Daddy. I've got good news. I have a date next weekend."

I think the King had an idea who she was going to tell him about since Madge had been around the house all day. "Er, that's great," he told her, "But I hope it's not that scrawny kid with snake hips who has been slowly destroying my prize magnolia tree."

I said, "You've got the right idea, Dad, but the wrong name. I heard his dad call him 'Grasshopper'."

"Wonderful," he muttered.

The next Saturday evening the grasshopper knocked on the door, which was inside our screen porch, and got no response. No one ever figured out why he ignored or didn't see the doorbell. Our parents had a bedroom window that opened on to the porch but they were getting ready back in their dressing area to go out and didn't hear the knocking.

The kid, in his frustration and desperation to gain entry to announce his presence to Madge, decided on a fatal solution. He struggled and was able to open the window to my parents' bedroom and proceeded to crawl through. I think the late afternoon sun made him unable to see what kind of room he was entering. In the meantime mother innocently left the dressing area in her bra and girdle outfit only to be confronted by a total stranger dangling from her window with arms flailing and groping to find a way in. Her shriek made him fall through the window and hit the floor. He was lucky Mother didn't take off one of her shoes and flail him with the pointed high heel. The date was nipped in the bud.

The best thing that could be said about this family catastrophe is that it had a boomerang effect. The King relinquished his court order and steady Eddie was reinstated to his original rank of chief boyfriend.

Sigma Chi Sweethearts (1954)

Back at school in the fall, I was ready for a new challenge. Classes still were mostly drudgery even though I accepted the fact that I had to put up with them. Elections for officers of Sigma Chi were scheduled in October and I was a candidate for president. On the day of elections, the president, J.C., came up to me after the votes were tallied. "Congratulations, you got the job, Bob. And you get the dog and Lady 'A'."

It took me a few weeks to fully understand his meaning. I had one week to move into the fraternity house away from my comfortable home quarters. As president, I got a private study room, a bunk bed in the 3rd floor dorm, three meals a day, and the dog, Siggie. Siggie was a white half-breed Collie with a black patch over one eye that made him look like a canine pirate. Unlike lazy Kydoo, this pup was always bright-eyed, tongue out, ready to go. He was famous on campus, and whenever he went with us, it was a sure way to attract girls who wanted to pet him.

J.C. hadn't been kidding. Somehow that pooch knew who was the official human top dog at the fraternity and from the day I took over the private study he stayed at my side like a faithful sidekick.

Lady 'A' was a different matter. The second day in my official role she stopped me for what would become a regular list of problems. Lady 'A' was the widow of a Presbyterian minister, and she accepted no nonsense. She fought a constant struggle to keep the house organized and figured the president should be on her side. One day she said very seriously,

"Bob, we have a big problem."

"What is it?" I asked. I hoped nobody had been arrested.

She pointed at Siggie. "We have got bugs and fleas all over the house and clothes and he is the cause." I swear Sig looked remorseful. "You better take him

Sigma Chi fraternity house

outside and give him a good bath before some of our members scratch themselves to death."

I hadn't realized dog bathing was part of the duties of a fraternity president so I decided to delegate, or at least share the job. Curley had been voted in as house manager and his job was to crack the whip on unruly inhabitants, fleas included, so I roped him into helping me.

The next few months were eye-opening. Now life wasn't just about solving my own problems, it was about feeling responsible for seven dozen young men, making sure they understood and projected the high values of the fraternity. I now realized how annoying our pledge class must have been to poor Ed King.

One night the phone rang at 11:00 PM. I was still up studying when someone called out, "Hey, Bob, sounds like your mother on the phone."

I went out to the hall and picked up the receiver. "Hello, Mom?"

"Don't give me that '*%&!$@&^&%*!!' Mom crap, this is Ethel Burnbridge, your next door neighbor!"

"Oh yes, Mrs. Burnbridge, what can I do for you?

"Get your lily white skull and bones body over here PDQ!" Slam went the phone. My ear reverberated. This was not the Ethel Burnbridge I knew. The first week as president I went next door to introduce myself and promote neighborly relations. I talked to the sweet little old lady for an hour about her flower garden and her grandchildren while we sipped tea and ate Streitmans Lorna Doone cookies.

I went over to find her waiting for me at her front door. Without a word she led me upstairs and pointed at her bedroom stained glass window and then at the wall behind her bed. The glass was shattered all over the floor and I could see three bullet holes making a perfect triangle in the wall. I wished I was back in New York, where it was safe.

I knew immediately who had done it. Every group has one member who just doesn't quite fit the mold and ours was a transfer student named Karp. He had belonged to the Sig chapter at his other school so we were obligated to take him in but knew he had a bad reputation, including the minor offense of taking a train locomotive for a joy ride.

I grabbed Curley and told him the situation as we went up to Karp's room. Karp was a big, friendly looking guy who grinned when we walked in. I asked, "Did you shoot some bullets out the window at the neighbor's house?"

His face became blunt and expressionless and he started to mumble, "Why, uh, why are you asking me?" We knew it was him.

Curley said, "What's it going to be, yes or no?" Again silence. There was no sign of weapons anywhere. The only possible hiding place in the room was a large locked file cabinet.

"Open it," I ordered. He did and there they were. One rifle, a 22 pistol, a 45 army pistol and another unidentifiable

imported pistol, plus at least four hundred rounds of ammunition.

I gulped and said, "Karp, you know better. No weapons on campus or the fraternity house. You have discharged a loaded gun and there is no excuse for your action. We are going to ask you to remove yourself and your guns from the premises by noon tomorrow. Any questions?" I hoped he wouldn't have any because I wasn't ready for a debate with a guy who could shoot his way out of the O.K. corral. He shook his head so we left him to contemplate the consequences on his actions. I breathed a deep sigh of relief that he seemed to be in a reasonable mood and just prayed no official campus honcho would find out about the incident.

The Friday after exams I faced another problem. I happened to look out of the second floor bathroom window at the four-acre U.C. parking expanse next to the house to see what was happening. For some reason there was a lot of noise and activity around a '51 Ford. I went downstairs and ran into Ike coming in the front door. "What in the world is going on over in the parking lot? Nobody ever congregates out there on Friday afternoons."

"J.C. decided to celebrate section change and make a few bucks at the same time. He went out and bought a trunk full of ice and about four hundred bottles of beer. His car is ready to bust its springs."

I wanted to let loose with a line of curses but restrained myself. My term as president would soon be over and I didn't want it to end in disaster. The school had a strict law against drinking alcoholic beverages on campus, and at any off campus college organizations including fraternities and sororities. If the University found out we were in trouble. I took a deep breath and marched out the door.

Normally the upperclassmen at U.C. reflected a sophisticated attitude, trying to appear unfazed to the world. When Ike and I arrived near the scene, those same upperclassmen were acting like primitive natives, dancing and wobbling about to the music from the car radio. Siggie, my traitor of a dog, was there too, waiting to lap up any spilled beer. A crowd of non-drinkers was gathering, amazed to see anyone who would dare drink on school property.

J.C. and his friends, Tiger and Birdlegs, were acting as

bartenders. I decided they knew the consequences of what they were doing and I didn't need to put on my official hat so I stayed away from the scene.

The story of the beer party spread through the campus. The next morning before I was fully awake someone yelled for me to pick up the phone. The voice on the other end asked, "Did everyone have a good time in the parking lot yesterday?"

I mumbled, "Why do you ask?"

"Because we are going to put an end to your program right now."

"Who is this?" I asked.

"This is Dean Brickup and be in my office at 9:00 AM Monday." He hung up the phone.

J.C. wandering through the hall looked at me and said, "You look pale, Mr. President. Any problems?"

"You'll be the first to know," I replied and went back to my room to contemplate my legacy as the president who got the fraternity banned.

Monday morning I faced the secretary of the Dean of Men, a pickle-faced woman who acted like she was guarding the President of the United States. She ushered me into the Dean's large dark-paneled office. He pointed to the chair directly in front of his giant desk. I sat down and waited. He was a bear of a man who had large, deepset eyes and thick black eyebrows that furrowed together when he spoke. The overwhelming authority of the man and the place made me shrivel in my seat before he even started talking. When he did, he let loose a tirade, "I am holding your fraternity responsible for the beer party in our 'C' parking lot next to the Sigma Chi house. I want to know exactly who was there and who were the ringleaders." He waited for an answer and when I couldn't find my voice, he spent the next half hour lecturing on the need for rules and order on campus, and on the penalties for those who didn't go by the book.

Finally, I had to speak up so I could get out of there. It felt like he would keep me until he talked himself out and I had no idea how long that would take. "No, no, Dean. You've got it wrong. First of all, let me tell you I heard about the party but I did not attend or partake in it. Secondly, I can promise you that my chapter would never be dumb enough to drink on campus. It was not a planned Sigma Chi social event and it's not my responsibility to find out who was there."

We were at a standoff. Without proof he couldn't do anything. He waved me out of his office in disgust and I headed back to the house determined to make J.C. share some of my misery and irritation. When he saw me he asked, "Anything happen?"

"Not this time, but next time you will have to charge more for the beer," I told him.

"Why?"

"Because next time you're going to need to pay a lawyer."

Lollapalooza (1955)

College was winding down. I had been booted from the Air Force Reserve because of asthma so I knew flying wasn't in my future. Luckily, the war in Korea was also winding down, so I didn't have to worry about spending the next few years slogging through Asian mud. I enjoyed my classes after I had a talk with Dean Pickering. He convinced me that even if I felt like I didn't need some of the education immediately, I would find it useful to have in the future.

I wasn't sure where the live nude model drawing class fit into the category of useful and valuable knowledge, but I wasn't going to argue that particular point.

The instructor, Reggie, taught the only real art class on campus. He looked exactly like a giant Toulouse-Lautrec, with goatee, wire glasses down on his nose and frock down to his knees. Like most artists with a student audience, he loved to expound on philosophy, the virtues of the abstract art revolution, the weather, whatever.

The best thing about the class in the beginning was glancing at the model, Florence. The worst thing about the class became really looking at Florence, again and again, week after week. Flo was about 45 years old with streaming bright, undyed red hair, light blue eyes and a sweet little round cherub face. The first time she took off her tattered chenille robe, she exposed a plump, curvaceous Florentine figure, all pink and rosy, like one of the Medici angels Michelangelo painted all over the Sistine chapel. Reggie adored every bit of her, thinking her the perfect artist's model, uncorrupted by the modern look.

They had a routine for class. She would ascend her platform, hold her robe tight and wait for his signal. He would walk over to the entrance, close the door, draw the curtain over the window in the door, and snap his fingers.

At first it was hard not to gawk but we soon looked at her as if she were only curves and colors, mixing with the smell of linseed oil and turpentine. We were the envy of the rest of campus though, particularly the engineering students who inhabited the building next to ours. The last class before spring break, the entire group couldn't settle down to work. We spent the first hour drawing and then putting down background paint on canvas when Reggie called for the standard 15-minute break.

I went outside with a few other students to have a smoke. I was surprised when my rather quiet fraternity brother Tom W. said, "I'm bored. Let's do something."

An idea had been kicking around in my head all term. "How about opening Pandora's box?" I ran back in to get some paper and a marker from my tackle box of supplies. We printed one sign that said 'Open House in the Art Studio Today' and another that read 'Welcome, Please Maintain Silence when Studio Class is in Session'. Tom took the first sign and darted across to the Engineering building. We waited until everyone else was in place and posted the second sign on the wall outside the studio door. Reggie looked over his glasses at us when we were the last ones in but he didn't say or suspect anything.

It only took about seven minutes before I heard the door open quietly. There were no girls in the Engineering department so those poor geeks were starved for anything female. Reggie didn't notice them. He was busy walking around doing his critiques of individual work. Florence, on the other hand, had nothing to do but sit motionlessly and keep an eye out for intruders. She belted out a scream, grabbed her robe, jumped off the platform and tried to hide behind one of the easels.

Reggie knew without having to take in all the details. He dashed towards the door, knocking over four easels before grabbing two of the infiltrators. "What are you doing here?" he screamed. One brave engineer said, "We just read the sign on the door that said 'Welcome'." Silence. You could have heard a brush stroke. The bell rang and we escaped to the freedom of section change spring break.

    Joining Dick, me and two other friends for spring break in Florida was Jordan, a character who had more conversation and enthusiasm than sense. We took off in Dick's '51 Ford convertible, determined to make Florida in 27 hours. It was a realistic estimate because Dick had just completed a full race overhaul on his engine.

    Jordan ate M&Ms, drank Pepsi's and yacked for the first five hours and then fell into a deep sleep. He reminded me of my old St. Xavier nemesis, D.J. I whispered to the other three, "Do you think he has all his marbles? How are we going to stand him for 22 more hours?"

    Dick, true to form, said, "I have a plan to keep that puppy awake, quiet and tired for the rest of the trip. Play along with me." He jammed on the brakes and Jordan's head snapped forward. "What's going on?" he mumbled.

    "Wow, look at that!" Dick screamed. "Did you see the size of that thing?"

    I had no idea what he was up to but I knew it would be good. Max and I stuck our heads out the window and looked back. "That was amazing!" I said. "I have never seen anything like it."

    Dick shook his head, "That's the biggest lollapalooza I have ever seen. It must have been six or seven feet long." We waited for Jordan to ask what a lollapalooza was but he didn't. Maybe he didn't want to admit he didn't know. All he said was, "I've never seen one before."

    Dick was quick. "I've heard they only live in Georgia and Florida. Maybe we will see some more." Jordan spent the next hour looking out the window but then I saw his head nodding forward. Dick slammed his brakes again, and we went through the routine, expressing amazement over the fearsome creatures.

    We turned south on A1A and skirted along the water's edge filled with bathing beauties on the left and a row of two story motels on the right. We found our spot, the 'Ole Spanish Motel'. It looked like it had barely withstood the last hurricane, missing shingles and shutters, the paint long ago worn off the stucco, but it was only one block from the famous Elbo Room Bar on the beach.

    The manager's nametag read 'Ruby' and her hair matched

her name, at least what I could see of it wrapped up in orange rollers. She looked us over and said, "Your suite has 2 bedrooms, living room, a kitchen, a screened porch, a bathroom, $5.00 a day in advance. The four of you will be nice and comfy." We didn't tell her we had three more friends showing up the next day. We had figured out with seven of us, it would only cost each of us 71 cents a day. Since we got here first the latecomers could divide the sofa, the floor and the porch among themselves.

Dick was used to going first class so I expected him to have a list of complaints about the dilapidated conditions but his main worry was the lizards. They were everywhere – the lampshades, the walls, the top of the refrigerator, hanging out. I guess he didn't like them watching him because he kept trying to shoo them out. After we got settled and went out to buy some snacks, Dick pulled over at a hardware store and bought a can of red spray paint. "What are you doing?" I asked, worried about a scheme involving paint.

"Just wait." We got back to the motel and Dick gave a squirt at the first reptile he spotted on the porch. "They turn green or brown depending on where they are. I want to be able to see the little buggers so they don't sneak up on me." Soon we had the most exotic looking chameleons in Florida at our place.

I had good intentions for my stay in Florida – to get some rest, sun, meet a few girls and get a start on my senior thesis on color psychology. Most of the time I was on the beach and

Dick holding first Polaroid with Haven, Polly, Jordan, Ike, Betty, Bob and Ruthie at Ole Spanish Motel.

couldn't concentrate on color psychology beyond analyzing good colors for bathing suits.

It was easy to make friends. Everyone was in the spirit of vacation. We met girls from all over and it was a snap to invite one to roam up and down the beach at night visiting different bonfire parties. One night I had a date with a girl named Ruthie, one of the 'interesting' girls, just quirky enough for me not to be able to understand what she was talking about. Studying anthropology at Ohio University she tended to look at people as if trying to categorize what tribe they belonged to. She only had one good leg; the other was encased in a cast from a stair accident.

For our date I hip hopped her down to a party the Betas were having – a huge pine and cypress wood bonfire on the beach. The smell of the smoke from the fire mixed with the damp salt air – an aphrodisiac I wanted to bottle and take home. We only stayed an hour or so and then Ruthie said she wanted to leave. I respected her request because I knew she was dead tired from limping and gimping around the soft sand all day. After I took her back to her room, I thought it would be a good chance for me to work on my thesis so I spent a few hours outlining it until I conked out about 1:30 A.M.

Sometime later, the screen door on the porch flung open and a laughing dancing couple came twirling through the apartment, into my bedroom and eventually out the kitchen door. It was so dark I didn't know who it was. Sixty seconds later they were back again, bumping into tables and chairs and back out again. When the door opened one more time, I was ready for them. I put my fingers on the lamp switch and waited. When they came through again, I turned on the light and they froze, momentarily blinded by the light. I was astonished to see Ruthie and one of the Betas, a guy named Gary. I guess he was more anthropologically interesting than me.

The last night we went out to eat at a drive-in. The roller skating waitresses zipped deftly between the cars, creating a show along with the food. We parked next to a chopped and channeled '51 black Mercury convertible being driven by a couple of real greasers. We eyed each other back and forth and finally the driver said, "What are you Ohio guys doing down in these parts?" This was a dumb question since the town was crawling with college students on spring break.

Dick said, "We're just down for a little winter vacation."

This they thought hilarious. "Yo all come to the wrong place, ain't no winter in Florida." We tried to ignore them but as we finished our burgers and black cows, the driver threw out a challenge to Dick. "Wanna race?"

Dick glanced at me, smirking, and then said, "My car's not running too well and it's not that hot, but sure, why not?" I knew this was a typical Dick set-up play. The guy couldn't wait to make us eat his dust. We followed him to an undeveloped construction area. I could tell the local had been there before, because he knew exactly where to start and finish without smashing into anything.

We lined up, his passenger counted to three and we were off. After a quarter mile Dick let him win by three yards. While they were gloating, Dick said, "That was pretty close, let's try it just one more time."

This time Dick was careful to win by just a few feet. Now the other driver was begging for a final heat. Dick said, "Naw, your car is just too good." After more pleading, Dick finally relented and agreed to one last run. On three Dick opened up both carbs, and then the big bore cylinders and racing cam screamed into action with a huge roar, and his back tires peeled a straight strip of rubber 40 feet long. When Dick was up to 50 miles an hour he shifted to second and our heads jerked back. After we hit 100 he throttled back and coasted until our challenger could catch up.

When their car came to a stop, they both hopped out. I got worried. They sauntered over and took up positions leaning on the sides of our car. The driver took out a comb and smoothed back the grease he called hair, sending little droplets over the hood of Dick's car. The other showed his teeth and sneered, "We ain't happy about being duped and set up. If we find you guys tomorrow we'll cut you up in little bits and sprinkle you in the everglades." Two switchblades appeared with a snap as if choreographed. We were convinced.

Dick said, "Good thing we are leaving tomorrow," gunned the engine and we drove off into the night.

We departed early the next morning for an uneventful trip back home, enlivened only by an occasional lollapalooza sighting. We stopped in northern Georgia for breakfast at a Texaco truck stop with a sign that read 'EATS'. Hand painted signs over the counter described the major choices: 'Hog Backs', 'Chitlins', and 'Fried Chicken Wings'. I wondered what they did with the other parts of the hogs and chickens. It was one of those places where if you don't smell it, it wasn't on the menu. We all ordered eggs and toast, except Dick, who ordered Wheaties with bananas and milk. While we were waiting I found a nickel in my pocket and chose *In the Still of the Night* by the Five Satins on the Wurlitzer juke box. We waited and waited and got a little concerned when our waitress, Pearl, dashed out the front door. Ten minutes later she came back in with a small package and said, "We all be ready in one mo' minute."

She served Dick first, putting a plate down in front of him with two bananas and two hot dogs all laying in a neat parallel pattern. He stared down at them and then said, "What is this?"

She looked puzzled, 'Thems yo bananas and wienies ya'll ordered. I'm sorry it took so long but I had to go down the street special to get them wienies." Dick controlled himself and took a bite so he wouldn't hurt her feelings.

It was our turn next. She brought out our three-egg blue plate special for 35 cents each. The eggs lay on one side almost overwhelmed by a mound of white goo. "Pearl," I asked, "Just what exactly is this white stuff?"

"Thems grits," she said, eyeing me like I was a creature from Mars.

"But I didn't order grits." I told her, not even sure what grits were.

"It just comes with it," she informed me, shrugging her shoulders. I ate them, but reflected she was more of a philosopher than she realized. A lot of things in life, good and bad, 'just comes' whether you want it or not.

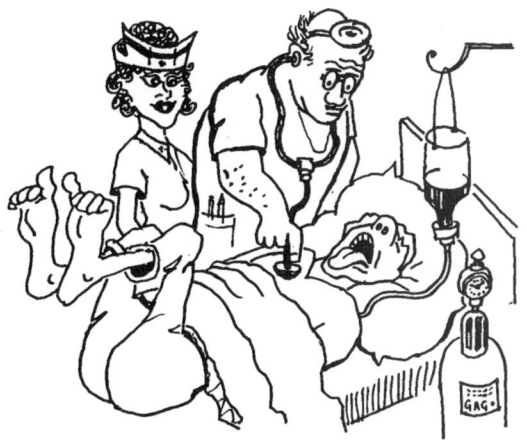

Unsplendor in the Grass

With degree in hand I was anxious to exert my artistic independence so I accepted the first and only job offered to me — by my dad. Many of my high school and college friends were getting married and needed their first apartment furnished. It was fun creative work but otherwise it was slim pickings. I didn't earn much by helping them choose light fixtures, paint colors, and Sears ready-made drapes, but the furniture and carpet sales made it worthwhile. Like automobiles in the '50s, there was a huge amount of cheaply made furniture. Tapered wooden legs were the tacky hot detail on chairs and tables. The high end goods like Baker and Widdicomb were untouchable for my friends. Even though Italian provincial with olive green carpet was all the rage, I tried to steer them into more classic furnishings.

Dad decided to further my practical education. One day he said, "Bob, today I am going to teach you how to sell. We have a 2:00 appointment at the Duboor Chemical Co."

At 1:50 we pulled into their parking lot. The plant was located about a mile west of downtown and looked like a massive jungle of plumbing pipes, stacks, tanks and buildings all interconnected with more ducts and tubes.

As we got out of the car, Dad said, "I really want this job. My bid is $17,000 to paint the entire exterior but I don't know if Mr. Duboor will go for it. He doesn't like Catholics." The Duboors lived down the road from us and I knew Mother was in the same garden club with Mrs. Duboor, but I didn't remember ever seeing them at any of my parents' summer parties in the ballfield.

We walked in and a secretary directed us to two armless wooden chairs in a dark hall. We waited for a half-hour with no sign of life. Finally at 2:30 we were escorted to C.P Duboor's office. He sat behind his desk, stern-faced. His son, C.P. Duboor, Jr. stood behind him, trying to look as serious as his father. I saw Junior Duboor every summer at the Portage Point Inn, had always liked him and knew he was not as tough as his father.

We shook hands but there was no chitchat about the weather or the Reds. No one offered to take our coats and C.J. motioned us to the two chairs in front of his desk, identical to the uncomfortable hallway chairs. The floor was uncarpeted and the room spartan.

Dad launched right into his prepared three-minute speech and then said, "We can do the whole job for $16,900." Mr. Duboor didn't speak. We sat in silence while C.J. and Dad stared at each other. I hadn't been aware that a good selling technique consisted of the type of staredown I used to have with Richard when we were in grade school.

Finally C.J. spoke, "You are the highest bidder so it's been nice to see you again." He stood up. "Before you go, tell me something, Mr. Greiwe. Ever since you got here your left hand has been inside your coat pocket. What the hell are you playing around with in there?"

Dad yanked out his hand, held up a black beaded rosary, shook it at Mr. Duboor and said, "I was praying to get this job." The C.E.O started back like he was being shown a shrunken head. Jr. C.P. broke up laughing but his father merely snorted, sat down, signed Dad's contract and handed it to him. "Now you get the hell out of here. I don't want to see you again till you finish the job, then I'll pay you."

I waited until we got to the car. "I don't get it, Dad. Why did he give you the job?"

"It doesn't matter that he doesn't like me. He knows his wife would give him a lot of grief if he didn't do business with the husband of someone she has to see at the garden club meetings."

Most businessmen go on vacation to relax after months of action-filled work. In my job I went on vacation to find some excitement. I was climbing the walls with inactivity and felt like a trip to somewhere. I decided to join the family for the annual trip to the Portage Point Inn and persuaded Dick to come along. The following week we left in two cars. The family together in one, and me in my car with Dick in the copilot seat.

Portage Point was perfect for beer drinking and bonfire festivities on the beach. But the best part of the old firetrap was the dining room staff. The owner, a 65-year-old bachelor named J.J., only hired the best-looking college kids so between the waitresses and the guests it was two girls for every guy.

The second best part of the spot was the hotel's own grass ball field a couple of blocks down the road, which had bleachers, a backstop and clay base paths. We found enough people to get up games every day. After looking over the potential of all the players, Dad decided to throw out a challenge to J.J, "We have enough hometown guests at the hotel who are good ballplayers, so go on notice that on Friday, Cincinnati will take on the rest of the world."

J.J. practically jumped up and down with delight. He announced the event before each meal and posted notices in the lobby. Even the cottagers three miles away got wind of it and by game day the ball field teemed with guests, staff, locals and sports enthusiasts from all over the north woods. It was fast pitch softball. J.J. had a 6'4" staff busboy from Michigan State as his pitcher. Dad had his rubber-armed son, Bob, as his pitcher from the Little King athletic program. My brother, Richard, played left field but could have covered the entire outfield himself if necessary. C.J. Duboor Jr. played center and Dad's buddy, Gus, played right field. The remaining infield was made up of a sturdy looking bunch of staff and guests from Cincinnati.

At 10:01, J.J. bellowed from the grandstand, "Where is Gene? We can't start this game without that cocky captain of the Cincinnati team." We didn't know either so we just stood in a group near first base. In a few minutes, Mother drove in alone, right onto the ballfield. She parked next to the pitcher's mound. This was such strange behavior for her I wondered if she was feeling all right. J.J. was already in a rage over the delay but seeing a car on his beloved ball field blew his fedora right off his sweaty bald head.

The rear door opened and a figure rolled out, got up, and

blew kisses at J.J. The crowd roared with hilarity. It was my Dad all dressed up in his special, never before seen 'Little King' outfit, robe and all. He looked exactly like the Little King character in O. Soglon's cartoons in the comics, right down to the pom poms on his hat. He was in his element. Dad pranced around showing off his robe and then marched over to third base to assume his official duties as royal hometown coach.

J.J. got his act together and shouted 'Play Ball' and I flipped the first batter a nasty little slider that almost burned a path across his stomach. It was a great game, nip and tuck all the way and by the tenth inning the game was tied up 12 to 12. Our first batter struck out; the second dribbled a wiener ball to the first baseman who plucked him out before he even got near the bag. It was my bat.

Pop yelled, "Come on, Bob, this is it, just get on." The third pitch was decent but slightly outside, just where I wanted it. I popped a soft blooper ball short between the center and right fielder and held first base. Brother Richard was hitting after me. He had enough power in his swing to put that ball beyond the cut grass into the marshes if he could tag it. The King was airborne with excitement. His monarch hat flew off and he stomped it unnoticed.

Richard liked the first pitch and belted it deep between the left and center fielder. By the time the center fielder got it, I was already headed to third. I thought I could make home plate but it would be close. I knew where the bag was on third but I was busy running as fast as possible and watching the outfielders getting ready to nail me at home. Unfortunately the Little King was also watching the throw and waved me in standing right in the running base path. It was a good thing Mother padded him with pillows because I hit him with full power on and knocked him clear over to the world team on deck bench. I quickly picked myself up and continued, thinking I

The Little King plays ball.

needed to be a hero so Dad wouldn't be mad at me for causing him to lose his dignity. I slid across home plate just in time.

That evening Dad showed up at the celebration party dressed in a new costume. Since his king costume had grass stains, he made his entrance wearing one of Mother's nightgowns. Under it he fashioned paper bags around his legs to look like pantaloons and to top it off he wrapped one of her nylon stockings around his head. He looked like a demented Arab.

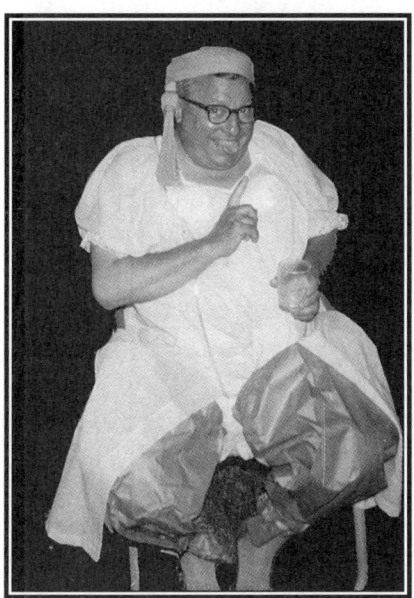

The Little King celebrating after the ballgame.

The week had been so great, Dick and I were reluctant to leave. Our weekly American plan at the Inn was up on Friday so Dick said, "Let's rent a cottage at 'Happy Landings' in town and have one final killer party there."

The family left and Dick and I moved into our new quarters to prepare for our bash. Since Dad's success with his costumes we decided to have a costume party also. We needed something for our guests to drink so Dick and I took a used five-gallon potato chip can, poured in cheap brandy, fresh thick cream and two bottles of creme de cacao to make it last longer. Our guests arrived but our Brandy Alexanders proved to be a major mistake because it put the festivities on fast forward within the first hour. Forty kids jammed into a single room cottage about 15' by 20' with two twin beds and a tiny bathroom. I decided to mimic Dad's look and wore some beach towels to go for the Sheik look myself. It was a popular choice, beach towels being about the only available costume material.

I began to experience the same dizziness I experienced as a child when I twirled and spun in circles so long until I could no longer stand. Things got blurry. Then I found myself lying outside, face down in the grass struggling to breathe – a combination of a grass allergy and too many alexanders.

Everything was quiet except for Dick's voice. "What's wrong? You OK? Talk to me."

I tried to answer him but the only answer I could give him was, "Take me to the hospital, I can't breathe." Dick dragged me to the car and we took off in the chill of the night. After he turned on the heater, I lapsed into a semi-conscious state again.

The beginning of the end

When I woke, a doctor and a nurse stood over me. "How do you feel? You came in last night with an acute asthmatic condition. Ever have it before?"

The pollen and Michigan mold caught up with me. I never expected to have it land me in a hospital. I nodded my head yes. Should we call your parents? I shook my head no. I was stuck in the hospital for two days, shot full of massive doses of allergy serum. By the third day of confinement, I had to get out of my hospital gown and out of the hospital. I thought about talking to the doctor but decided I didn't want to take the chance he would keep me there. I called Dick; "I need you to pick me up at the rear door at 4:00 this afternoon." He was willing. I wrote the doctor and nurse a nice thank-you note and gave them my phone number and full address to send the bill. AT 3:55, I threw on my grass-stained clothes, and scampered down three flights of stairs and outside to the waiting getaway car.

Ten hours later we pulled into my driveway. I got my gear and walked into the kitchen. Dad sat at the table in the breakfast room waiting for me. "We got a call from the hospital asking if we knew our son had gone AWOL. Also, just what kind of party did you have? I got a call from the owner of the Happy Landings cabins. You left behind your white bucks and he wanted to know exactly how those shoes made footprints all over the ceiling."

A View from 4000 Feet

Dick and I thought we needed more legitimate excitement than some of our past hijinks so we decided to learn to fly. After a few lessons at Lunken airport, I realized it wasn't what I expected. The navigation and landing of those Cessna trainers were challenges but the takeoff and flying around in practice circles was as exciting as driving on an empty country road. Dick loved it though and called me up one Saturday as I contemplated a nap in the hammock, "How about if we hop in a plane and wing it? I need to log ten more solo hours before I can get my permanent license. It's a perfect day for flying." I couldn't turn him down. He made it sound like it would be fun.

At Lunken airport we climbed in a Cessna 170 he had reserved. After we took off I passed the time trying to figure out which roads we were flying over. Dick practiced a few required moves and then leveled off at 4000 feet. He asked, "Have you ever been in a stall?"

"Negative, captain." I answered, not really paying attention because I was enjoying the view.

"I'm going to increase my air speed flying level, then pull the stick back until the nose of the plane is pointed straight up. The engine and prop will continue to turn but the plane will fall into a stall straight down backwards, eventually pancake out right side up and then go into a nose dive." He had my attention. "It's important in the dive that I don't try to pull the stick back too abruptly in a panic. At least that's what the manual says. I have to ease it out of its descent."

"Dick, that doesn't sound like a descent. That sounds like a plunge straight to earth."

"You'll love it and I need to practice."

I tried to sound persuasive. "That sounds like a great aeronautical learning experience for you but is there any chance you could take me back to Lunken?"

"It's no big deal. Tighten your seatbelt." My stomach rumbled a warning and then the next thing I know I was sitting on my back looking straight up. It happened just like he said, the plane became motionless. I looked over at Dick. He was motionless too, his hands off the wheel, his eyes closed and his head tipped to the side. I was pretty sure that wasn't in the manual. We started to fall backwards, did the pancake bit and slowly fell into a dive position. Dick was out cold and wouldn't wake up no matter how much I screamed. Maybe the gravity forces pressed the blood from his brain when he picked up speed and pulled the plane into an abrupt climb, but I did not have time to wonder. I tried to remember what he told me about pulling the stick back without panicking. Luckily my hands were so shaky I could barely hold the stick, otherwise I would have jerked it right out of the socket. As we leveled out, Dick woke up and took over as if he had just been taking a catnap.

When we landed and came to a stop Dick asked, "Are you okay, Bob?"

I answered by opening the door and throwing up outside on the runway.

Bob – happy to be back on solid ground

Greasing a Pig on a Pole

It was time for a real fishing trip, no more Spike's Mud Puddle Lake for Dick and me. To make it a real event, we invited three other friends – Ike, Max and Junebug, all friends from college.

Put-In-Bay on South Bass Island in Lake Erie had a grand fishing reputation. We took two cars up to Port Clinton, Ohio to catch the ferry. The boat to the island only held 14 cars and we didn't want to pay for both of ours so we crammed everything into Dick's car and left Max's in the parking lot. The town of Put-In-Bay had one main street with restaurants, bars, gift shops and sleeping facilities that stretched no more than two blocks.

Since this was a serious fishing trip, we dumped our gear in our rented 'A' frame and went to meet our charter guide waiting for us in his 22' Lyman. When we pulled out of the harbor, a steady soft rain caught us unprepared but the conditions were ideal for catching small mouth bass and perch. By the time we pulled back into the dock at 3:30 we had two 50-gallon garbage cans full of fish. Charlie, our captain, took it to be cleaned, frozen, and packaged for the six of us.

Sunday the rain stopped but we decided we didn't need more fish so we took a passenger ferry over to see Lonz's winery on Middle Bass Island, for some world famous Ohio State vino. The winery was impressive, an imposing traditional fieldstone castle standing on a bluff overlooking the lake. The wine itself left something to be desired. As we sat out on the terrace admiring the view, a dark-haired petite girl walked by and tripped over the uneven flagstones. Her cabernet sauvignon spilled all over Max's neck and down onto his white sport shirt.

"Ooohhh," she squealed, "Let me fix that." She tried to wipe it off with her hands but red wine on a white shirt doesn't wipe off. "I'm really sorry, how can I make it up to you?" she asked, batting her eyelashes.

Max, ever smooth, said, "Have dinner with me." She looked very interested but then she said, "I'm here with a friend so I can't leave her." She pointed and I could see an attractive girl leaning over the wall. I piped in, "She can have dinner too. We'll all go together." It was settled quickly. The six of us picked up Bobo and Claire at their hotel in Put-In-Bay and drove them to a local fish restaurant about two miles from downtown. The restaurant was a style of architecture I had never seen before, a wooden cone-shaped building. It was like eating in a giant circus tent. A steel pole about 25' feet tall supported the center of the building. We quickly found out why the joint was so packed with locals.

The crowd would start chanting someone's name and then the chosen one would walk up to the pole, plant his feet wide, jump, grab it and try to climb to the top. If they actually made it all the way and planted their shoes on the ceiling, the crowd cheered wildly. I guess there wasn't much other entertainment in town. We ate, drank, talked and laughed for a long time. Near the end of the meal, Dick nudged me with his elbow and opened his right hand. He had four butter pats nestled in his palm.

I had known Dick long enough to know exactly what he was going to do and I also knew the trouble that would follow. "Please forget it. Don't even think about it." He gave me his patented devilish grin and stood up. I knew I could not change his mind so the best role for me would be to supervise the situation so we could leave with our heads intact. I motioned to the waiter to get our checks ready and passed around the word to our bunch we would need to leave soon and in a hurry.

As Dick made his way to the center, a few locals clapped half-heartedly so everyone at our table stood up and cheered loudly to encourage him. Dick stopped two feet from the pole and then took a mighty leap. He managed to grab it about nine feet off the ground, wrapping his legs around it to keep from sliding back. He tried to hold tight with one hand, the other clenched in a fist, but he couldn't make it very far. Finally, he slid back down; both hands now wrapped around the pole. When his feet touched the ground, the crowd booed. Dick shrugged his shoulders and walked back to the table.

The next competitor rose. He must have been a local favorite because the crowd set up a loud stomp and cheer chant for him, yelling, "Go, Porky, Go!" I could tell from his attitude he had done the climb before. We moved to the cash register, paid the bill and then stood by the door to watch one last time. The initial leap didn't have much to recommend it but the man's bulging upper arms held onto the pole in a vice grip and he struggled up about halfway. He hung there for a moment and then slowly slid to the floor, his face clenched in a red knot. The crowd was silent. When he reached the bottom, he yelled, "Who is the jerk that greased the pole?" A few in the restaurant looked at us. We took off out the door and hopped in Dick's car. As we pulled out of the lot, I turned around and saw a bunch of fellows run out the front door.

When we got back to town, the rest of the guys went off to bed while Max, Bobo, Claire and I walked around town, unwilling to end the evening. Finally Claire said, "We have to go. We need to get up early to catch the ferry so we are on time to catch the bus for Dayton."

Max must have liked Bobo more than I realized because he

Max and pilot of Tin Goose

said, "I have a great idea. Forget the ferry. Let's take the Island Airline flight back to the mainland and then Bob and I will drive you back to Dayton." The next morning the four of us climbed in the 18-seat Ford trimotor plane and took off. BoBo and Max cozied up in the single seat behind us and Claire and I heard only whispers on the short flight.

When we landed, Max tossed me the keys. "You drive, Bob." He and Bobo hopped in the back seat and were embracing even before I got the engine warmed up. After 150 miles they were still in the same clinch and I wondered when they would come up for air. I liked Claire but not enough to get involved in a romance 50 miles north of Cincinnati.

My dad always taught me to be sincere and honest with girls. He would say, "Don't lead them on if you aren't interested." For me that meant stay out of the back seat or you could end up with a commitment you didn't want or expect. I thought Max was getting himself into a very awkward situation.. Claire and Bobo weren't the kind of girls one could just kiss off and run from, but I also knew Bobo wasn't Max's type at all. When we got to Dayton, the first stop was Claire's house. I walked her to the door, promised to write and kissed her goodbye.

After I got back in the car I saw Max straighten up, wipe off the lipstick, brush his fingers through his hair. I wondered what he was going to tell her. We drove by a new huge Presbyterian Church and I heard Max say, "Nice looking liturgical edifice. By the way, what church do you go to?"

"Saint Cecilia. I'm Catholic, you know," Bobo replied, fluffing her hair.

Max jerked back like he had been bitten, "Catholic! I can't get serious with a Catholic! My folks would disinherit me. They would kick me out of the family. No one in my family has ever dated a Catholic."

She was beaten. No one we knew dated out of their faith or ethnic group. If Max said he wasn't Catholic, she had no choice but to back away. The girl was angry, though. We pulled up to her driveway and she climbed out and then leaned back in the window for a parting shot, "You are the rudest, crudest, and most narrow-minded boy in the world. I am sorry we ever met. And I hope I never see you again."

She flounced away and Max got into the front seat. He settled back and said, "I could never date a girl called Bobo."

Box o' Tricks (1956)

It was to have been a quiet and cozy triple date far away from the madding crowd downtown. "This sounds too good to be true," I told my sister, Madge, Eddie, Johnbo and his date, Ann, and a new friend for me named Barb. "I heard about a small country bar and restaurant in Kentucky with a live band. Supposedly the best part is a dance deck overlooking the Ohio River and the moon is out tonight."

Eddie said, "That sounds great. Where is it?"

"I'm not sure but it's about ten miles down river just past a town called Bromley in Kentucky. It was easy to find the roadhouse and we spent a great evening crunching chips, sipping beer and doing the bunny hug on the deck in the warm night air. The combination of the Japanese lanterns decorating the deck and the barges, steamboats and occasional pleasure cruisers added a festive touch to the view.

My date was quiet throughout the evening but was soft and romantic when we swayed to the trio's rendition of The Capris' *There's a Moon Out Tonight*. After a few songs of slow hugging music, the band picked up the tempo with the Ink Spots' version of *I Don't Want to Set the World on Fire*. Barb didn't like the faster music and everyone else had danced enough so we decided to make our way back to Cincinnati.

As we drove back through the town of Bromley, a police car hidden in a dark side street pulled out behind me when I passed. He flashed his lights to let me know to pull over. After showing him my driver's license, I said, "I really have no clue why you picked me up."

Box o' Tricks 218

"You went through a stop sign back there."

I said politely, "I'm not questioning you but would you mind showing me that sign because I honestly did not see it."

We followed him back a block where he showed me an 18" square piece of tan cardboard with the letters STOP written in black marker. It was nailed to a large tree and blended right in with the bark. I couldn't believe it and I let my temper show. "Are you giving me a ticket for going through a handmade unofficial stop sign?"

He was waiting for that and barked, "Don't get funny, Mister. Follow me back to court at the firehouse."

Not very graciously I stomped back to the car and trailed him to an old one-story brick firehouse. Everyone else waited in the car while the cop and I walked in the front garage-type door, past a couple of ancient La France fire engines and through an open doorway to a long, narrow back room. The town mayor/fire chief was holding court behind a temporary card table all dressed up in a sweaty white t-shirt.

"Well, young fellow," he said, spitting his tobacco in a tin can next to the table, "What do you have to say for yourself?"

I pleaded my case to no avail, knowing they weren't about to listen to reason. He waited for me to finish and then said, "If you want to argue this, you can return next week when

The Bromley Fire Crew

court will be in session for traffic violators. You pay 20 dollars tonight or you sleep in our jail."

I nearly exploded but didn't want to sleep in anyone's pokey jail. I paid the $20 and walked out the door to the fire engine area. Near the door I spotted the firemen's gear all neatly lined up. I needed to take some action and I wanted to get back at the so-called officials for taking my 20 dollars. I decided the fire chief's hat would do nicely, tit for tat. I had to solve one problem first. The door to the kangaroo court was open and the gloating officer and mayor still sat watching me.

I walked back in to the rear 'court' room and closed the door behind me. Fumbling in my pockets I asked, "Have you seen my driver's license? I think I left it on the table." While they searched around, I pulled it out of my back pocket, acting as surprised as if I had pulled a rabbit out of a hat. I walked back out, opening and shutting the door behind me.

There was an empty cardboard box underneath the coats so I grabbed it, filled it with an old fire hose, a pair of rubber gloves, put on the Chief's helmet and dashed outside.

I opened the passenger door and tossed the load on Ann and Johnbo's laps. Gunning the Olds we raced away, everyone but Barb laughing and joking. Eddie said, "Just wait til that fire bell rings and that jerk can't find his big-shot helmet." As I turned to give him a response, I could see my date doing a slow burn.

"What's wrong, Barb?" She gave me a ten-minute searing lecture that felt like a slow roasting at the stake. I realized there might be some consequences to what I had done and regretted that spur of the moment act.

The next night I came in from work late to find everyone already at the dining room table. Mother sat stiffly in her chair and said, "Bobby, we have something to discuss." She always called me Bobby when I was in trouble. The very name made me sound more juvenile than Robert or Bob. "I got a phone call today and they said you could be in big trouble. I'm told you are the prime suspect of the Bromley Kentucky Police Department on a robbery charge involving firehouse equipment and a special helmet. Is there any truth in these charges?"

"Yes, its all true." Dad perked up, swallowed something and leaned forward. Unlike Mother, he enjoyed a good story.

"Why would you pull a stupid stunt like that?" she asked,

exasperated.

"For a good reason and I'll tell you why." I worked up to righteous indignation. "Madge was there, she'll confirm everything I tell you. That Bromley cop arrested me for going through a homemade stop sign that none of us could see at night. Then they gave me the choice of paying 20 dollars or spending the night in jail."

She said, "Tomorrow I want you to go back over there, give them their equipment and clear your name of these charges."

I had no intention of doing that. "Let's not be too hasty, Mother. They can't be positive I'm the one who took it. They had to pick up a bunch of guys Saturday night who were probably just as unhappy as I was. I know it was a stupid thing to do but they will use it as an excuse to make me a boarder in their town jail."

Dad chuckled, "I agree. Let's not throw the boy into the flames." Mother pursed her lips and knew she had lost the battle.

Off the Hook

There was a clear path to marriage in those days. You met a girl you liked, you dated, you gave her your fraternity pin, you gave her an engagement ring, and then her mother took over. Simple. Everyone knew the rules. If you stepped off the path, though, it felt a little like standing around in gym class waiting to be assigned a partner for square dancing. Who would be left by the time your turn came? Would you be stuck with a girl strong enough to swing her partners off their feet?

Of course there were drawbacks to the easy pathway. Some of my friends seemed to find themselves married before they realized what happened. One moment they would casually put their arm around a girl at a party and the next moment someone would be throwing rice in their face. And sometimes it worked out amazingly well. I envied those married couples at parties who spent the evenings smiling at each other from across the room as if they shared a secret. But sometimes disaster quickly followed the wedding. I had a friend who married his dream girl only to wake up and find a nagging stranger in a housedress following him around waving ads for new appliances.

How could you know before the final 'I do' rings through the church? How could anyone know from a few months of dating who could stand the trials of married life? Can sitting next to someone at a movie give you a clue how they will endure endless hours on family car trips, complete with fighting children in the back seat threatening to throw up on each other?

To add extra pressure to my dating life, the newly marrieds tried to add others to their ranks with the fervor of Marine recruiters. Newlyweds seemed to think it was their mission to marry off all their single friends. They pretended they wanted everyone to be just as happy. I suspected the real reason was to increase the number of souls who could discuss lawn mower intricacies and new surprises to add to tuna casserole. My married friends had decided my new girlfriend, Betty Jo, or BJ for short, was the one to bring me into the ranks and I found myself pressured into thinking they might be right.

Betty Jo laughed at my jokes and she could tell a few herself. She had the poise and looks that came from being elected college homecoming queen and she had a beautiful voice, as languid and soft as a lazy summer stream. Listening to her made me forget my troubles and want to drift along with her.

We had dated for a few months and time seemed to be closing in. I felt like I should be able to make a decision about us but couldn't quite bring myself to picture the future. One night I went to pick her up for a late dinner, wondering how I could really know. I pulled up in the driveway and got out. Her folks were sitting on the front porch watching the day end. Would Betty Jo and I ever sit in such compatible silence? Did I want that much silence? And would she be able to put up with me if I wanted a little more excitement? As I walked up the steps, it came to me. I could do a simple test to find the real BJ behind the smooth, smiling face.

Back in those days you could dial your own phone number and it would ring to any other phones in the house. This quirk was mainly exploited by children calling their parents to ask if they had Prince Albert in a can. I had another, more useful idea. I knew Betty Jo had her own phone in her room because we spent quite a few hours talking about nothing. I put my fingers to my lips and said quietly, "I want to see if I can get that beautiful daughter of yours to hurry up. Can I use your phone in the kitchen?"

Her mother looked puzzled but waved me in. Her father shook his head as if it was a hopeless thought. I was careful to open the screen door slowly. Luckily, it didn't squeak too badly.

The phone sat on the kitchen counter. I hesitated for a moment and then picked it up and dialed. When it rang I heard BJ's voice. "Mom, can you get that? My nails aren't dry.

Mom?" I could picture her waving those lovely long nails around. Was I ruining a beautiful manicure?

It rang a couple more times and then BJ gave in and picked it up.

I jumped right in after her hello. "Hi, Betty Jo. It's Bob. I'm down at the Pilot Inn having a few beers." Of course there were no juke box noises, no crack of pool balls. This was turning into an IQ test as well.

"I don't understand," she said, not so softly. "We had an eight o'clock date."

"Well, I've got this problem." I heard the screen door open and close and I knew at least one of her parents was close enough to hear. I plunged ahead anyway. "Some buddies of mine are here from out of town and I'm going to show them some of the local spots."

"What are you trying to tell me?" Now she began to sound more like my sixth grade teacher standing over me as I tried to explain how Billy Walsh's math book got glued to his desk.

I was committed to finish this little atomic bomb of an experiment. "I've got to go. I'll call you tomorrow." I hung up the phone. Dead silence from upstairs.

Standing in the kitchen I was anxious to see her response. Would she remain upstairs and mope? If so, I would yell up the stairs, 'April Fool's'. Would she head down the stairway? If she did, she would discover soon enough that I was not at the Pilot Inn after all.

The slam of the phone upstairs reverberated down into the kitchen and rattled the spoon collection hanging next to me. The spoon from Texas decorated with tiny longhorns fell to the floor.

I turned around and looked into the hallway. BJ's mother stood there, a look of horror on her face. This was a bad sign. And then the Fury came down the stairs, the thunder of high heels almost drowned out by the screaming and the long hair swirling. BJ didn't see me, and her mother made shushing noises, to no avail. The Fury missed the signal and continued the tantrum until I began to fear the heavens would open up on us. I decided to stop the racket before the neighbors called in the police so I stepped into the hallway and BJ's face changed instantly. She registered the hoax, and smiled sweetly but didn't say a word. I thought to myself, don't move, BJ, please don't open your mouth. You are so beautiful, I want to forget you just the way you are.

    I found out later the real truth of the episode. She had been planning to get rid of me anyway and my trick gave her the perfect opportunity.

Looking for "Miss One"

After B.J., I felt like hanging upside down from a maple tree in the yard and trying to see the world from a different perspective. I had been trying to find the right girl for years but each time I thought I was getting close, the romance would fizzle.

There was one bright spot in my life – my family. I enjoyed living at home with the Little King and Mother and knew they liked having me around. I could run errands, do odd jobs, keep things lively and entertain my little sisters. Life was still good, secure and comfy. Even thought the bumper crop of good looking college girls was slowly disappearing, I still didn't feel completely burned out.

I dismissed Gloria Glockenspiel after high school because I had developed great respect for my mom's guidance and opinions. My mind was open to any suggestion and one day I said to her, "What did you think of Sally, the girl I brought home for dinner last Friday night?"

"She was very pretty with a good sense of humor, but other than that, she didn't impress me one bit."

Okay, so Mom was picky but then so was I. She said, "My friend from school is coming to town next week with her daughter. I have met her before and she's a lovely girl. You might consider taking her out."

"No chance, Mom, she might get cold feet after she sees me." While I respected Mom's opinion I drew the line at being set up on a blind date by my mother.

"You might be right. I'm probably the only woman that

could put up with you."

This wounded me. "I'm not that bad."

"With your reputation, you would be lucky if any nice girl would consider you."

"Hey, I want you to know that I've gone out with a hundred different nice gals in the past ten years."

Mom gave me a smile of understanding and said, "I can understand the large turnover."

"Look here, Mom, you and Dad have both given me everything. A nice home, a wonderful education, a job; what can I do around here to help you out and repay you?"

"Leave home." Mother had been watching too much Jack Benny. Her timing was getting too good.

One summer evening with no warning, my world changed forever. It was going to be a day to remember and little did I suspect why. Once in a blue moon I know that feeling I get when I walk into a crowded space. It's a strange sensation that something was right, or it wasn't. I couldn't put my finger on it. My former girlfriend Maddie's parents were having an engagement celebration cocktail party for Happy and his bride to be, Susan.

The event was held in their old wooden frame homestead on Mooney Avenue and by the time I got there, the party had spilled out onto the front veranda.

After greeting Maddie's parents and offering my congratulations to the happy couple, I settled into a steady conversation with Maddie's younger brother, Billy. Bill and I were good friends from college days when he was my designated "Little Brother' while a pledge in Sigma Chi.

"Haven't seen Maddie in a few years. Where is she now?" I inquired.

"Her husband is in the Air Force and they are stationed up at Wright-Patterson Field in Dayton."

"And your little sister, Kay. Is she still in nursing school up in Dayton?"

"Yes," Billy said, "She'll be going into her last year next month."

"Wow, time sure flies. Too bad she and my sister, Madge, had to miss this big family party."

I noticed several guys standing around I didn't recognize. They looked like they could be serious competition if any

Dad, Bob doing photo of photographer, Kay, Dick and Dinnie at Happy and Susan's engagement reception.

good looking girls showed up. "Who are those fellows?"

"Oh, just some Ivy Leaguers who are in Hap's wedding party."

Just then the screen door at the front entrance opened and a girl looking like Kim Novak stepped carefully down onto the porch floor with a tray full of drinks. All the eastern eyes and mine turned front and center. I started to ask, "Who in the world....," when Bill interrupted.

"I was just getting ready to tell you that Maddie was stuck up at the Air Force Base with no wheels but Kay here got a ride."

The sight and scent of her were so overpowering, my legs almost collapsed. The curves on her set off an explosion in my brain. I took the tray from her and said, "Hi, Kay. Remember me, I'm Bob. I'll help with the drinks."

"Sure, I remember you. How could I forget?"

I thought to myself, "Wow, that's one of the nicest compliments any girl ever gave me."

She continued, "I'll never forget staying overnight at Madge's a few years ago when you lived up east. We snuck down to your rec room in the basement and stole a listen to those filthy dirty song records you brought back from New York City."

"Oh." Well, that's one way to make an impression. "I forgot about those."

Strike one. She's not buying my line. I went out to the kitchen to butter up the chief umpire. Her mother was busy in the hot kitchen laying out hors d'oeuvres. I kept busy helping make drinks and passing out canapés to redeem myself.

A while later I cornered Kay in the hallway and asked, "When this is over, how about you and me going out?"

"We won't have time. I have a ride back to Dayton at 9:00 PM."

"That's okay. Just for a half-hour. Please?"

A little while later the party was over, we cleaned up. I grabbed her hand and we took off. We drove to the golf driving range by Lunken Airport and I got a few of my clubs out of the trunk. "Let's hit some golf balls." It wasn't typical but what else could we do? I was a little old for a shake at the maltshop.

Her golf drives were erratic but her demeanor was perfect and I couldn't stop looking at her face. Her skin was as creamy white and smooth as a pearl. I could barely concentrate enough to look down at the ball before hitting it. We made it back home in time for her ride back to school and parted not knowing when we would see each other again.

Over the next few days I contemplated the events of the evening. Kay had all the qualities I could fall in love for. She was smart, beautiful, humorous, talented, happy, caring and fun to be with. She had one trait that I thought was very rare. She felt a sense of responsibility to think about others and help them before herself. A few nights later I fell asleep thinking about her again. Sometime later, I woke with a start. I opened my eyes and was amazed to see a blue moon shining directly in on me through my window. It was a misty night and the moon glowed with a faint electric blue color like the distant light of a neon sign.

I'm going to marry that girl, she's perfect, I thought. Someday at our wedding, I told myself, I'll stand up and tell all my friends and family that I had the whole idea figured out to a tee after the first date. Then I thought of the skeptical looks appearing on the faces of Dick and Hap. I knew they would never believe me. I needed some way to prove to Kay that I loved her from day one.

I got out of bed, turned on my desk lamp and composed a

letter. In the morning I mailed it to myself. When it arrived back at our house a day later I promised myself I would keep it unopened until the big day.

We started dating but to see her, I had to drive my '54 Mercury 120 miles round-trip to the St. Elizabeth Hospital dorm in Dayton. Kay's off days from nursing were seldom and short. Months could go by without setting foot on her Mooney Avenue front porch to pick her up and see her parents. Except for a few engagement parties for Hap and Susan, ours was strictly a long distance romance. I was crazy in love and the trips gave my life a shot in the arm.

On a typical date in Dayton, our time was limited and that meant the activity list was brief with no time to cut figure eights. One night I picked her up at the dormitory and we headed straight for our favorite Polynesian restaurant, the Mai-Tai. Sitting among the sound of waterfalls, under bamboo-laced ceiling with errant palm leaves swaying overhead, I would start the night off with, "How did your day go?"

"I helped the doctor in the E.R. today fix someone up after a fight. He had a fishhook in his eyeball and it had been pulled out of the socket enough so it was hanging by a few ligaments." She calmly sipped her drink and I knew that here was a girl strong enough to face life without flinching.

After dinner we had only a scant amount of time to kill so I would head for the Great Miami River near the hospital. It flowed between two 20-foot high slanted concrete embankments, which helped control seasonal floods in the low areas. We found a secret maintenance road that led down to the flat slab on the water's edge. The reflection of the moon on the water was very romantic and I was so in love, I didn't even notice the bunker effect of the concrete embankment.

Over the next few months I grew as attached to that spot as my own room, so much so that I forgot it didn't belong to us. One night late in the fall, the car windows had steamed up enough to give a tropical lagoon-like effect but we were disturbed out of our reverie by a pounding on the window. A very tough looking policeman stood by the car.

I rolled down the window and he barked, "This is private city property and you are trespassing. What are you doing down here?"

"Watching the submarine races, sir, but they're over now

and we are just leaving." I started the car as he peered out on the river with a puzzled look on his face.

"I don't think you can see the periscopes anymore but it was a great race. Have a good evening, officer." I hightailed it out of there leaving him scratching his head.

I proposed to her one evening at 11:57 in my car in front of St. Elizabeth's dorm and she quickly accepted in order to make her deadline with the night nurse. The next order of business was to get permission from her father and mother. I made the appointment, went to their home and was ushered into the living room. Her father, Walter, ran a strict home operation with Kay's three brothers and two sisters. He had been a fighter pilot during WWI and still looked like he could have easily faced down the Red Baron. The missus was a quiet, sweet woman who usually looked a little tired from keeping house for the eight of them.

He sat in the big 'Daddy' chair striking his pipe ashes. Since there was no "Mama' chair, Kay's mother sat down beside me on the sofa looking content to give her legs a rest. I could tell from the questionable look on their faces, they had no clue why I was even there. I thought I would work up to it slowly. "How's your golf game?" I asked, thinking this might establish a common bond between us.

"Fine," Walter answered. He looked at me strangely. "Say, what brings you over here?"

I decided just to forget the small talk. "I just wanted to ask both of you for permission to marry Kay."

The missus smiled approvingly but Kay's father started to utter some deep down guttural sounds with jaw flapping. After finally composing himself, he put on a very dignified act and said, "I don't think that would be a very good idea." I looked at Kay's mother's face but she didn't speak and looked at the ceiling. I couldn't speak either. Two minutes later I crawled out of there with my tail between my legs.

The next day I hopped in the Mercury after work, pulled out the overdrive lever and let her rip to Dayton. When I picked Kay up, she seemed remarkably calm and happy considering I had had the insides ripped out of me and tromped on. As soon as she got in the car, I said, "I couldn't believe your father refused my request."

"Don't blame him, he didn't know we were even dating

steady, much less getting married." This was a minor detail I would have liked to know before I made an idiot out of myself.

"I thought you told your parents about us."

"I told my mother about a month ago."

"What did she say?"

"She wasn't too happy either."

I couldn't believe it. "Why not?"

"She thinks that you like to travel a lot by yourself in your car." I hadn't considered that as a major drawback to approval.

"Well, I do, and most of the time I'm driving back and forth to Dayton to see you." Now what was I going to do? I didn't know how to convince her parents I was worthy of their daughter.

"Oh, I forgot to tell you. They both gave us their blessing and approval when Dad called me last night." She smiled and I was convinced I had truly met my match.

Piece of Cake (1957)

I knew it was possible for my future-in-laws to have second thoughts about me but I didn't think Kay would. The wedding was scheduled to start at 10:00 AM Saturday morning the 28th of September, 1957. It was the same big gothic St. Mary's Church where I tweaked little Bo Hassel almost 20 years ago. As I stood with my seven groomsmen in the same location, waiting for Kay and her parents, I was afraid it would turn out to be another bad luck deal in the same spot. My watch said 10:10 and I knew it was right. The most embarrassing thing that could happen at anyone's wedding is for the bride to do a 'no show.' All sorts of things were going through my head: Would she change her mind? What happened since I saw her yesterday? Who has she been talking to and what had they told her about me?

Old Father Schmidt had been through too many weddings to show any patience for tardy brides. The organist had worn out the pre-march music and the friends and relatives were turning their heads looking for the main attraction to show. At 10:15 Schmitty had enough, he clicked his heels, did an about face at the main altar, and started the mass without Kay.

That was the final straw. I went nuts trying to imagine why she stood me up. Then my realistic side kicked in and I realized that maybe it was some simple little human error. It was now 10:20 and I was more agitated at the performance of the Pastor than Kay. I was ready to go up to the altar to plead for more patience when I glanced back and saw the rear church doors open to a stream of light. To see her translucent wedding dress float in was like welcoming the spirits of all the weddings past.

Two hours later after a ceremony that sped by like a dream, we were seated for brunch in a large dining room at the Maketewah Country Club. We both had large families so by the time the bridesmaids, ushers, aunts, uncles and parents were seated, there were more than four dozen highly attired relatives and friends. My brother, Richard, was Master of Ceremonies and he was in rare form. He had been up all night with his wife, Missie, who had delivered a baby boy at 6:00 AM that morning. Lack of sleep added an edge to his speech, needling me about not being married earlier, about being fickle, and about being a reckless and fun-loving proverbial bachelor.

I stood and answered him. "This may come as a shock to most of you but everything my brother has just said about me is true and possibly even worse." I probably should not have said that because, when I did a quick glance over at my new in-laws, you could tell they were thinking, "How could we let our Kay marry such a clod?" I could see it on their faces. I continued, "I knew the day I met this girl I would marry her." That comment really stirred things up.

Catcalls started like I was a magician unable to do a trick. Someone called out, 'That's easy to say now, Bob." And these were my loving friends and relatives? It did act as the perfect setup for the moment I had waited 13 months for. I carefully removed the sealed envelope from my tux jacket, handed it to Kay and said, "Kay, notice that the envelope has never been opened. It is postmarked a few nights after our first 45-minute date last year. I wrote the letter and mailed it to myself for safekeeping. I would like Kay to read it now."

Kay had a smooth crisp voice like a radio personality and I knew it would be more effective from her. She stood, opened the envelope and read through it, ending with my last paragraph: 'But here is my prediction – fortunately it won't take a lifetime to find the right girl, and as a matter of fact I had my first date with her Sunday night. Her name is Kay Hadley. May God help both of us to make the right decision.' Signed Bob Greiwe.

The room was silent and then applause broke out. My father-in-law seemed slightly relieved but I knew I was still on trial.

Leaving the reception

Dick, Hap and the rest of the wedding party were whispering to each other and I knew exactly what was going on. At other friends' weddings, I was always the one leading the pack to decorate their cars and disrupt their getaways. I had followed Hap and Sue all the way to the airport and up the steps of the DC-3, hitting them with bursts of club soda from a dispenser. He was ready to get even.

When brunch was over, 200 more people came to the reception along with a five-piece band. The bourbon and scotch flowed and the cigarette smoke danced right along with the rest of us. At the end I changed downstairs and waited for Kay to appear. She came down in a trim elegant navy suit. The crowd followed us out the front door, the ushers were salivating about getting even with me, but they had a problem, "Where's the car?" I heard one ask.

"He doesn't have one here, I drove him to the church," Richard said.

Hap and Dick scurried over to my parents. "Where's he going? How are they going to get there?"

Mom and the Little King just shook their heads. "You know Bob. We're lucky he told us he was dating Kay much less where he's heading now."

Kay and I walked out to the parking lot with a hundred followers. I felt like the pied piper. A faint 'dat dat dat' sound grew louder and all of the sudden our helicopter appeared between two giant maples. It was a sweet experience. The pilot landed 30 feet away and opened the door for us to get in. My little sisters, Liz and Conky, started weeping. Dad hugged Mother and I got a huge lump in my throat. We said all our goodbyes and ducked under the swirling blades of the chopper.

Our honeymoon was a blur of travel. The helicopter took us to the train station, the train took us to New York, a taxi took us to our hotel, a plane took us to Bermuda and then we roared around the island on motor scooters until it was time to do the whole trip in reverse.

Escaping the wedding crowd

The Bubble Bursts (1958)

Time sped by. In 1958, we had a baby, a second on the way and I was busy. Besides being the best thing that ever happened to me, I had great respect for every little subtle and tactful suggestion Kay made about our relationship. Instead of nagging she would say, "Bob, do you think you could get home a bit earlier than 5:00 from your Saturday golf game?" or "Will you let me know which Sundays you won't be racing the Porsche so we can do something with the family?"

There was no doubt about it, my weekly Saturday golf game was improving. I did convince the boys to get a 7:30 AM tee-off time instead of 10:30 to please Kay. But the sports car races on Sunday were different. There was no way I could tell the chief steward when he should drop his checkered flag and the simple solution to stop racing just didn't occur to me.

After Kay and my baby daughter, my next love was racing my Convertible Porsche. My Castle Park friend, Gasoline Clive and another friend, De Camp, and I, founded the Consolidated Sports Car Club, and soon after we were being invited as guests to the big SCCA Sports Car Club of American speed events. The first competition was held at the new Kenwood Shopping Mall in the days when it had 50 acres of parking and only a few stores. The host SCCA club laid out a third of a mile gymkhaha course that was designed by placing about a hundred orange cones. The layout required constant upshifting, down shifting, double clutching with toe and heel, and braking. Each was an individual race against the clock for the best time.

When it was my turn, I faced the course. The orange spots ahead of me looked like a lake full of bright fishing bobbins, and at 3500 RPM I popped the clutch and let her fly. The field got so confusing; I missed the course half way through but continued on to the end for the practice. "No time" the steward at the finish line yelled. I thought, what a loser I am, how could I fail not to memorize that layout before my turn? I didn't know what made me think I was going to breeze through the orange maze without careful study. My only consolation was everyone got two runs at the course and they took the time on their best run only if they managed to stay on track. I was determined it wouldn't happen again. Fear of failure is a great motivator. Hate could also work well because I hated losing more than I loved winning.

I studied the pylon layout, then waited my turn for another two hours. It was a day to numb the senses. The reflections and the heat bore down on the black pavement and I could see squiggles of hot thermals spiraling off the lot in the distance. At times the straight pipe exhaust noise was deafening and the odor of fuel mixtures and carbon monoxide was enough to make my eyes water. But the cars, like Auston Martins, Alfa Romeos, Austin Healeys, and Triumphs more than made up for it.

We finally lined up for our final run. I was second to last driver for the day. Jack McCarty waited behind me. He was one of the best racers SCCA had on the track. When it was my turn, the clock started and I peeled out like there was no tomorrow. A pure rush of adrenaline flowed through my veins and I was oblivious to everything around me except those orange devils. At every turn and corner my tires were almost at the point of losing adhesion except when I skidded to a stop after crossing the finish line. I turned to get the answer from the two timers behind me but they were in a deep huddled talk about something.

McCarty ran last and they gave his time immediately on completion at the finish line – 59.47 seconds. That was the best time of the day. The event was over but I didn't know where I stood. The chairman of the race climbing up on a chair and shouted through his bullhorn. "The best time of the day – Bob Greiwe, with a time of 59.34 seconds."

It was one of the highlights of my life because it was the first trophy I won and it had a little gold Ferrari mounted on

The Bubble Bursts 238

First Place SCCA trophy

top. When I showed it to Kay later at home, she just smiled and said nothing. When I showed it to the Little King at the office, he acted surprised. A week later I showed it to my mother. She picked it up and from the look in her eye I could tell she wasn't impressed.

A few months after the Kenwood Mall excitement, Kay announced the tacky race trophy collection gathering dust on the shelves in our living room represented a lapse in interior decorating judgement. "These mementos of hair-raising speed are poor evidence and a bad representation of the kind of image I want my friends and family to have of us."

I replied, "It seems to me that I've reached that age which should grant me a small amount of right of eccentricity."

She didn't answer and went back to the kitchen. Her comments bothered me. Was she trying to send me one of her subtle messages? Was she upset?

I found out soon enough. We were driving home from my parents' house one night through Madeira. I was following some old slowpoke and approaching the railroad tracks. Right before the tracks, I was overcome with impatience and zipped passed him as he slowed down to go over the rails.

Kay grabbed her armrest. "You are not supposed to pass another car while crossing railroad tracks," she hissed.

I was just about to explain why I just had to pass the car when I saw a police car headed directly toward me. I couldn't see through the window in the dark but suspected it might be Tag 'em Willie. He passed, did a quick U-turn, put on his flashing red light, and started to chase us. Nothing improves my driving like a police car following me and this one was gaining fast. If it really was Willie, I was sure he would make my life very tough. He wouldn't realize I was no longer a teenager. I decided one of the biggest risks in life is doing nothing. Before he got too close, I hit the brakes and stopped. "Kay, quick, switch seats with me."

Her mouth dropped open. "Are you crazy?"

"No," I said. "I don't have my driver's license on me. Do you have yours?"

"Yes." she said and didn't argue when I reached over, dragged her across my lap and plunked her in the driver's seat. Five seconds later the flashing lights pulled up behind us and stopped. I could tell by the way Kay was sitting up stiffly that her nose was out of joint with me. As I slunk down in the passenger seat, Willie appeared at her window. Kay rolled it down and he peered in.

There was silence for about 15 seconds. He looked at me and then he looked at Kay. "I could swear it wasn't you driving back there." Again, not a sound. He pointed his finger at us both. "Don't ever let me catch you passing on the railroad tracks."

Kay replied with clenched teeth. "Thank you." She rolled up the window and drove home without a word.

My suspicions were right about her being upset. It was just a matter of time before it happened. Kay said, "Bob, the baby is asleep and we need to talk." We went into the living room and sat together on the loveseat. She reached for my hand, looked me square in the eye and said softly, "We have a serious investment problem."

"Like what?"

"We have no money."

"What?"

"It's worse. We are 13 weeks of your salary in the hole."

"Why didn't you tell me sooner?"

"I couldn't. You are never home and that's the second problem. With golf on Saturday, racing on Sunday and your watercolor painting in the basement at night, it gets pretty lonely up here with the baby."

I sat there stunned for a moment. "It isn't the end of the world," I stammered. "Give me a couple of weeks to solve some of the problems and in a few months I promise you I'll have everything under control and fixed."

"I've got a surprise you are going to like."

"I'm reluctant to ask." After that I was afraid she would pull out a hammer and finish me off. She handed me a big flat box. I was hoping it wasn't an overcoat; I was already getting hot under the collar. I tore it open. Anything had to be better. It was a Jack Kramer signature wooden tennis racket with genuine cat gut strings. "I love it."

She said, "With this you can pick up where you left off in high school. It will only take a fraction of time compared to your other sports."

Only Kay would sweeten my disappointment by giving me a great present. She finally made me understand I was going in the wrong direction and pushed me back into sanity. The golf clubs were permanently put to rest while the racket came to life. My old Porsche 'Porky' never won another race, but he and I got plenty of jollies when I felt the streets were frog free. The artist's paint and brushes were temporarily stored away in the basement. They would definitely have their day in the sun again, and I hoped it would be soon.

The financial problem was something else. I just couldn't turn it one way or another very easily. The next week I roamed around the office trying to get inspiration. One of the interior designers, George, stopped me. He was a squeaky little guy with a thin slick mustache who looked like a retired jockey but who had tremendous artistic talent.

"Bob, I have too many clients all of the sudden. How about taking one off my hands?" he asked, sounding like he really needed a favor.

It was manna from heaven. "Who is it?"

"It's Pete Schmidt in Kentucky. He owns some nightclubs and is raking in the money. You ever been in Glenn Schmidt's Rendezvous on 5th Street?" I had, and while it didn't show much sophistication I could see where the owner would be getting rich off it.

I couldn't believe my good luck but then I started to think. "Say, George, if it really is such a good opportunity, are you sure you want to pass on it?"

"I just don't want to drive back and forth to Kentucky all the time. I'm having trouble with my car. Let me go find their phone number." He left before I could question him further.

I found Dad in his office. "Dad, what do you know about Pete Schmidt in Kentucky?"

He leaned back and lit a cigarette. "He's a tough character. Why do you want to know?"

"George just passed him off to me as a client and I want to know why."

Dad's answer opened my eyes wide. "Pete Schmidt built the original Beverly Hills Club casino in Southgate, Kentucky in the '30s. Because it was so successful, the Cleveland mafia syndicate took special note. In February 1936, 'Red' Masterson and Ed Garrison set a blaze and the club burned to the ground. Fourteen months later, Schmidt rebuilt the new Beverly Hills Country Club into the most elaborate and profitable supper club casino in the midwest. The syndicate decided they had to have it and did everything to hassle Pete into selling it to them. At one point mobsters with submachine guns stole the club's bankroll. Pete retaliated by hiring gunmen to combat the syndicate's pressure but finally surrendered and sold the club to them in 1940. I wouldn't want to get on his bad side."

"That is just great," I thought to myself. I needed the work but I wasn't sure this was the ideal type of client. I had to take it on though, because the bills were piling up. Dad must have been watching my expression because he asked, "Is anything wrong? You haven't been looking or acting like yourself lately."

"Just life, at this point. Sometimes too much of a good thing goes bad."

"I know just what will cheer you up. Your mother and I have a surprise for the whole family next weekend. A little trip will take your blues away. I'm going to call Kay and talk to her first and then I'll tell you the details."

I was so distracted by my problems that I didn't even care about a weekend trip. I didn't think that was enough to help. On Wednesday I drove down to Kentucky for my first meeting with Mrs. Schmidt. As I pulled into the driveway of the large brick colonial overlooking the Ohio River, the first thing I saw was a big "KEEP OUT" sign and a large hound dog sleeping next to it. I wondered if the saying 'mean as a hound dog' had any truth to it. As I got out of the car, he opened one eye and showed a few teeth. I looked around for a place to run in case he decided to try to take a chunk out of my leg. A gardener was trimming some hedges on the side of the yard and I called out. "Is this dog going to bite me if I walk by him?"

The gardener turned to me and I realized he was the biggest gardener I had ever seen. His nose had been rearranged enough times to resembled a Stowe ski run and his hands looked big enough to rip small trees out of the ground. I knew he did more around the place than yard work.

"Naw," he said. "Just don't act scared when you walk by."

This was good advice but tough to follow. I held my briefcase so the dog would chomp on it first if he decided I wasn't walking nonchalantly enough. I made it to the front door and rang the bell.

The housekeeper answered the door. I thought I was back at the Hi-D-Ho Club looking at Madam Rita's sister. She didn't look like any housekeeper I had ever seen before but then I realized the Schmidts probably had trouble keeping help. Mrs. Schmidt came down and showed me around. She was pleasant, a big German-type with a friendly face. We chatted and walked around looking at the rooms she wanted done. After we had seen the downstairs and we headed upstairs she said, "I want you to redo our bedroom but my husband gets home late and is sleeping in there right now. We can just peek in so you can get an idea of what it looks like."

She opened the door and stood back. I peered into a dim room with the shades drawn. When my eyes adjusted to the light, I could see Mr. Schmidt asleep on his stomach, totally naked. He had a large pistol clasped in his right hand.

She shut the door quickly. "Did you have enough time to get any ideas?" she asked. "What should we do first?"

"Buy him some underwear."

The Last Best Resort (1958)

We arrived at the French Lick Hotel in southern Indiana on a Friday afternoon. The Little King had managed to round up the whole family for the surprise trip and my spirits lifted a little when I looked up at the front of the old hotel. It hadn't changed all that much since my grandfather, J.H., made his pilgrimages here to take the healing spa waters. The hotel still served guests bottles of 'Pluto Water' from its famous mineral springs and provided tennis, golf, shuffleboard, and croquet for the hardier types.

After dinner my brother-in-law, Eddie, my brother, Richard, and I went outside for a walk to investigate the carnival in progress on the other side of the railroad tracks. The small fairs that traveled through the rural Midwest in the '50s were mostly run by what we called gypsies. There were no rides, just canvas tent booths strung with lights set up on Main Street. Most the booths had some sort of target game and the rewards were displayed to entice all ages. Stuffed animals, kewpie dolls and toy cars were the sucker bait.

I noticed no one at the carnival carried any prizes except for some kids with small balsa wood airplanes that started to disintegrate the moment someone held them up in the air to catch the nonexistent breeze. We walked around studying the setup. You could throw a ball at six stacked white bottles, pitch darts at balloons, or throw a baseball at a metal target button on the rear end of a donkey. Teenagers crowded around the most popular game, shooting air rifles to try to hit metal ducks moving back and forth.

French Lick Hotel

We watched the shooting gallery for a while. The man running the booth appeared to favor the Stanley Kowalski look right down to the sneer on his face and the pack of cigarettes rolled up in his dingy striped tee shirt.

Not one kid managed to knock over a duck even when a shot pinged right on one of the bird's vital spots. With the carny out front hustling sales, I was able to slip in the rear of the tent to see why his ducks wouldn't flip over when hit. To win the grand prize, you needed to hit and flip over 12 ducks with 12 shots. When I looked at the back of the setup I could tell why he had no winners. There were strings tied to most of the quackers so they couldn't tip more than an inch.

The three of us decided to check out the rest of the games. The wood bottles barely wavered whenever anyone hit them so we figured they had lead in their bases. The balloon dart game was 90% back wall and 10% balloon. On the mule game, if you didn't throw an 80-mph fastball and hit the button dead center, the ass refused to kick back a doll in your face.

"This is making me irate. It takes a lot of nerve for these guys to steal good money from people," I said.

"Bob, you know carnivals are like this everywhere. You

The Last Best Resort 245

didn't just fall off the turnip truck. Don't worry about it." Eddie replied.

But I couldn't stop thinking about it. I should have spent time pondering my other problems but here was a situation that needed a quick solution. I hit upon an idea but for once I worried about what Kay would think. That night, back in the room, I asked her, "There's a slight chance I may get in trouble again, but it's for a good cause. Will you give me some advice?"

"Now what do you have up your sleeve?" she asked as she brushed her hair.

I carefully explained the plight of the poor downtrodden locals being snookered by the carnies.

Kay asked the obvious question. "Why do you care so much?"

She had me there. I just needed to do something with a little constructive excitement. I didn't say anything while I tried to think up some plausible reason.

Kay rescued me. She sighed and said, "Okay, go ahead and do what you want but don't tell me the details. Be careful and whatever you do, make sure no one gets hurt."

I lay awake that night thinking of the details. Saturday morning as we were walking to the tennis court I said to Eddie, "I have an idea to get back at those lowlifes at the fair. Are you game?"

"What do you have in mind?"

"What would make their skin crawl? Only somebody official, right?"

"Yeah, but I don't think we should tell them we are local law enforcement. The local police chief wouldn't be too thrilled with us. Plus, we don't have any uniforms."

"Just leave it to me. I need to know if you will go along."

"Okay, okay. You know you can count on me." Good old Eddie. Just what a brother-in-law should be. The sun seemed to brighten and every stroke I took on the court went deep and in bounds.

Saturday night, while we sat in the main dining room I could hardly concentrate enough to eat. Mom said to me, "Bob, why do you keep lining up the peas on your plate and then scattering them around. You are a million miles away." Kay, bless her, just smiled at me.

"Nothing, Mom. I am just thinking about our tennis game

today." When we finished, I pulled our waiter aside. "George, I have to ask you for a favor. I need to borrow your union badge tonight." I pointed to his jacket where he wore the official looking silver badge clipped to his lapel.

He pondered this for a few moments.

"I guess I could, Mr. Bob. I won't get in any trouble over this, will I?"

I slapped him on the back. "Not at all, George. I wouldn't do anything to get you in trouble." I hoped I was right. "Plus, I need two more if some of your buddies would lend us theirs. Why don't you go ask and I'll wait for you near the kitchen door." I slipped him a five-dollar bill as an extra incentive. He went off shaking his head at the peculiarities of hotel guests.

Dad had been watching. As the ruler and host of the group, he considered it his prerogative to know what everyone was up to at all times. I knew he was so curious he could hardly stand it. He came over and said, "What's going on, Bob?"

"I'll tell you later, Dad. Something you might appreciate tomorrow." The badge problem solved, it was time to tackle the next issue. I decided Eddie and I didn't look authoritative enough to pull this off ourselves. Dad would have jumped at the chance but he looked too much like a jolly round elf to be taken seriously. I needed my brother, Richard. He was taller and older looking than me. I knew convincing him to take part in this serious joke would be as tough as asking him to parachute out of an airplane, but I also know I could be persuasive when I had to be. I cornered him in the lobby. Surprisingly, the mineral water must have gone to his head because he agreed right away.

We walked our wives back upstairs to the game room and then met again on the front porch, all of us dressed in suits and ties. I gave Eddie and Richard their badges and we each fastened them inside our wallets next to our drivers' licenses. We stood for a moment looking at the carnival lights in the distance. Even from the hotel I could smell the faint odor of cotton candy and popcorn. Eddie said, "I don't know, Bob. I don't think we are going to fool anyone." He was right. We looked like three fraternity brothers ready to take our dates to the homecoming dance.

"I have an idea. Wait here." I went back inside to the coatroom. The gal at the coat check was filing her nails, looking like she was about to expire from boredom. "Joan," I said, looking at her nametag. "My friends and I need a favor. We would like to borrow three dark colored hats for a little while." I put my hand on my heart. "I swear I will bring them back in perfect condition." I winked, hoping that would seal the deal. She didn't even bat one of her lengthy eyelashes as she rustled up three chapeaus.

"These gentlemen aren't going to need their hats tonight. They are all elderly and I am sure they have already gone to bed." She held three fedoras out in front of her. I never realized a coat check girl could put a face to a hat so quickly but I figured it was a sign things would go well.

I carried them out on the veranda and we put them on. Eddie's and Richard's fit fine but mine was so big it came down to my eyebrows. I decided to keep it, hoping I would appear more menacing.

The carnival was much more crowded than Friday night. Farmers stood around in groups, dressed in clean overalls and checked shirts, discussing the weather and the crops. The wives strolled about in floral print dresses, lacking only their hats to look spiffy enough for church. Kids darted everywhere. My pant leg nearly took a hit from a mustard-laden hot dog clutched by a speeding child escaping from parental captivity.

Dad, Bob, Richard, Missie, Madge, Liz, Kay, Mom, Eddie, Conky holding Jenny, Rick in foreground.

"Three balls for a dime, try your luck, show the little lady you are a winner!" The donkey man waved a large stuffed purple bear at us and then decided we didn't look like takers.

"Shoot the ducks and win a big panda. Show them all what a good shot you is."

I said, "He's the one we want. Let's get Mr. Duckman." The three of us walked side by side up to his counter and flipped our wallets open in unison. Our credentials flashed 12 inches from his face.

"FBI here, Mister," I said, in the deepest voice I could muster. "Agent Joe Hoover here." Eddie turned a snort into a cough. "We've had this entire show staked out since you set up and I gotta tell you, you're all in big trouble. Everyone here is operating a rigged gaming device in favor of the house." I stopped to carefully look at my watch. "Sir, I'm going to give you and all your relatives here exactly eight minutes to clean up these games or we are going to shut down the entire carnival. We will put out a federal arrest charge that will land your troop in jail for an extended period of time until your case comes to court."

The sweat rolled off that guy until I thought the snake tattoo on his arm would lose its skin. "Yes sir, yes sir," he said. "I'll take care of it right now, yes sir." He poked his head through the adjoining booth and mumbled something to the donkey man. We walked up and down long enough to see each worker pass the information down the line. When it looked like they all had the message, we slipped back in the shadows out of sight under a row of maple trees to watch. "Don't you think calling yourself Joe Hoover was taking it too far, Bob?" Eddie said. "I nearly choked."

"I was hoping the guy would think I was old J. Edgar's son. You know, add a little more oomph to our act."

"I just hope we don't have a pack of angry fellows pinning us up to the dart toss," Richard said.

Fifteen minutes later, giant stuffed bears were being paraded around the fairgrounds by excited kids, teenagers and more than a few adults. "I think we have seen enough. Let's hightail it out of here before one of these gypsies get wise to us." Maybe the Hoover bit had been overkill. I didn't want to explain to Kay any bruises or split lips. When we got back to the hotel, Richard and Eddie headed upstairs to their rooms. I wandered around on the veranda, too keyed up to sleep.

Down at the end of the porch, I could see the glow of someone's cigarette bobbing up and down as a rocker squeaked back and forth. It was Dad, keeping watch for me. "What's all that terrible roaring noise over at the carnival games?"

"It's bears, Dad." I joined him in another squeaky rocker and told him the story. I hoped he wouldn't disapprove. It had occurred to me when we were walking back to the hotel that it was a felony to impersonate an officer of the law.

He replied, "Hey cowboy, I think you are back in the saddle again. I was worried about you last week. Sitting here in this old inn reminds me of 35 years ago at the Banff Springs Hotel with Bob and Jack. Did I ever tell you about that?"

Only a dozen times, I thought, but I didn't really mind. I listened to the story again, chuckling at my dad's inventive mind. When he finished, he said, "I felt like my life was just beginning then. Life's been good for me and I want you to enjoy yours." I reflected on my own life for the past two decades, always walking on thin ice that separated right and wrong, rational and foolish, safety and danger. Either way the decisions and chances taken were fast paced life experiences that tested my sense of judgement for the future.

The two of us rocked away in the cool night air, watching the fireflies blink on and off, listening to the quiet.

Epilogue

Bo Hassel (Chapter 5) - Retired white bearded Catholic priest who does abstract painting.

Bobby Thompson and **William Clark** (Chapter 9) - Both family relatives were soldiers killed in WWII.

Maddie (Chapter 12) - Lovely mother of nine children.

Tony (Chapter 12) - Married three times with children - now divorced and living in Florida as priest and pastor of a Catholic Church.

Jim Bunning (Chapter 15) - Is in the Baseball Hall of Fame. Former United States Congressman and Senator from the Commonwealth of Kentucky.

Dick (Chapter 16) - Married Dinnie, moved to Chicago and had five boys. We met every year for holidays or trips. He passed away in 1998 and is dearly missed by all.

Happy (Chapter 17) - Married Susan, retired, and divides his time in Cincinnati, northern Michigan and Ocean Reef, Florida. We still spend time together with family, parties and tennis.

Mitch (Chapter 22) - Is the senior editor of National Geographic Magazine in Washington, D.C.

Jack (Chapter 23) - The security guard at Frisch's Mainliner is now CEO of Frisch's Restaurant and Hotel chain.

Gus and Polly (Chapter 26) - Both killed when their airliner crashed in Indianapolis.

Neil (Chapter 28) - Last reported address was Atlanta Federal Penitentiary.

Irish (Chapter 34) Vice president of Cincinnati real estate firm

Curley (Chapter 34) - Retired full bird Air Force Colonel still plays senior championship softball.

Ike (Chapter 35) - Former U.S. Marine captain. Regional vice president of Mutual Benefit Life and most outstanding group manager in USA.

Tom W. (Chapter 35) - One of the internationally famous founders of the Pop Art movement - lives in New York City.

J.C. (Chapter 38) - Still selling refreshments. Is owner of largest popcorn making machine company in the world.

Max (Chapter 39) - Comfortably retired former owner of five mattress manufacturing companies.

Junebug (Chapter 42) - Former Air Force jet fighter pilot and retired Vice President of a large Cincinnati Bank.